The Economics of Everglades Restoration

For Batya

and also

Chana Leah, Avraham David, and Meital Peninah

The Economics of Everglades Restoration

Missing Pieces in the Future of South Florida

Richard Weisskoff

University of Miami, Coral Gables, USA

Edward Elgar

Cheltenham, UK • Northampton, MA, USA

Published by
Edward Elgar Publishing Limited
Glensanda House
Montpellier Parade
Cheltenham
Glos GL50 1UA
UK

Edward Elgar Publishing, Inc.
136 West Street
Suite 202
Northampton
Massachusetts 01060
USA

A catalogue record for this book
is available from the British Library

Library of Congress Cataloguing in Publication Data

Weisskoff, Richard.
    The economics of Everglades restoration: missing pieces in the
future of South Florida/Richard Weisskoff.
        p. cm.
    Includes bibliographical references and index.
        1. Environmental policy—Economic aspects—Florida—Everglades.
    2. Ecosystem management—Economic aspects—Florida—Everglades.
    I. Title.
    HC107.F62E848   2004
    333.91'8153'0975939—dc22

                                                                2004047121

ISBN 1 84376 224 2 (cased)
        1 84376 242 0 (paperback)

Printed and bound in Great Britain by MPG Books Ltd, Bodmin, Cornwall

Contents

Acknowledgments

First, thanks to my wife for her unceasing support and encouragement.

I would also like to thank a great many other people who gave their time, data, and ideas to this project. Dick Pettigrew, Chairman, and Bonnie Kranzer, Executive Director, the Governor's Commission for a Sustainable Florida; Carl Woelcke and Dick March at the South Florida Water Management District (SFWMD) and Grace Johns at Hazen & Sawyer; Captain Ed Davidson, former Chair of Florida Audubon and dive master in the Keys; Buffalo Tiger, tribal elder of the Miccosukee and all-around guide; Chip Abele of Southern Facilities, master developer; George Treyz and Fred Treyz, father and son team at REMI, Amherst, MA, regional model-makers; Scott Lindahl and Doug Olson at Minnesota IMPLAN Group, patient tutors; Attorney Dexter Lehtinen, fearless counselor and teacher; Joe Browder of Washington, DC, measured advocate and environmental consultant; Richard Marella at US Geological Survey (USGS), Tallahassee, water guru; Mike O'Connell, now at the South Florida Regional Planning Council, formerly at the Florida Agency for Workforce Innovation (once known as the Florida Department of Labor and Employment Security), creative economist and keeper of the Region's REMI model; Tom Lodge, ecological advisor; and Jim Murley, Director of the Catanese Center for Urban and Environmental Solutions at Florida Atlantic University and an early supporter of regional modeling.

At the University of Miami, thanks to Ruthanne Vogel (now librarian of the Palmer–Trinity School) and Craig Likness, guides to the Everglades Collection at Richter Library; Alberto Montero-Valdes, curator of the Law School's Everglades Litigation Collection; Professor Ron Hofstetter, research biologist and long-term Everglades investigator; Dr Don DeAngelis, biologist and Everglades computer modeler.

Thanks also to Bill Hunt and Eric Rosch of the US Army Corps of Engineers in Jacksonville who helped me get started and to Russ Reed during the work on the Restudy; Dick Ogburn at the South Florida Regional Planning Council and Ping Chang, now at the Southern California Association of Governments; in Tallahassee, Ed Montonaro (now at Florida State University) and Frank Williams of the staff of the Joint Legislative Management Committee, and Barry Pitegoff of Visit Florida; at the University of Florida (UF) in

Gainesville, Professors Yasushi Toda in the Economics Department, Dave Mulkey and John Reynolds of the Institute of Food and Agricultural Sciences (IFAS); Wally Milon, now at University of Central Florida; Carol West, Dave Lenze, and Stanley Smith of the Bureau of Economic and Business Research (BEBR); in Belle Glade, Jose Alvarez and George Snyder at the UF/IFAS Everglades Research and Education Center; in Canal Point, Barry Glaz at the Federal Plant Breeding Station; and Stan Bronson, Executive Director of the Florida Earth Foundation.

Financial assistance was provided by the University of Miami for a year-long sabbatical leave in 1997–98 which allowed me to begin this study and two small grants from the Provost's Research Fund for data, software, and local travel. Thanks to David Benjamin and Robert Farmer of the Third Planet Foundation for their support in sending me to Urban 21, Global Conference on the Urban Future, in Berlin in July 2000, and for their help with the present volume to support educational outreach work in South Florida concerning sustainable development.

Completion of the research would not have been possible without a grant from the Department of the Interior, Everglades National Park (ENP), under the Critical Ecosystem Studies Initiative (CESI). Thanks to Bill Perry of ENP for his patience and encouragement. Thanks also to the Center for Ecosystem Science and Policy (CESP) of the University of Miami for support in preparing the final manuscript for publication

Alexander Moltchanov and Sherry Bartz, students in UM's Economics Department, helped process the two land-use studies for the 13 counties used in Chapter 10. Pamela Blackman, Liu Yang, and Jin Yan of the Department of International Studies and Yue Xu of the Economics Department helped compile the agricultural censuses and early tourist statistics used in Chapters 12 and 14.

Thanks to Helena Solo-Gabriele, Dan Meeroff, Alice Clarke, Tom Tanner, John R. Meyer, Robert Burchell, Rick Edwards, Gary Fauth, Tim Withee, and Tom Goodman for their comments on earlier drafts.

And special thanks to Mrs Barbra Imberman, round-the-clock typist; Chris Hanson, master map-maker; and Marcia Stevens, typesetter.

Disclaimer: No one acknowledged above should be held responsible for anything in this study.

Finally, I would like to recall the memories of four colleagues who were especially kind to me: Peter Rosendahl, Vice President for Environmental Affairs at Flo-Sun, Inc., who guided many a class of mine through the sugar mills, fields, and warehouses. He graciously opened the industry to us and us to his industry.

Dave Anderson, research economist at IFAS in Belle Glade, had made his own bold projections of population growth of South Florida and generously arranged for me to present a staff seminar at the Everglades Research and Educational Center.

Paul Larson, engineer and consultant to the rock miners of South Florida, was the first to calculate the magnitude of Everglades surface water lost to tide every year through the canals. He opened our eyes to what could be saved.

Ken Trager, economist for all seasons, ran the REMI model for the state's Joint Legislative Committee and then moved on to reform the State's Employee Pension Fund. He opened his home to me in Tallahassee and showed me by his example how data could be made to answer the people's most pressing economic questions. He was unfailing in his view that serious economic modeling should be brought to South Florida.

May this book also be a parting thank you to these intrepid colleague-investigators.

Abbreviations and Acronyms

AROG	average rate of growth
ATLSS	Across Trophic Level System Simulation
BEBR	Bureau of Economic and Business Research
C&SF	Central and South Florida (Project)
CERP	Comprehensive Everglades Restoration Plan
CPI	consumer price index
CPS	*Current Population Survey*
EA	Economic Area
EAA	Everglades Agricultural Area
em	employment
ENP	Everglades National Park
EU	employment update
FLUCCS	Florida Land Use, Cover Classification System
fsa	*Florida Statistical Abstract*
GEC	Gulf Engineers & Consultants, Inc.
GEER	Greater Everglades Ecosystem Region
GIS	geographic information system
HH	households
IMPLAN	Impact Analysis for Planning
IWR-MAIN	Institute for Water Resources–Municipal and Industrial Needs
KSV	Kissimmee River Valley
LEC	Lower East Coast
LWC	Lower West Coast
mgd	millions of gallons per day
MSA	Metropolitan Statistical Area
NOAA	National Oceanic and Atmospheric Administration
pop	population
PS	Public Supply (water)
q	output
REIS	Regional Economic Information System
REMI	Regional Economic Modeling, Inc.
RF	Rest of Fresh Water
ROF	Rest of Florida
saus	*Statistical Abstract of the US*

SF	South Florida
SFWMD	South Florida Water Management District
SIC	Standard Industrial Classification System
TESS	Threatened and Endangered Species System
UEC	Upper East Coast
USACOE	US Army Corps of Engineers
USDA	US Department of Agriculture
USGS	US Geological Survey
wmd	water management district

... There, where the birds nest,
The stork with its home among the cypresses ...
...
The young lions roar after their prey,
And seek their food from the Almighty.
The sun rises, and they are gathered in,
...
Man goes forth to his work ...

Psalm 104

1. The Professor and the Corps

One hot summer day in July of 1997, as the US Army Corps of Engineers was passing the two-thirds mark in drafting its plan for restoring the Florida Everglades, an economics professor from the University of Miami flew to Jacksonville. He hitched a ride downtown to his appointment with several officials at the Army Corps' Regional Headquarters. His mission was to alert the Corps' planning staff about those economic factors that he thought were missing from their Everglades Review Study, also known as "the Restudy," for short.[1] Without considering certain economic factors, he would argue, the plan could not possibly succeed.

The Professor presented the staff with a summary of the region's economic growth. He explained how Florida's official population forecasters tended to underestimate the likely future development of the region. The Professor was most concerned that the anticipated $4 to $5 billion of public spending for Everglades restoration would itself lead to even more economic growth and the further undoing of the Everglades, contrary to the intent of the entire undertaking.

No one was adding up all the pieces of what was happening in South Florida, the Professor argued. New housing, new shopping malls, new stadiums, new hospitals, and new schools were all being constructed on newly-drained lands. Tourism was growing. Miami and Ft Lauderdale were leading ports of departure for an increasing number of cruise ships. The roads were already clogged with trucks and passenger cars, and even more so during the busy winter months when the "snow birds" – those who live part-year in South Florida – drive or fly south to flee the cold northern winters. The regional economy seemed to be bursting at the seams.

All this growth threatened the Everglades, the Professor said. Pure drinking water was needed by the cities and suburbs. The farmers felt threatened by both the needs of the expanding cities and the demands of the environmentalists. The South Florida Water Management District, together with the Farm Bureau and the sugar and vegetable growers, had been locked in almost constant combat with the US Attorney's Office, the Florida Audubon Society, Everglades National Park, and the two Indian tribes over the responsibility for maintaining clean water in the Everglades region.[2] The growing cities needed to fill the marshy lands with crushed foundation stone, which was mined from the deep quarries near Everglades National Park. The wisdom of constructing these open pits so close to the Everglades was being questioned. On almost every front, the needs of the modern economy were clashing with the goal of restoring the health of what remained. Would there be enough pure water at the right time for all the parties to realize their goals? Surely, an economic model was needed to see how *all* the pieces of the complicated South Florida puzzle added up!

The Professor showed the officials of the Army Corps a copy of his book describing the economic model he had developed and applied to Puerto Rico.[3] This might be of interest, since the Corps' Jacksonville district also had responsibility for many federal projects on that island. Twenty years of rapid growth and 2000 tax-exempt factories had not succeeded in reducing unemployment, the Professor explained, because they had never *added up all the pieces*. As new jobs were created in industry, agriculture was allowed to collapse, destroying old jobs. Only his complete economic model revealed how all of that society's efforts at "development" had barely kept the Puerto Rican ship afloat. Better to look at the whole picture, he said.

The Professor was motivated by a more current, more chilling scenario, which he feared was being replicated in South Florida. In the early 1980s, almost all of the Latin American economies had defaulted on their loans to the international community. The collapse of their economies, now called the "Debt Crisis," plunged nearly half the entire continent's population into poverty, simply because *no one had been adding up the pieces* at the highest levels of government. No one had been summing the individual loans that the different international banks, liquidity-rich with petrodollars recycled by the oil producers, had extended to a wide range of public and semi-public agencies in each country. As one borrower after another failed, their contracted debts were passed on to the national government, the guarantor of the individual loans. Starting with Mexico in 1982, almost every national treasury collapsed from the "surprising" accumulation of obligations.[4]

As the nations defaulted, trade and aid stopped, and their economies crashed into what was to become the "lost decade" of despair and depression. In place of the once buoyant if irresponsible prosperity came a new era of drug trafficking, civil war, and political instability, the results of which are still being felt today.

Here in South Florida, the Professor explained, it is the ecosystem that is overburdened, not the economy. There are so many new projects being undertaken, and each project needs water, land, and energy. Each creates employment and draws new people to Florida. Each employee has a family, and every family needs a home, at least one car, air conditioning, a school for the kids, a place to shop, police and fire protection, fresh water, and a connection to a

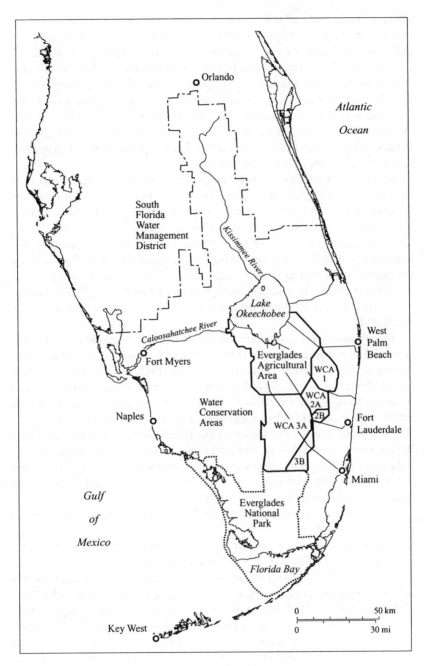

Figure 1.1   Major Features of South Florida

sewer or septic tank. All this creates even more economic growth, and on top of this, we are going to put in billions to save the ecosystem! How do we know the added billions won't sink the ship we're trying to keep afloat?

The officials listened attentively. But, Professor, they said, economic considerations are a low priority on this project. Our objective is to restore the Everglades. The economic impacts with which you are concerned – whether the economy, indeed, will be blown apart by restoration spending of such magnitudes – may be legitimate. Yes, we have heard of "economic impact studies," which is what you are proposing. The Corps has applied this analysis to much smaller projects in other regions.

At that, the Professor showed them a report on the economic impacts on the Upper Mississippi River System – 76 counties in five states – of recreation spending which generated $1.2 billion and supported 18 000 jobs. But the South Florida project to restore an entire ecosystem was, in fact, the biggest single project of its type *ever* to be undertaken by the Corps and one that required planning 50 years into the future. Everglades restoration was already the largest single project in the world.[5]

But, Professor, the officials asked, was there ever a case of an economic model accurately forecasting the outcomes in the situations such as you've mentioned?

I can think of three, he replied. In my own model of Puerto Rico, I estimated seven different trajectories, the slowest of which proved to be less than one percent off on a ten-year projection. Second, Professor Leontief's "World Model" developed for the United Nations in the mid-1970s correctly identified future trade imbalances in Latin America, but the collapse occurred a decade earlier than expected. Third, a later study by Duchin and Lange using the "World Model" showed that the optimistic future envisioned in the Brundtland Report, *Our Common Future*, was simply not realizable unless major changes were to occur. Their nitty-gritty economic studies which projected the current world economy just did not support the rosy vision of world growth being compatible with environmental preservation.[6]

But, Professor, all those studies took years to complete. We have but months remaining!

That's very true, the Professor replied. The model that I developed as a young professor at Yale together with a team of three grad students took two years to build. But that was twenty years ago! Over the last decade, the US Forest Service has made available a very similar model, called IMPLAN – Impact Analysis for Planning – and this can be applied to any county or group of counties in the United States with the click of a mouse. What took my team two years of hard labor can now be computed for the counties in the Everglades area in just a matter of minutes. The Professor then demonstrated the IMPLAN software by modeling the impact of a change in farm sales on jobs and income on Dade (now Miami-Dade) County.

But, the Professor cautioned, this model computes great detail for only one year's impact. If we want to know the possible economic course for the next 35 years, then there's another system, called REMI – Regional Economic Models, Inc. – which might be used. The REMI model captures the dynamic effects and the feedbacks of big expenditures: how the new employment will affect housing, migration, and transport, for example, and what the demographic and racial composition of the region will look like. This is the tool we should be using. It is powerful, insightful, but very expensive. Up to now, only the Joint Legislative Management Committee of the Florida Legislature uses this model to evaluate the economic impacts of new laws and taxes.[7] Their model is for all of Florida, and we need a model of the South Florida region.

Professor, the officials explained, our budget prohibits us from doing too much analysis, and there is little time left. Just last year, Congress amended the original Water Resources Development Act. They want the final report by July 1999, which means all the analysis has to be finished by August 1998, and here it is, almost August 1997!

Besides, the Corps has never been asked to do this type of economic modeling before. Traditionally, we had been required by law to compute a benefit–cost ratio for each new project to show the public that all the benefits from flood protection, water supply, navigation, and recreation exceed the costs of constructing and operating the proposed project.[8]

But this is ecosystem restoration. The value of a restored environment – saving species, preserving wetlands, recreating habitats – these are all unknown or inestimable, so the need for a benefit–cost ratio has been suspended. According to our regulations, our responsibility is limited to the *new* economic development that might be caused on the national level by restoration spending. The other factors that you mention are quite outside our mandate.[9]

But, the Professor responded, no other organization has the oversight or scope of vision you are charged with. Each Florida county has its own "comprehensive plan" which it draws up for itself. The state is broken into "regional planning districts" that are groups of counties, but the Everglades ecosystem embraces 16 counties that fall under the jurisdiction of five different regional planning councils. Only the boundaries of the South Florida Water Management District, not the county lines, were drawn with the whole ecosystem in mind, and the Water Management District is the *local* sponsor of the entire project. Besides, it is the Army Corps, not the Water Management District, that is charged with planning the next 50 years. If you don't include an economic model of the region, no one else will.

Professor, the officials answered, your case is compelling. The public interest might well be served by a study such as you urge. But we have neither the time nor the resources to consider all the factors you would have us take on…

The Professor went on. The restoration of an ecosystem can't be successful without considering all the human participants and the consequences on the people. The State of Florida itself is promoting the growth of agriculture, tourism, and new industrial and commercial development. Retirement communities and trailer parks are expanding. Tax incentives and energy prices favor new construction and sprawl, and these press against the Everglades. The runoff from the cities is discharged into the estuaries. This kills the offshore fishing industry and destroys the barrier reef. In times of emergency, the city runoff has been back-pumped into the Everglades. The problem of urban growth and the challenge of Everglades restoration are a single problem. They must be planned together!

Upstream from the Everglades are sugar lands, beef and dairy cattle, citrus, vegetables, and greenhouses. Public policy now promotes their expansion, which causes a problem downstream. The problem of agricultural growth and the challenge of Everglades restoration are a single problem. They must be planned together!

The Professor had gleaned his material from attending the public hearings of the Governor's Commission for a Sustainable South Florida. The Commission, a unique phenomenon in the annals of ecological restoration, had taken a motley crew of stakeholders and opposing interests and charged them to act like nothing less than the ecological conscience of South Florida.

The official responsibility of the Commission was to recommend steps to achieve a healthy ecosystem, a sustainable economy, and healthy communities. The Commission members came from all corners of the South Florida landscape – small farmers and giant agro-business leaders, real estate developers and rock miners, water managers and city mayors, environmental groups and the two Indian tribes, forty members in all, many of whom were more accustomed to seeing one another on opposing sides of a courtroom.

The Commission, its sub-committees and staff had been holding monthly hearings on the Everglades Restoration Project and had drafted its own "Conceptual Plan," which was intended to be advisory to the Army Corps' Restudy. The Conceptual Plan consisted of seven recommendations and forty preferential options, and these reflected the unanimous vote of the stakeholders regarding the future restoration.[10]

Several months prior to his visit to Jacksonville, the Professor had also challenged the Governor's Commission to concern itself with economic modeling of the region, not just hydrological models. Secretary of the Interior Babbit had also appeared before the Commission, and, in front of a huge aerial photograph of the ecosystem which hangs permanently in the Water District's auditorium, the Secretary had spoken passionately of his apprehension over the clash between the expanding coastal metropolises of South Florida and the Everglades preserves in the interior. Our Professor was merely bringing the concerns of the Governor's Commission and the themes of the stakeholders right into Corps' headquarters.

Within three months, the Jacksonville District did contract Dames & Moore, one of the top engineering companies in the United States, which in turn contracted David Miller & Associates, a Washington DC consulting firm to perform the required socioeconomic studies for the Restudy. And, the Washington firm did hire the Miami Professor to draft a proposal to study the regional economic impacts of the restoration. That proposal was finished in October of 1997, and in a two-day meeting at the Jacksonville office, each of the key elements of the Professor's proposal was rejected by the Corps, the consulting firm, and the Water Management District.

The Restudy would not re-examine the long-term population forecasts or the possible impacts of an increase in tourism, recreation, and non-commercial fishing that might result from ecosystem restoration. It would not study the impact of the project on minority peoples, migrant farm workers, or the Native American Tribes. It would not look at the importance of seasonality on the economy and the influx of part-year residents. It would not examine the impact of alternative crops that would tolerate more flooding. Nor would the Restudy examine the economic incentives that attract people to the region or the nature of the South Florida lifestyle, both of which are ultimately responsible for increasing stress on the environment.

Instead, the economic mandate would be simply to undertake an inventory of the region's economy and examine a few measures of growth. The regional "impact study," which our Professor was formally commissioned to do, would be restricted to those impacts that would result directly from the restoration spending itself, that is, the new pumping stations, bridges, storage wells, and land purchases, plus changes due to reductions in farm land and enhanced water supply. The broader and more basic questions – what would happen to the economy if the ecosystem were improved overall or if it were allowed to degenerate? – would not be addressed.

The Professor returned to Miami determined to find a sponsor for the study he thought South Florida truly needed. He phoned a number of private foundations active in the environmental field. Foundation Alpha was encouraging. "Send us immediately a letter with your proposal, and we may be able to get back to you within the month." Foundation Beta was less exuberant. "The Everglades is too political. We used to work there, but the scene was too controversial. Call Foundation Alpha; they finance Everglades work."

Foundation Gamma sponsored research only on narrow issues of pollution. Foundation Delta didn't see the value of economic studies. Foundation Epsilon funded research only on marine fishing, and Foundation Zeta only financed land purchases. Long-term economic studies? Putting the pieces together? Why not the Water Management District? Why not the Army Corps? they asked.

Only one foundation trustee told the Professor what would take years for him to understand, namely, that the viewpoint he was taking – that the economy must also be "mapped" in order to rescue the environment – was not yet a part of conventional thinking. The foundations would have to be educated.

Six more months passed. Foundation Alpha finally wrote back that they were getting out of the Everglades business. They wished the Professor luck in finding support.

In the meantime, the Professor made a bold but costly decision. If nobody else would compute the missing pieces of the regional economy, then he must, on his own. Of the two computer programming tools needed to do the job, the Army Corps had decided on the IMPLAN, the simpler and less costly one; the Professor needed REMI.

The Professor called the REMI company, explained his project and mission, and privately ordered the REMI model for the broad Everglades area out of his earnings from the Army Corps' exercise. George Treyz, REMI's founder, and recognized as the "dean" of applied regional economic modeling, explained that economic models do not respect the environment; they have no ecological footing or foundation, aside from an amenity variable which is subject to some discretion. The economy simply grows. There is no limit or constraint due to space or water or air.

Could the REMI economic model assist in computing the land and water required by an economy? the Professor asked.

Perhaps, the Dean answered, but that's up to you. REMI doesn't go that far. It's just an economic model.

The Professor eventually flew to Amherst, MA, and apprenticed there for a week to learn the intricacies of the model and its requirements. He would use both IMPLAN and REMI models to test for the missing pieces, an ambitious research program that would require some time to complete.

The Professor's REMI model grouped the Everglades counties into four drainage basins, corresponding roughly to the four planning regions within the South Florida Water Management District. A fifth region, consisting of all the other counties in the state, would allow the Professor to replicate both the economy of South Florida and the entire state. In that way, the future of the Everglades region and Florida as a whole might be compared.

But, it turned out, neither the REMI model nor IMPLAN proved to be a crystal ball. As other researchers have also shown, the national statistics scaled down to the relevant county had to be adjusted with local data and local employment forecasts. Various pieces, the Professor found, were missing from these "off-the-shelf" models.

The Professor believed that these high-powered computer models would alert the public and private agencies involved in restoration to the urgency of including the economic dimension. Beginning in February 1998, he summarized his first results for the monthly Governor's Commission meeting in Homestead, FL, and then formally presented it to the scholarly community in the plenary session of the Twelfth International Conference on Input–Output Techniques in May 1998 in New York City.[11] He gave seminars using REMI and IMPLAN for the Audubon Society, the Water Management District, the South Florida Regional Planning Council, and at the Institute of Food and Agricultural Sciences (IFAS) at the University of Florida in Gainesville and its Research and Educational Centers in Belle Glade and Ft Pierce. When he challenged the newly-formed Governor's Commission on the Everglades on the need for economic studies, the best that a sympathetic Commissioner could do was to refer his questions to the technical agencies that were, in fact, charged with promoting growth, not with examining the consequences of it. These agencies had already been lobbied; their position was already known. The public agencies, the environmental groups, the universities, the foundations – nobody seemed interested; nobody seemed to be listening.

For all the talk of "economy and environment" on the national and global levels, the reluctance to undertake this type of research in South Florida meant that it must be a very important topic indeed! The working assumption on the local level seemed to be that economic growth was not to be studied, challenged, or questioned.

To accomplish these tasks would be a very difficult assignment. The Professor would need to use both the IMPLAN and REMI models to map out the interconnections within the urban and rural economies. He would have to know the history of the "missing pieces" and make projections of their futures. All these adjustments would then be entered into the computer model of each region in hope of gaining some insight into their combined effects for the next 30 years. Only once the economic model was adjusted and projections made, could he then begin to compute the connections between the economy and the environment, as those connections are not a built-in feature of the economic models.

Who had been responsible for making projections of water needs? Who was looking out for South Florida? The more the Professor investigated, the more curious he became. The various forecasts of water consumption done by outside consultants tended to be based on "boiler plate" models that used "official" but conservative estimates of population growth and "national coefficients" or averages for water use, not local or measured relationships between people and their real needs.[12] If either of these were low – the population projections or the water use per person – then the whole ecological future of South Florida would be understated. The prospect of a successful Everglades restoration would be compromised because no one was adding up the pieces or forecasting their trends correctly!

Yet the local economies in all corners of South Florida seemed to be booming. Real estate, construction, tourism, farming, banking, transport, shopping centers: people were moving in from all over America and the Americas. The cities and the farms that surround the Everglades were all growing at a dizzying pace – inland from both the east and west coasts, southward from Orlando and northward from the Keys. If we could "add up" all these "normal" growth pressures and then lay the Everglades restoration plan on top, the Professor thought, then this computation might provide a hurricane warning, as it were, of the fast-growing economy and its storm surge of stressors on the environment.

In the meantime, the Army Corps' Restudy for Everglades Restoration was nearing completion. The "Planning Team" had drawn on the participation of scientists and engineers from a wide variety of agencies, all of which gave their approval to the Restudy once their objections to the plan were met, often by the addition of new "components." In the end, it looked like the interests of Everglades National Park, the Florida Fish and Wildlife Commission, the South Florida Water Management District, and the various environmental protection agencies could be harmonized, or at least minimally satisfied, to get the plan completed and off the ground. This was, after all, a new era in the greening of the Army Corps of Engineers. Not only was the Corps now involved in fixing the ecosystem, which it had single-handedly drained, diked, and ditched, but all this was done openly with much public and professional interagency participation. The mission of the Army Corps was no longer to create fresh farmland from marsh, but to restore marsh and protect Everglades National Park.

The Army Corps' Restudy was completed by October 1998 and presented in a series of public meetings around the state in the following month. The report itself, 3000 pages long, available as a single CD-ROM and on the Corps' website, www.evergladesplan.org, is a triumph of complicated engineering and multi-disciplinary collaboration. The Restudy is fundamentally a hydrologic plan to improve the environment, together with the agricultural and municipal water supply, in an 18 000-square-mile region that is home to more than six million people and destination for some 25 million tourists each year. The area also provides pasture for over 600 000 cattle and irrigated soil for 47 percent of America's sugar cane and 38 percent of the nation's citrus trees.

The main goal of the Restudy was seen as the restoration of the quantity, purity, and timing of the waters flowing into Everglades National Park, which, after Yellowstone, is the second largest national park in the lower 48 states and the only World Heritage Site in the US declared "In Danger" by UNESCO. Everglades National Park, also a World Biosphere Preserve and a Wetland of International Importance, is the remnant of a once-vast flowing marshland, a unique and subtle set of habitats formed by the confluence of temperate and tropical climates. The park holds probably the largest number of species of flora and fauna of any protected area in the United States today.[13]

By the end of 1998, the environmental groups had mobilized their political forces behind the Restudy. The costs of the project – which had risen to $7.8 billion – were to be split between Florida and the US Congress, with the state's burden to be shared with the local sponsor, the South Florida Water Management District, which also has the power to tax and sell bonds. But before the Restudy could be submitted to Congress in July 1999, local backing had to be secured.

A new Republican governor of Florida, the son of a former president, took office in January 1999, and promised support for the Restudy. For the first time in a century, the Republicans controlled both houses of the state legislature as well as the executive branch. Governor Jeb Bush appointed a new czar for economic development, charged with laying the groundwork for new pro-growth policies in South Florida, and a new environmental czar to coordinate policies for restoring the Everglades. No one saw a contradiction.

With the state apparatus squarely behind the Restudy, local governments, the major environmental groups, the Indian tribes, and regional stakeholders all lent support for the plan that seemed to promise so much to so many parties.

Then, in January 1999, long-suppressed criticism of the Restudy by Everglades National Park scientists was leaked to the press. The scientists' report, which had been kept secret by Park Service and Corps of Engineers officials, said the Restudy would actually cause more harm than good to Everglades National Park and other natural regions of the Everglades. On February 22nd, five internationally distinguished US ecologists issued an open letter and met with Secretary of the Interior Babbit, stating their doubts as to the effectiveness of the Restudy's recommendations. Better to delay the whole project by six months so that objective, non-involved professionals could review the program, they pleaded, rather than proceed full steam ahead.

The dissenting ecologists doubted the ability of the Restudy to restore the natural water flows to Everglades National Park. They argued that in the future the region would find itself in a similar situation as in the present – dependent on water managers who would have to choose between dividing the waters among the many users within the region.

Conceptually, the Restudy was also seen as misguided and misdirected. Everglades National Park, in whose name the restoration was being undertaken, would not be the primary benefactor, but rather the recipient of last resort of the $8 billion project. Had the scientists examined the economics of the restoration proposal, they would have had even greater doubts.

The presidential election of November 2000 focused new attention on Florida, and by December 2000, the passage of the Water Resource Development Act (WRDA) brought all the historic compromises to a single table. The promise of a full Everglades restoration came into reach. The Restudy now became the "Plan." The proposal had become a program, and both the federal and state governments committed themselves to financing and getting the "Plan" underway. A scientific oversight panel, whose creation was written into WRDA 2000 to satisfy those outspoken environmentalists who took issue with the overall thrust of the Everglades restoration plan, was to be set up, and "assurances" were to be formulated regarding the quantity of water that would be reserved for the natural system.[14] Again, it looked as if economics presented no inherent contradiction to the Everglades Plan. Restoration had become a technical question of "getting the water right," meaning, its timing, volume, quality, and distribution. These are, it is thought, engineering, scientific, and ultimately legal, not economic questions.

Here, then, in this book, are the Professor's findings, the economics of Everglades restoration, and what these missing pieces mean for the future of South Florida.

NOTES

1. The full title is "The Central and Southern Florida Project Comprehensive Review Study."
2. The initial suit was filed in October 1988 as *United States v. South Florida Water Management District*, US District Court for the Southern District of Florida, Case No. 88-1886-Civ-Hoeveler. The documents may be found in the special Everglades Collection of the University of Miami's Law School Library and on its website: www.law.miami.edu/library/everglades/litigation.
3. See Weisskoff (1985).
4. See Lissakers (1991) for analysis. For estimates of the share of poverty on the continent, see Weisskoff (1993).
5. *The Integrated Financial Plan* (May 1997) published by the Working Group of the South Florida Ecosystem Task Force had already counted close to $1 billion of project appropriations associated with different restoration activities throughout the region and $4.5 billion as the total requirements to complete all the projects at that time.
6. See Weisskoff (1971) and (1976) for the original forecasts and (1985) for the retrospective on Puerto Rico. See Leontief, Carter, and Petri (1977) for the "World Model," esp. Ch. 14, "Balance of Payments Problems," Tables 60, 62, on anticipating the Debt Crisis. See Duchin and Lange (1994), Ch. 1, on testing the vision of the Brundtland Report, published by the World Commission on Environment and Development (1987).
7. See, for example, Trager (1991) and (1999).
8. See US Army Corps of Engineers (1991).

9. See US Army Corps of Engineers (1996).
10. See Governor's Commission (1996).
11. Published as Weisskoff (2000) using only the IMPLAN model for all of South Florida.
12. See, for example, Gulf Engineers and Consultants (August 1996), which used the standard IWR-MAIN Water Demand Analysis Software.
13. On Everglades National Park as a World Heritage Site, see http://whc.unesco.org/pg.cfm?cid=31&id_site=76; as a World Biosphere Preserve, see http://www.unesco.org/mab/wnbr.htm; as a Wetland of International Importance, see http://ramsar.org/types_mangroves_present.pdf. On the Park itself, see http://www.nps.gov/ever/ and http://www.everglades.national-park.com/info.htm#wor.
14. See Doyle and Jodrey (2002).

PART I

Findings and Forecasts

2. Forecasting the Future Economy

INTRODUCTION: A SYNOPSIS OF THE BOOK

"The Everglades were dying," Marjorie Stoneman Douglas began the last chapter, "The Eleventh Hour," in her 1947 book, *The Everglades: River of Grass*. Then came "Forty More Years of Crisis," as she called the "Afterword" of the 1988 edition, wherein she narrated the construction of the Central and South Florida Project. Are we not now in the closing moments of that last hour?

Today, as the Everglades restoration gets underway, it is suspected that the benefits may reach the remaining natural system only toward the end of the restoration period, say, by 2030. But if growth continues upstream and in the surrounding area, even this outcome may be unlikely.

The Everglades, in short, may be facing a "lose–lose" situation, not "win–win," as is commonly portrayed. If the economy grows and all the financing is available for restoration, the Everglades lose because the growing demands on the environment will undermine the effort to save it. The cities lose because they continue to grow at a reckless and hothouse pace without making provision for their own future water supply and need for space. Agriculture may also lose in the long run unless it makes adaptations for the fragility of the ecosystem and for the downstream dangers caused by its runoff. In short, everyone – the people of South Florida as well as the sponsors and donors from the rest of America – loses due to the rate and style of growth while claiming all the while that their efforts are restoring the Everglades.

If, on the other hand, the plan falls short for whatever reason – cuts in federal or state funding, technological failure of the aquifer storage and recovery (ASR) wells, a series of overwhelming tropical storms – then the economy of the region may stagnate and, with it, true Everglades restoration.

In either case, the Everglades currently face a losing battle. To summarize, if the plan does proceed and the economy continues to grow at an historical rate, then the environment loses due to the intensity of growth that will be documented in this book. If the plan fails, even if the economy slows, the environment still loses, because it remains in its present state of collapse.

There is at present a trade-off between economy and ecology. The ecosystem is in a no-win game as long as the economy continues to use land and water and generates waste and pollution in the proportions that we are experiencing today. Only a radical change in the conservation of land and water, as well as how we treat society's wastes, can reverse that. Indeed, if the economy could treat the ecosystem as the fragile entity it really is, then as we modify our lifestyle and material needs with that in mind, we probably could live amicably with nature and with growth.

The major theme of this book is that the economic growth of the region has been a missing piece in planning Everglades restoration. This is somewhat ironic since it has been the growth of the South Florida economy that created the crisis in the Everglades in the first place. To correct this omission, this study began by applying a "ready-made" REMI economic model of the region in order to forecast the dimensions of the future economy. But this, too, was found to be lacking, for four important pieces are still missing from the pre-packaged models, namely, a complete accounting of the trends in agriculture, investment, tourism, and the newly-committed spending on Everglades restoration itself.

Once these "missing pieces" were added to the economic picture, then our computer simulation models were able to make more reliable projections for the future. But this end point – the economic forecast – is actually the starting point for the rest of the book.

In Part I, we present the results of the economic forecasts (this chapter, see below): how many people and jobs and how much output are to be expected by 2035, and how our forecasts compare to other projections made by "official" sources.

These economic projections are then immediately applied to gain insights on two important issues: the future demand for water (Chapter 3) and the future demand for urban land in the region (Chapter 4). A similar procedure is followed in both chapters. First, the historical relationships between the economic variables and water and land, respectively, are estimated and then these measured statistical relationships are applied to the economic forecasts to make projections of *future* water demand and *future* demand for urban land.

These three chapters – projections of the economy, the demand for water, and the demand for urban land – are presented up front rather than at the end of the study due to the urgency and their central role in the current debate regarding these issues.

Once these Findings and Forecasts are laid out (Part I), then the reader is introduced to the Economy of the South Florida Ecosystem (Part II), the details of the Economics of the Missing Pieces (Part III), and conclusions for Changing the Future (Part IV).

Part II, the Economy of the South Florida Ecosystem, consists of six studies reviewing the basic issues that underlie the regional economy and its ecological setting: the role of the economy as the primary stressor of the Everglades (Chapter 5); a statistical review of the South Florida economy (Chapter 6); a brief history of the great public works which have resulted in the "carving up" of South Florida (Chapter 7); a comparison of population growth of the regions (Chapter 8); a quantitative study of agriculture (Chapter 9); and estimates of the value of ecosystem services in the region based on two recent land use surveys (Chapter 10). Much of the statistical information presented in these background chapters is published here for the first time.

In Part III, the Economics of the Missing Pieces, the reader is introduced to the comparative strengths of the two regional economic models that will be used in the forecasting process, REMI and IMPLAN (Chapter 11). Estimates for each of the missing pieces are then made based on the different sources of available information: income generated by agriculture (Chapter 12); the components of investment (Chapter 13); tourist spending (Chapter 14); and all expected spending on Everglades restoration (Chapter 15). Each of these chapters examines the various data sources and how the economic model is corrected for each of the missing pieces – the results of the insertion of ALL the missing pieces having already been presented up front in Chapter 2.

The conclusions, Changing the Future, in Part IV, summarize the empirical findings of the economic models and the general implications of the compatibility of ecological well-being and economic growth.

BASIC METHODOLOGY

The greater Everglades ecosystem covers the major parts of 13 full South Florida counties, which are, for modeling purposes, grouped into the four sub-regions corresponding to the four different water basins and planning areas of the South Florida Water Management District (SFWMD). The four sub-regions are: the Lower East Coast, which includes the population centers of Miami, Ft Lauderdale, and West Palm Beach; the Lower West Coast, a ranching and vegetable-growing region with the sprawling cities of Naples and Ft Myers; the Kissimmee River Valley, with its dairy herds and southern suburbs of Orlando (which lies outside our region); and the Upper East Coast, a citrus-growing area with the cities of Stuart and Ft Pierce. A fifth sub-region, the "Rest of Florida," consists of the 54 remaining Florida counties. A REMI economic model was constructed for these five sub-regions from historical data for the years 1969 to 1996, and this computer model was the basic tool of analysis.

The four South Florida sub-regions were also summed to form a single consolidated South Florida region, which, added together with the Rest of Florida, formed an economic model for the entire state. For the purpose of forecasting, our basic economic tools consisted of the five sub-regional models and the two "consolidated" regional models. The counties and the grouping of the economic models are shown schematically in Figure 2.1a and in map form in Figure 2.1b.

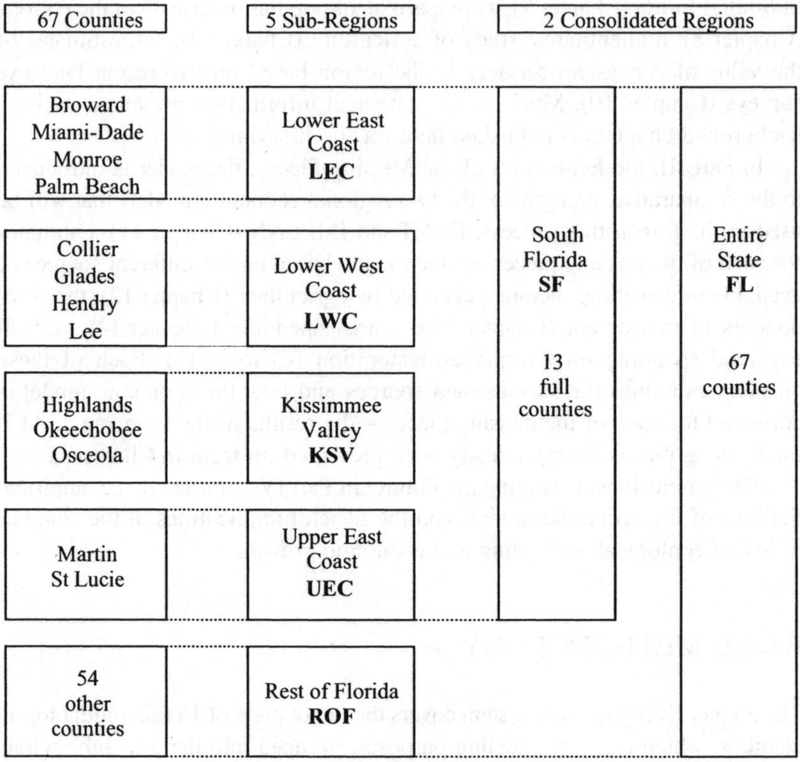

67 Counties	5 Sub-Regions	2 Consolidated Regions	

Broward Miami-Dade Monroe Palm Beach	Lower East Coast **LEC**	South Florida **SF**	Entire State **FL**
Collier Glades Hendry Lee	Lower West Coast **LWC**	13 full counties	67 counties
Highlands Okeechobee Osceola	Kissimmee Valley **KSV**		
Martin St Lucie	Upper East Coast **UEC**		
54 other counties	Rest of Florida **ROF**		

Figure 2.1a   Composition of the Regional Models

The REMI model for each of the five basic sub-regions was programmed "at the factory" and provides a stable and slow-growing trajectory for the future years – in this case, 1997 through 2035 – for 14 basic economic sectors[1] and the hundreds of economic and demographic variables available for each sub-region. The fundamental model is known as the REMI control or "REMI base," and it is intended to project the growth of each of the sub-regions in the absence of any exogenous shocks or major new projects. The REMI control is used as the yardstick for comparing the economy "with" and "without" any given program or policy, for example, new spending on a factory or a change in tax rates.

But this internally-generated growth path captures only the ongoing activities whose impacts gradually play out in the future years. In order to permit the introduction of other data that are found at the state or county level, REMI equips its models with an "employment update" (EU) option that allows the analyst to incorporate independent forecasts of employment growth for the 14 basic sectors for each region.

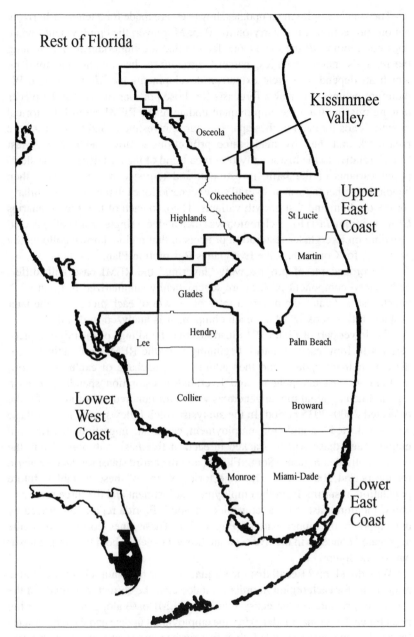

Figure 2.1b   South Florida Counties and Regions in the Economic Model

The state's employment updates, however, are made for a ten-year horizon, but our projections must carry on to 2035. Moreover, the employment update does not capture *all* the exogenous factors that are important in determining the region's major activities, namely, agriculture, investment, and tourism, which all depend to a great extent on developments *outside* the region. We therefore estimated our own forecasts for those portions of each of the pieces that are missing from the employment update of the REMI control. Historical growth trends for each of these pieces – farm, investment, and tourism – were measured, and then we made three projections – slow, medium, and fast "pace" relative to the historically-observed trend of the past decade. The slow-paced variants of the farm, investment, and tourist components were then bundled together to form an overall slow scenario for each region, and similarly for the medium and fast growth variants. Then, to each of the three scenarios (slow, medium, fast) for each region was then added a single profile of expected spending on Everglades restoration projects in that region, known colloquially as CERP, for Comprehensive Everglades Restoration Plan.

The procedures of progressively "layering" the REMI base with differently-paced component profiles are schematically summarized in Figure 2.2, which also indicates the different rates of growth of each piece, and the later chapter in this book in which each component is analyzed in detail.

The lower part of Figure 2.3 illustrates the "bundling" of the missing piece variants to form each scenario, beginning with the REMI base, adjusted for the employment update, and then adding each package of exclusively slow, medium, or fast components and Everglades restoration spending in each region. Each regional model generates values for hundreds of variables for the projected 2000–2035 period. In the analysis which follows, only four of these will be selected – population, employment, economic migration, and regional output – and these will be tracked in each of five basic sub-regions and the two consolidated regions (South Florida and the entire state) for each scenario for the period 2000–2030. The trajectories of one of these variables, future population, resulting from the employment adjustment and the three scenarios (slow, medium, fast) for the consolidated South Florida region, are traced by the graph in the upper part of Figure 2.3. These lines correspond to the aggregated concepts in the five separate boxes labeled in bold type in the lower part of the figure.

Why do all this? Recall that the ultimate goal is to obtain reliable economic projections for each region in order to understand the correct magnitude of the economic pressure on the ecosystem. The REMI base alone is but a starting point for each regional model. After the employment update and the adjustments for each component are added, then two further questions shall be addressed: which of the alternatives – the slow, medium, or fast – is more likely, and how do these projections, based on adding the missing pieces to a regional economic

| **Regional Control** "REMI base" | The basic REMI forecast, given for 1997–2007 for all regions. Our starting point. (See Chapters 11–12.) |

| **Employment Update** EU | Set new employment totals for 14 sectors for 1997–2007 for all regions, from Fl. Labor Dept. (Chapter 12). |

Farm			3 sub-pieces: projections of (1) farm income; (2) farm employment; (3) indirect farm inputs computed from IMPLAN models of the 4 regions; for 2000–2035, all regions (Ch. 12).
S	M	F
slow	med	fast
1%	2%	4%
aver. growth rate		

Investment			3 categories: residential and non-residential construction and producer durables, each adjusted for differences from REMI EU base for 2000–2035, all regions (Ch. 13).
S	M	F
slow	med	fast
0.25	0.5	1.0
historical trend		

Tourism			Increase tourist spending on 6 categories of expenditure due to new visitors for 2000–2035 for all regions (Ch. 14).
S	M	F
slow	med	fast
1%	2%	3%
aver. growth rate		

| **Everglades Restoration** CERP | Allocate programmed spending for construction, real estate fees, engineering services, operation & maintenance (O&M) (excluding land purchases) for 2002–2035 for all regions (Ch. 15). |

Figure 2.2   Missing Pieces and their Adjustments

model, compare to the forecasts currently being used in the region? Once these basic questions are answered, we shall then use the new economic forecasts to estimate future water use and the demand for urban land.

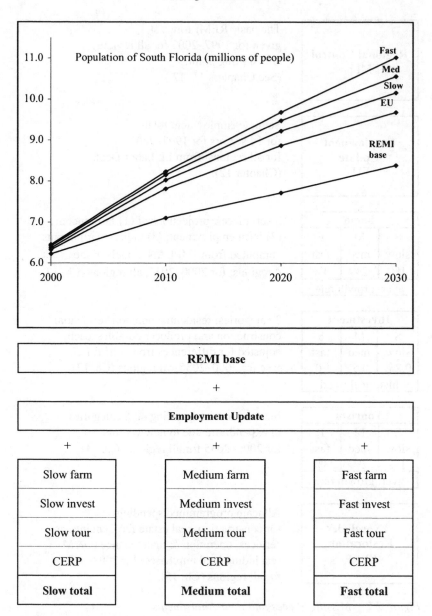

*Figure 2.3   Projecting the Final Scenarios and the Missing Pieces
to 2030*

OVERALL RESULTS OF THE SCENARIOS, MAJOR REGIONS

Tables 2.1 and 2.2 summarize the trajectories by reporting the results of the beginning and ending year (2000 and 2030) for four variables (population, employment, economic migrants, and regional output) for the five program scenarios (REMI base through fast growth) in all seven regions.

We shall walk the reader through one set of results and then summarize the features for the remaining regions. Top Panel A in Table 2.1 refers to the entire State of Florida. Line 1 gives actual statewide totals for year 2000 population, employment, economic migrants,[2] and regional output measured in constant 1992 prices. Line 2a gives the basic, unadjusted REMI control forecast for the year 2030 for each variable, along with the percentage change from the year 2000. Line 2b gives the impact on the statewide variables due to employment updating for each of the five underlying regions according to Florida Department of Labor's ten-year employment forecasts, aggregated to correspond to the REMI's 14 sectors. This employment update model results in a significant increase over the unadjusted REMI base for 2030 in the population, employment, and output variables, but a negative change in the number of economic migrants.

The employment update model (line 2b) then serves as the new base onto which the three different growth scenarios are built. These results appear in lines 2c, d, and e. The final population for 2030, then, lies between 26.6 and 28.7 million people or an increase ranging from 66.2 to 79.8 percent over the year 2000 population. Employment by 2030 is projected to be between 12.3 and 13.6 million, an increase of 37.1 to 51.9 percent over the figure for the year 2000. New economic migrants could range from 33.8 to 140.8 thousand, and regional output is projected to rise from 100.8 to 129.1 percent in real terms over the year 2000 base.

For South Florida (Panel B in Table 2.1), which is the sum of four sub-regions, the increases in population, employment, and regional output are of the same order of increase over the base as in the all-Florida model (Panel A). The range of the projected population for South Florida is between 10 and 11 million for 2030, employment between 4.7 and 5.2 million, and regional output double or more the present level.

Turning now to the results for the four basic regions of South Florida (Table 2.2), we note that the population of the Lower East Coast (LEC) in Panel A, which consists of the three heavily populated counties of Miami-Dade, Broward, and Palm Beach plus Monroe (the Keys), is projected to approach 8 million people. Employment could reach 4 million, and regional output could more than double.

Table 2.1 Summary of Final Scenarios, Florida and South Florida, 2000 and 2030

	Population		Employment		Economic migrants		Regional output	
	thou.	% chge. row 1	thou.	% chge. row 1	thou.	% chge. row 1	bill $92	% chge. row 1
A. Florida								
1. Actual, 2000	15 982	—	8 951	—	98.1	—	515	—
2. Models, 2030								
a. REMI base	22 123	38.4	10 103	12.9	24.1	−75.4	820	59.0
b. Empl. update	25 388	58.9	11 699	30.7	21.2	−78.4	994	92.9
c. Slow growth	26 557	66.2	12 272	37.1	33.8	−65.5	1 035	100.8
d. Medium growth	27 530	72.3	12 820	43.2	63.3	−35.5	1 088	111.1
e. Fast growth	28 732	79.8	13 599	51.9	140.8	43.5	1 181	129.1
B. South Florida								
1. Actual, 2000	6 444	—	3 465	—	9.8	—	212	—
2. Models, 2030								
a. REMI base	8 391	30.2	3 840	10.8	2.1	−78.6	331	56.1
b. Empl. update	9 691	50.4	4 474	29.1	−1.2	−112.2	403	90.1
c. Slow growth	10 160	57.7	4 702	35.7	5.0	−49.0	420	98.1
d. Medium growth	10 559	63.9	4 919	42.0	14.3	45.9	441	108.0
e. Fast growth	11 021	71.0	5 208	50.3	41.2	320.4	475	124.1

Sources:

Line 1 (Actual 2000): Population from Census; employment from REIS CD-ROM (May 2002); economic migration from BEBR, fsa 2001, T. 1.75. "Net Migration Flows" based on IRS filing data. Regional output from REMI base.

Line 2.a. from REMI control.

Line 2.b. adjusted from data from Florida Department of Labor.

Lines 2.c–e. adjusted for all "missing pieces" at different rates of growth (see Chapters 12–15).

Table 2.2 Summary of Final Scenarios, Four South Florida Regions, 2000 and 2030

	Population		Employment		Economic migrants		Regional output	
	thou.	% chge.	thou.	% chge.	thou.	% chge.	bill $92	% chge.
A. 1. LEC actual, 2000	5 090	—	2 819	—	-5.9	—	180	—
2. a. Models, 2030: base	6 420	26.1	3 099	9.9	4.8	-181.4	281	56.1
b. Empl. update	7 355	44.5	3 581	27.0	1.2	-120.3	341	89.4
c. Slow growth	7 551	48.3	3 681	30.6	1.2	-120.3	350	94.4
d. Medium growth	7 807	53.4	3 836	36.1	10.0	-269.5	367	103.9
e. Fast growth	8 098	59.1	4 036	43.2	28.4	-581.4	394	118.9
B. 1. LWC actual, 2000	739	—	388	—	14.3	—	19	—
2. a. Models, 2030: base	1 081	46.3	446	14.9	-1.0	-107.0	30	57.9
b. Empl. update	1 309	77.1	549	41.5	-0.6	-104.2	39	105.3
c. Slow growth	1 478	100.0	635	63.7	3.6	-74.8	44	131.6
d. Medium growth	1 586	114.6	678	74.7	3.6	-74.8	47	147.4
e. Fast growth	1 716	132.2	748	92.8	5.9	-58.7	54	184.2
C. 1. KSV actual, 2000	295	—	113	—	3.5	—	5	—
2. a. Models, 2030: base	445	50.8	139	23.0	0.3	-91.4	9	80.0
b. Empl. update	489	65.8	152	34.5	0.3	-91.4	10	100.0
c. Slow growth	560	89.8	183	61.9	2.0	-42.9	11	120.0
d. Medium growth	557	88.8	180	59.3	1.8	-48.6	11	120.0
e. Fast growth	582	97.3	190	68.1	3.0	-14.3	12	140.0
D. 1. UEC actual, 2000	319	—	145	—	-2.2	—	7	—
2. a. Models, 2030: base	445	39.5	156	7.6	-1.9	-13.6	11	57.1
b. Empl. update	538	68.7	192	32.4	-2.1	-4.5	14	100.0
c. Slow growth	575	80.3	207	42.8	-1.8	-18.2	15	114.3
d. Medium growth	602	88.7	221	52.4	-0.8	-63.6	15	114.3
e. Fast growth	630	97.5	237	63.4	1.0	-145.5	17	142.9

Sources: See Table 2.1.

27

The Lower West Coast (LWC), Panel B, consisting of the two coastal counties of Collier and Lee plus the two interior counties of Hendry and Glades, is projected to grow faster than the other regions, reaching a population between 1.5 to 1.7 million and employment between 635 000 to 748 000 by 2030. Its regional output is projected to grow by 132 percent in the slow growth scenario to 184 percent in the fast growth scenario.

The two other sub-regions, the Kissimmee Valley (KSV), Panel C, and the Upper East Coast (UEC), Panel D, are of similar economic, but not geographic size. The KSV consists of the three interior counties, which stretch from Lake Okeechobee to the suburbs of Orlando, while the UEC consists of two coastal counties, Martin and St Lucie. Both sub-regions are primarily agricultural, with year 2000 populations around 300 000 and employment ranging from 113 000 in the KSV to 145 000 in the UEC. In the fast scenarios for both regions, population is projected to almost double, employment to rise by two-thirds, and regional output to increase by 140 percent.

The contributions to employment from the different components for the slow scenario for all Florida and South Florida are given in Figures 2.4 and 2.6, respectively. Note that despite the steep historical climb from 1969 to 1997, the latest historical year of our data, the basic model then slows down on its own after 1998, suggesting that *internally*-generated growth provides only a limited impetus for the future growth of the regional economies. The correction for employment update provides the biggest boost from 1997 to 2010, and thereafter, its forecast of employment also tapers off. The forecasts for the missing pieces of farming, investment, tourism, and Everglades restoration (CERP) result in modest increments in employment "on top of" the employment update base. (The contributions of each component for each scenario and each region are given in Appendix Tables A.1–A.3.)

Figures 2.4 and 2.6 trace the broad sweep of the years 1969 to 2035. The trajectories for the years 1996 to 2035 are magnified in Figures 2.5 and 2.7, which trace the contributions to *new* employment by each component for Florida and South Florida, respectively, for the slow scenario. The "notch" or steep decline in the year 2001 for the *increase* due to tourism reflects the 9/11 events when tourism spending stagnated, but did not fall. The topmost overlay for Everglades restoration reflects the net contribution that this spending will make to employment once the state and regional tax contributions are subtracted.

The contributions to growth by three of the missing pieces (farming, investment, and tourism) for the three growth scenarios for the single year 2030 are summarized in Table 2.3. For all of Florida (columns 1–3), farming is responsible for almost a majority of the increase in both population and employment in the slow scenario (column 1, lines A.5 and B.5). By contrast, it is investment in the fast scenario (column 3) that contributes 51 percent of the new population and 56 percent of the new employment (lines A.6 and B.6), while the share of farming falls from 49 percent to around 27 percent for both population and employment (lines A.5 and B.5) and the share of tourism rises from 13 percent to 21 percent for population and to 16.5 percent for employment in the fast scenario (lines A.7 and B.7).

In South Florida (Table 2.3, columns 4–6), the conclusions are similar. The share that farming contributes to both new population and employment falls from 51 percent for the slow scenario to around 29 percent for the fast scenario. The share that investment makes to the increase in population rises from 36 to 45 percent and to the increase in employment from 37 to 51 percent from slow to fast scenarios. The major difference between the two regions is the more pronounced rise in the share of tourism in South Florida. In both regions, tourism contributes around 13 percent of the increases in both population and employment in the slow scenario. This share rises to 26 percent for population and 21 percent for employment in the fast scenario for South Florida compared to less dramatic increases in the statewide model. The composition of each of these components and different rates of growth will be examined in detail in Chapters 12 through 14.

The trajectories of population growth resulting from the medium and fast scenarios for all Florida are shown in Figures 2.8 and 2.9, respectively. The adjustment for employment update plus the differing impacts of the missing pieces set the overall population onto more steeply inclined paths than the flatter REMI-base, especially in the years until 2012. For the single year 2030, the numerical and percentage contributions of the major components in the statewide model appear on the left side of Panel A of Table 2.3.

COMPARING POPULATION AND EMPLOYMENT PROJECTIONS

How credible are the population and employment projections generated by the regional economic model? To what can they be compared? The Bureau of Economic and Business Research (BEBR) of the University of Florida in Gainesville publishes decennial population projections for all Florida counties until the year 2030 for three demographic scenarios (low, medium, and high),[3] and annual employment projections on a county basis through the year 2015.[4] In Table 2.4, we compare our REMI-missing pieces population projections, identified in bold print with a prefix "W" (for Weisskoff) and "slow," "med," or "fast" for each of the six regions for the decade benchmark years, 2000 through 2030. The population series in roman type, labeled "B" for the corresponding regions, are BEBR's "low," "med," "high" for the same years. It should be recalled that the BEBR population series are demographic projections based on births and deaths, plus an overlay for historical immigration.

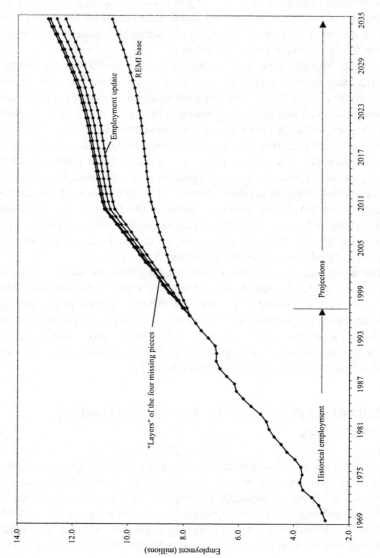

Figure 2.4   *Employment Projections for Florida at Slow Rates*

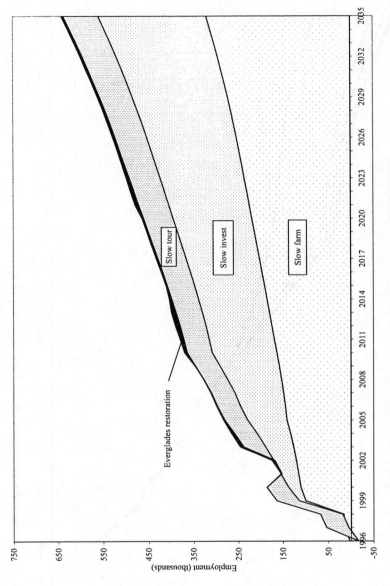

Figure 2.5   Florida: Differences from the Employment Update, 1996–2035

Slow tour

Slow invest

Slow farm

Everglades restoration

Employment (thousands)

750
650
550
450
350
250
150
50
-50

1996   1999   2002   2005   2008   2011   2014   2017   2020   2023   2026   2029   2032   2035

31

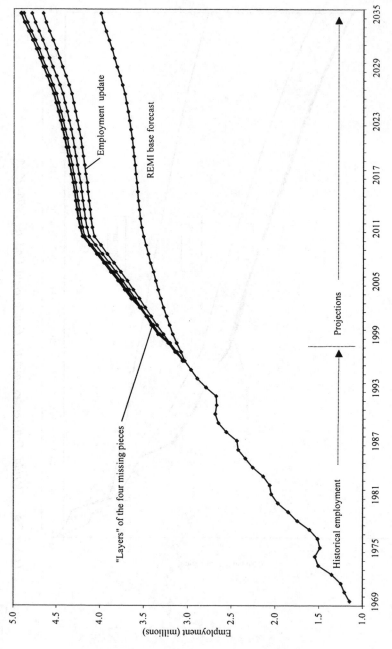

Figure 2.6   Employment Projections for South Florida at Slow Rates

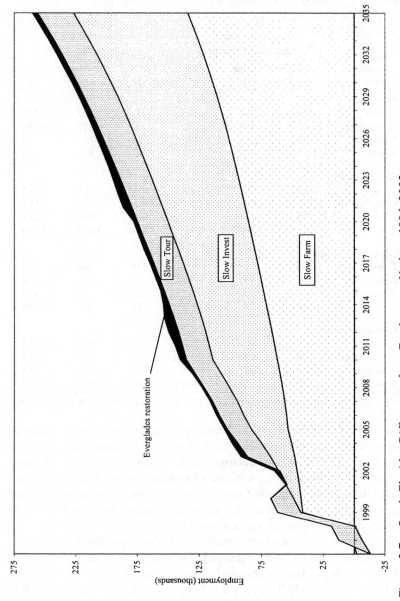

Figure 2.7 South Florida: Differences from Employment Update, 1996–2035

Table 2.3 Contributions to Growth by the Three Components, 2030

Economic variable and missing piece	Florida increase from employment update			South Florida increase from employment update		
	slow (1)	medium (2)	fast (3)	slow (4)	medium (5)	fast (6)
A. Population (thou.)						
1. Farm	566	794	960	235	313	391
2. Investment	438	884	1691	167	322	593
3. Tourism	158	458	686	60	227	340
4. Sum	1162	2136	3337	462	862	1324
Distribution (%)						
5. Farm	48.7	37.2	28.8	50.9	36.3	29.5
6. Investment	37.7	41.4	50.7	36.1	37.4	44.8
7. Tourism	13.6	21.4	20.6	13.0	26.3	25.7
8. Sum	100.0	100.0	100.0	100.0	100.0	100.0
B. Employment (thou.)						
1. Farm	280	417	515	114	162	208
2. Investment	215	490	1067	82	177	371
3. Tourism	73	209	313	28	102	152
4. Sum	568	1116	1895	224	441	731
Distribution (%)						
5. Farm	49.3	37.4	27.2	50.9	36.7	28.5
6. Investment	37.9	43.9	56.3	36.6	40.1	50.8
7. Tourism	12.9	18.7	16.5	12.5	23.1	20.8
8. Sum	100.0	100.0	100.0	100.0	100.0	100.0

Source: REMI model adjusted for employment update and each missing piece. See Appendix A.1.

While revised annually, the basic demographic information can be confirmed only at the decennial census years, and these serve to readjust the long-term projections. (The BEBR methodology will be reviewed in Chapter 8 below.)

Our REMI population projections, by contrast, are the product of demographic data plus economic and non-economic migration components. In that way, our scenarios, comprised of various components for each region, can generate more jobs which, in turn, require that more workers (and their families) be "drawn into" the region, resulting in a higher population. The BEBR projections are intended to be extra-inclusive; that is, their range is so vast so as to include the widest possible performance of all of Florida's 67 counties. For the whole state, BEBR's forecasts for the year 2030 range from 21.6 to 27.1 million and for South Florida, from 7.9 to 13.0 million. The low estimates in past years have generally proved unrealistically low, and the low estimates for the year 2010 will probably be surpassed by the middle of the present decade. The medium forecasts are generally taken as most probable, and the high as less credible.

In the case of our own projections, our slow scenario corresponds to a "severe recession" scenario, as the growth rates of the components were set to be a quarter or a third of the historically observed rates. The medium is slightly less than the recent trends, and the high is a continuation of the recent trends. Continuation of the recent Florida boom is a likely scenario if all the units of government can manage to promote growth through new combinations of policies, incentives, and public investments. Here it is our intent to show the *consequences* of the pursuit of such policies, which are being successfully implemented at the present time.

The finding that our economic projections are broadly consistent with the state's demographic projections gives us confidence in our method. It also warns that the state may be understating the true pace of long-range growth, which is more consistent with the historical economic record than with their long-range demographic forecasts.

For all of Florida, our slow population exceeds BEBR's low and medium projections for 2030, and our medium and high forecasts exceed BEBR's high (Table 2.4, top panel). But for South Florida and for three of its sub-regions, our three trajectories tend to be grouped together, with our slow being higher than BEBR's medium and our high being lower than BEBR's high. Only in the large LEC (Lower East Coast) does our slow projection fall below BEBR's medium figure for 2030.

The finding that our high estimate, which I tend to favor as the more realistic trajectory, is lower than BEBR's high, puts a realistic "upper cap" on BEBR's otherwise "open-ended" forecast. (We shall examine the implications of these population projections on water demands in Chapter 3 and the need for urban land in Chapter 4.)

A series of sketches illustrates graphically the findings of Table 2.4. In Figure 2.10, the record of Florida's historical population is plotted for 1970 to 2000 in solid lines and three BEBR trajectories from 2000 to 2030, labeled "B-high," "B-med," and "B-low," are plotted in dashed lines. In Figure 2.11, the period 2000 to 2030 has been magnified and my own low, medium, and high projections in solid lines are superimposed. While my medium and high forecasts for all Florida (Figure 2.11) fall above BEBR's high for the first two decades, they all taper downward with my low projection for 2030 falling below BEBR's high.

When the same comparison is repeated for BEBR's forecasts aggregated for our 13 South Florida counties (Figure 2.12) and our own forecasts superimposed in solid lines for 2000–2030, then we note their "grouping" between BEBR's medium and high throughout the period (Figure 2.13). The same relative effect may be noted in the four sub-regional sketches. In all cases, our

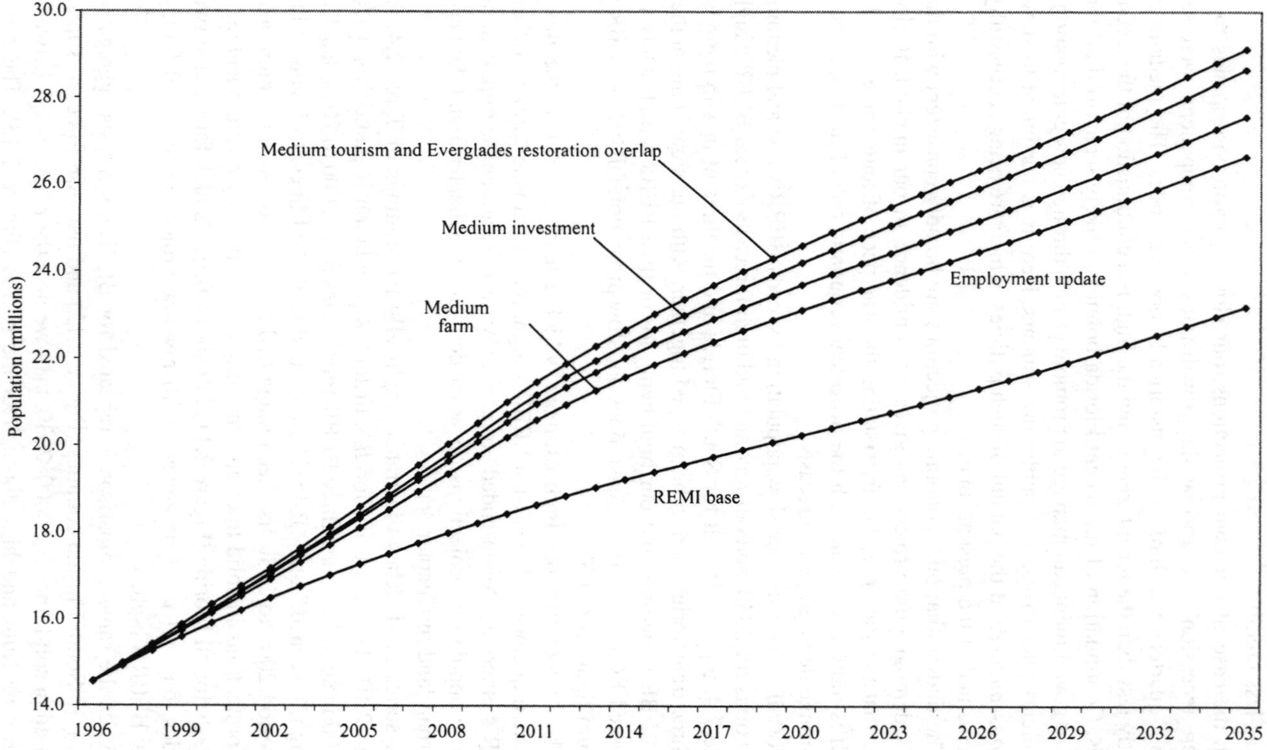
Population (millions)
30.0
28.0
26.0
24.0
22.0
20.0
18.0
16.0
14.0
1996
1999
2002
2005
2008
2011
2014
2017
2020
2023
2026
2029
2032
2035
Medium tourism and Everglades restoration overlap
Medium investment
Medium
farm
Employment update
REMI base

Figure 2.8 Florida Population Growth: Medium Rates, All Missing Pieces

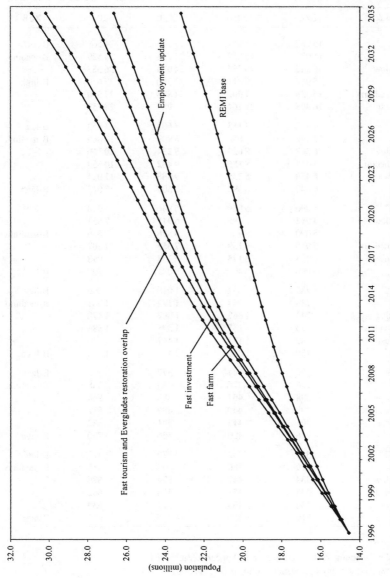

Figure 2.9   Florida Population Growth: Fast Historical Rates, All Missing Pieces

37

Findings and Forecasts

Table 2.4   Comparisons of our Population Projections to BEBR, 2010–30

Weisskoff	2000	2010	2020	2030	BEBR
FL	15 982	17 847	19 773	21 568	B-low
	15 982	18 867	21 793	24 529	B-medium
W-slow	**16 245**	**20 754**	**24 024**	**26 557**	
	15 982	19 811	23 590	27 050	B-high
W-medium	**16 338**	**21 002**	**24 598**	**27 530**	
W-fast	**16 405**	**21 164**	**25 088**	**28 732**	
SF	6 442	7 113	7 603	7 853	B-low
	6 442	7 654	8 909	10 089	B-medium
W-slow	**6 367**	**8 029**	**9 224**	**10 160**	
W-medium	**6 417**	**8 156**	**9 482**	**10 559**	
W-fast	**6 450**	**8 235**	**9 688**	**11 021**	
	6 442	8 390	10 605	13 015	B-high
LEC	5 090	5 526	5 846	5 998	B-low
W-slow	**4 992**	**6 105**	**6 911**	**7 551**	
	5 090	5 939	6 826	7 656	B-medium
W-medium	**5 010**	**6 159**	**7 055**	**7 807**	
W-fast	**5 025**	**6 195**	**7 173**	**8 098**	
	5 090	6 491	8 081	9 799	B-high
LWC	739	892	1 010	1 090	B-low
	739	954	1 172	1 381	B-medium
W-slow	**743**	**1 069**	**1 302**	**1 478**	
W-medium	**773**	**1 135**	**1 395**	**1 586**	
W-fast	**789**	**1 173**	**1 467**	**1 716**	
	739	1 050	1 403	1 793	B-high
KSV	296	344	377	393	B-low
	296	375	459	538	B-medium
W-slow	**298**	**407**	**490**	**560**	
W-medium	**299**	**409**	**489**	**557**	
W-fast	**301**	**413**	**501**	**582**	
	296	420	566	730	B-high
UEC	319	352	370	373	B-low
	319	386	452	515	B-medium
W-slow	**334**	**447**	**524**	**575**	
W-medium	**335**	**451**	**538**	**602**	
W-fast	**336**	**455**	**549**	**630**	
	319	430	555	693	B-high

Sources:

W-slow, medium, fast projections from Appendix Tables A.1–3.
B-low, medium, high projections from BEBR, fsa 2002, T. 1.41.

projections fall between the medium and high by the end of the period. In the Lower East Coast and the Kissimmee River Valley (Figures 2.14 and 2.16), the grouping is toward BEBR's medium; in the Lower West Coast (Figure 2.15), the three are spread evenly between BEBR's high and medium. In the Upper East Coast (Figure 2.17), the three exceed BEBR's high in 2010 but are distributed between BEBR's medium and high by 2030.

A similar sketch for BEBR's employment forecasts from 1996 through 2015 is shown in the dashed line in Figure 2.18 with our low, moderate, and high forecasts in solid lines. All our projections are higher than BEBR's for all years, due perhaps to a difference in definition and database. However, when the rates of growth (rog) implicit in BEBR's forecasts are applied to the REIS (Regional Economic Information System) employment base – which is also used by the REMI model, then this "new REIS–BEBR hybrid" yields a trajectory that coincides with our medium and high projections for all Florida (Figure 2.19) but exceeds our high forecasts for the Lower East Coast (Figure 2.20). Again, the proximity of our figures to the state's forecasts lends support to their credibility in that the models are derived with totally different methodologies.

The drawback of the REIS–BEBR hybrid is that it is a short series, ending in 2015. Using our own decade points for all Florida employment from Table 2.1 and Appendix Table A.1, we plot the results for our three scenarios in Figure 2.21. This figure begins in 2000 and broadens the range of the all-Florida trajectories until 2030. Note that the REIS 2000 data correspond to our high projection (that is, fully corrected for employment update and the missing pieces), and the REIS–BEBR hybrid falls a little above our low forecast for 2010. In the decade 2010–2020, employment growth is projected to slow but resumes a stronger upward movement by 2030.

Having compared our forecasts to the state's own estimates for similar concepts in the available overlapping years, we now turn in the next two chapters to the implications of this "future economy" on the demands for water and urban space.

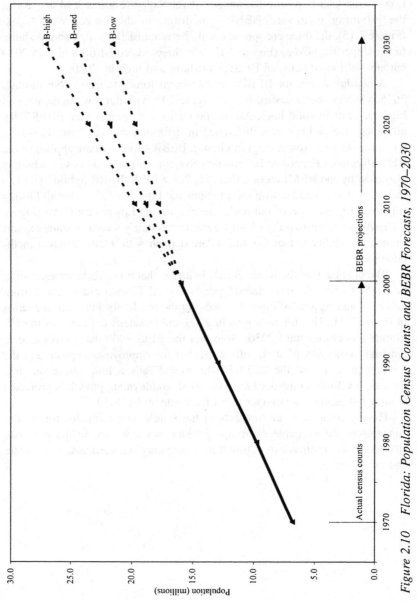

Figure 2.10   Florida: Population Census Counts and BEBR Forecasts, 1970–2030

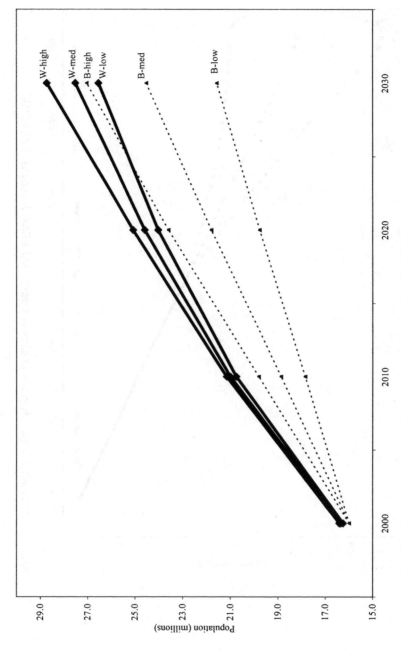

Figure 2.11   Florida: Comparison of Population Forecasts, 2000–2030

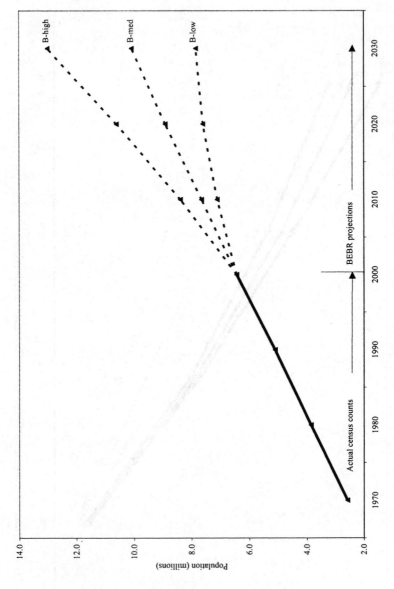

Figure 2.12   South Florida: Population Census Counts and BEBR Forecasts, 1970–2030

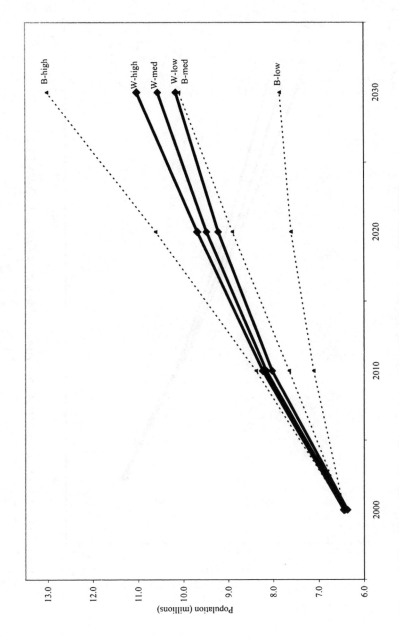

Figure 2.13   South Florida: Comparison of Population Forecasts, 2000–2030

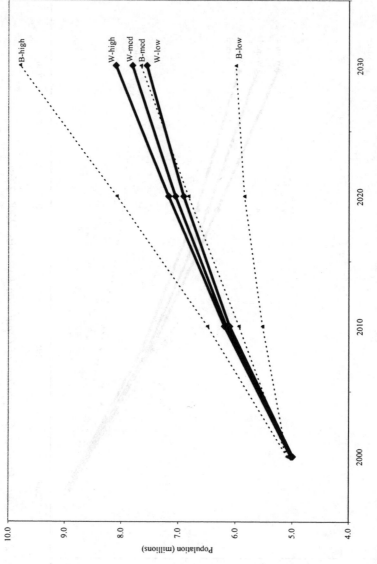

Figure 2.14 Lower East Coast: Comparison of Population Forecasts, 2000–2030

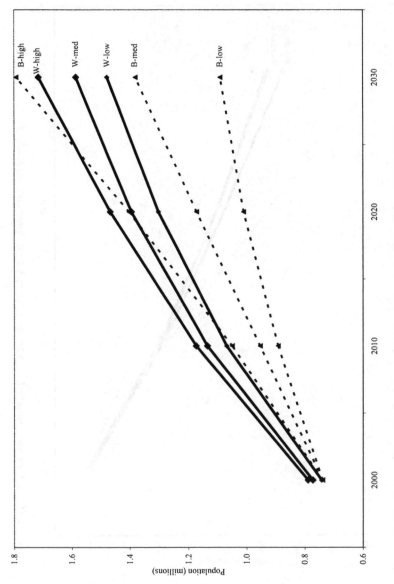

Figure 2.15   Lower West Coast: Comparison of Population Forecasts, 2000–2030

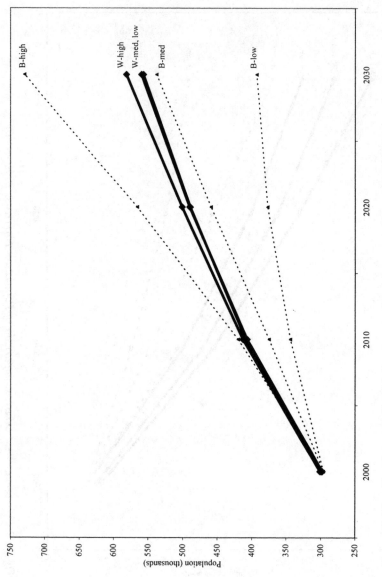

Figure 2.16   Kissimmee Valley: Comparison of Population Forecasts, 2000–2030

46

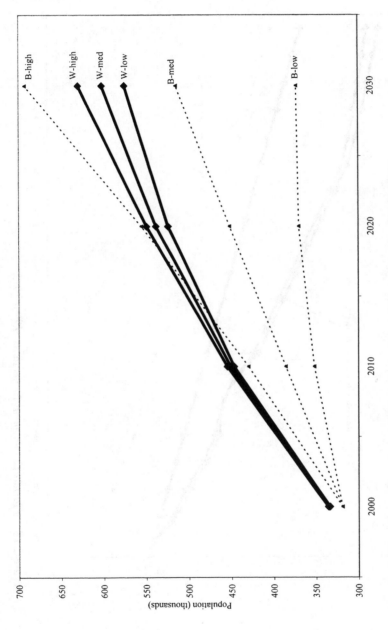

Figure 2.17   Upper East Coast: Comparison of Population Forecasts, 2000–2030

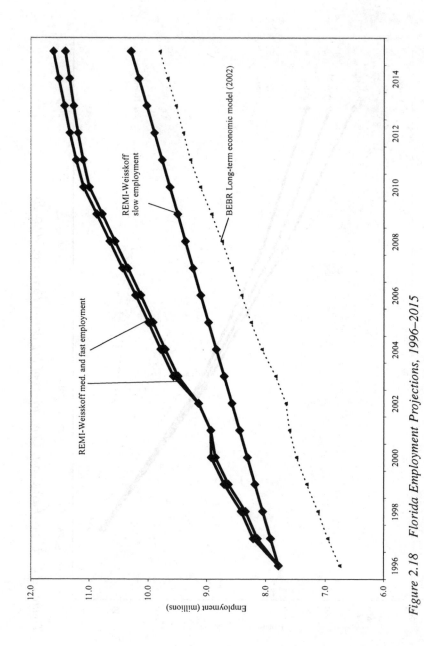

Figure 2.18   Florida Employment Projections, 1996–2015

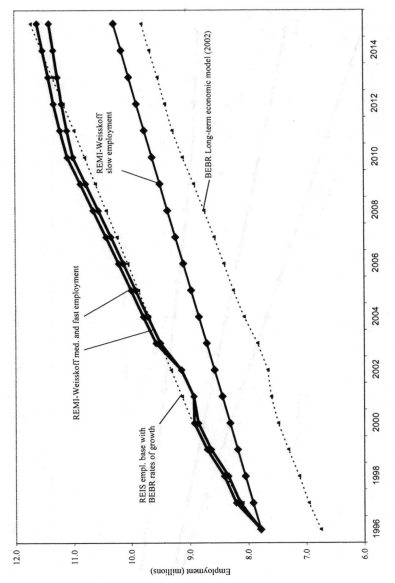

Figure 2.19   Comparing Florida Employment Projections

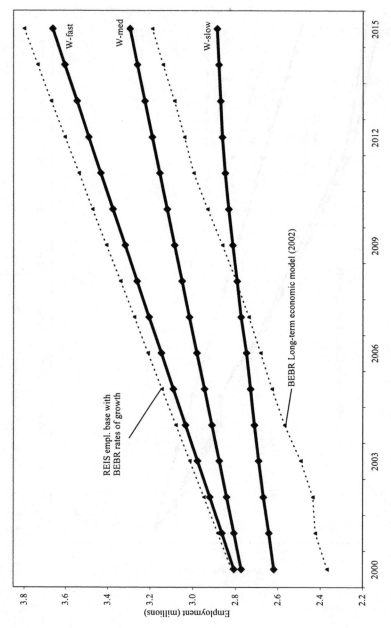

Figure 2.20   Comparing Lower East Coast Employment Projections

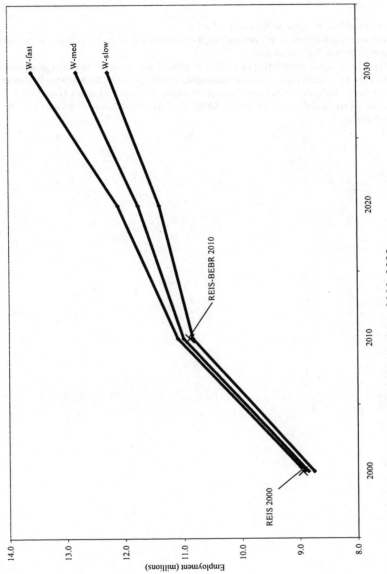

Figure 2.21   Florida Employment Projections, 2000–2030

51

NOTES

1. The 14 sectors are given in Appendix Table F.1.
2. The annual number of people moving into the region due to economic reasons, as opposed to military transfers and retirees.
3. These are released every spring in BEBR's Population Studies series and are reproduced in the annual *Florida Statistical Abstract* (fsa) which usually appears by the following December.
4. The latest employment projections for counties appear in BEBR's *Florida's Long-Term Economic Forecast 2002* (2002a), vol. 2. BEBR has announced that it is discontinuing this publication.

3. Forecasting the Demand for Water

THE GENERAL METHOD

In the previous chapter, we projected the population, employment, immigration, and output in seven regions for three different levels of activity by including "missing pieces" in the REMI standard regional economic model. In this chapter, we use those projections to estimate the amount of freshwater the future economy will require.

In order to do this, we must first estimate the trends in the historical relationship between water and the economic variables. Once these requirements of "water per person," "water per employee," and "water per dollar of output" are estimated, then projections of the future demand for water can be made using the population, employment, and outputs from the earlier chapter. We shall sum the economic projections of the first four basic regions (LEC, LWC, KSV, UEC) to construct the "South Florida" region, and, with the addition of the fifth basic region ("Rest of Florida") that includes all the remaining counties, we will estimate demands for an "All Florida" model as well. We shall concentrate on the medium and high-level forecasts for the main three economic indicators.

We shall divide total water needs into two parts, public supply (PS), that is, water delivered by the public utilities, and all other freshwater uses ("rest of the fresh"), the latter consisting of six groups of users: (1) domestic self-supply; (2) self-supply for commerce, industry, and mining; (3) agricultural self-supply; (4) recreation and landscape self-supply; and (5) power generation. All freshwater withdrawals will be considered. Excluded is all saline water, which is of considerable importance in power generation in the coastal counties.

Our method is to connect observed freshwater use, expressed in millions of gallons per day (mgd), to the three different economic measures – people (the population), jobs (employment), and money (gross regional product or GRP, in 1992 dollars). Ideally, water use in each economic sector should be coupled with the appropriate economic variable that best "explains" its historical record. For example, residential water demand depends primarily on the population. Water use in the transport sector (cruise ships, airport) and mining (rock quarrying) could be related to employment or output of those sectors. In this study, however, we were not yet able to estimate *sectoral* coefficients for water for each region. Instead, we estimated the "*total* population–*total* water," "*total* jobs–*total* water," and "*total* output–*total* water" relationships for each regional economy over time. We then use these "technical coefficients" and their changes to estimate total future water demands.

FORECASTING PUBLIC SUPPLY

We began by aggregating *water use data* for "PS" (public supply) and "rest of the fresh" for 1970 through 2000 for all the counties corresponding to our five basic regions. Then, for each five-year interval from 1970 to 2000, we estimated coefficients for water per person, water per job, and water per $GRP. We then projected these three sets of economy-wide coefficients for each region for the period 2010–30 on the basis of the rate of change observed in these coefficients in the latest four periods. Extensive use was made of the most recent and historical USGS data for the counties.

Projections of the technical coefficients were made on a case-by-case basis for each region, adjusting the future coefficients to trends measured from the data for the previous decades. A further adjustment was made for increasing the *coverage* of public water supply to a greater share of residents in a region, reflecting growing urbanization and the widening outreach of the utilities to the more remote residences.

The results of PS are given in Table 3.1 for the five basic and two aggregated regions. For each region, the historical supply of water in mgd for the years 1970–2000 appears in the central column. Alternative projections of water demand for the years 2010 through 2030 using employment (em), population (pop), and output (q) at each two levels, medium (m) and high (h), are arranged horizontally in ascending order from left to right for each region.

Three benchmarks from other forecasts are also introduced as boundaries for our estimates. The codes, "usgs-m" and "usgs-h," refer to the latest USGS forecasts for 2020 for each region[1] and are themselves based on BEBR's medium and high projections of population, respectively. The "sfwmd" estimates for 2020 are taken from the latest Water Supply Plan for each South Florida planning region.[2] The county forecasts for individual counties within each region have been aggregated to correspond to the counties in our four regions.[3]

Two extreme patterns can be discerned from these results. In the case of the State of Florida model (lowest left-hand panel), the USGS-medium and USGS-high estimates set the outer boundaries within which all our estimates fall for 2020. Close to this pattern are the cases of the LEC and SF in which only the "employment-medium" ("em-m") results are lower than the "usgs-m" for 2020, and the "usgs-h" forms the upper bound. In the LEC, however, the single "sfwmd" estimate (1215 mgd) for 2020 is close to the high end, whereas for SF, the "sfwmd" estimate (1361 mgd) is close to the lower boundary.

A second pattern is illustrated in the KSV, the Kissimmee Valley region, in which the three benchmarks, ("usgs-m," "sfwmd," and "usgs-h") are *all* lower than any of the forecasts made with the economic model. This could be due to our difficulty in estimating the true "water-output coefficients" for a primarily agricultural region. Or, our model could be giving a clear warning that the economic trajectory can be expected to generate more demand for water than currently expected.

In four of the regions – LWC, KSV, UEC, and SF – the single "sfwmd" forecasts for 2020 all fall close to the BEBR medium ("usgs-m") range, whereas *our* projections, based on employment, output, and population, generally forecast *much higher* levels of demand. Only in one case, that of LEC, are our economic forecasts almost all lower than that of the "sfwmd."

This analysis should make us comfortable and uneasy at the same time: comfortable, because our projections do fall in the same ballpark as both USGS and "sfwmd;" uneasy, because the USGS is based on conservative BEBR population forecasts that have been since updated and on fixed water per person coefficients that have been changing over time. Moreover, the range of the USGS estimates is so wide, reflecting the range of the underlying BEBR population estimates, that they offer little guidance as to practical policy. The single "sfwmd" forecast per region for 2020, on the other hand, falls toward the *lower* bound of this wide range, while our economy-based forecasts tend to fall near the high range – except in the case of the LEC.

In conclusion, therefore, our estimates suggest that the demand for public water supply is likely to increase to a much greater degree than is presently expected.

Three figures illustrate the findings of Table 3.1. In Figures 3.1–3.3, we have plotted the historical series of Public Water Supply for 1970 to 2000 in solid lines and the six different forecasts in the small-dashed lines from 2000 to 2030. The six forecasts for each region are derived by applying the three economic variables (population, output, and employment) to the forecasted coefficients of "water per economic variable," each at two levels of growth (medium and high). The result is therefore a range of forecasts that, in Figures 3.1–3.3, is compared to the benchmarks given by the USGS, represented by the hollow diamonds, and the "sfwmd," represented by the black circles.

In both the LEC and SF (Figures 3.1 and 3.2), only the PS forecasts based on employment-medium fall below the 2020 forecast made by "usgs-m" (the lower diamond). By comparison, the forecasts made on the basis of output-high fall far below the upper boundaries of the "usgs-h," represented by the upper

Table 3.1 Public Supply (PS) History, 1970–2000, and Forecasts, 2010–30, All Regions (mgd)

Region

Lower East Coast (LEC)

Year	em-m	usgs-m	em-h	pop-m	q-med	pop-h	sfwmd	q-h	usgs-h
1970	372.0								
1975	500.8								
1980	624.6								
1985	674.3								
1990	695.2								
1995	795.8								
2000	882.2								
2010	1041.7		1086.7	1130.8		1072.5		1175.3	
2020	1056.7	1139.6	1143.1	1195.5	1214.9		1303.3		1532.1
2030	1098.5	1238.0	1252.7	1297.5	1299.4				1497.6

Lower West Coast (LWC)

Year	usgs-m	sfwmd	em-m	q-m	em-h	pop-m	pop-h	usgs-h	q-h
1970			15.8						
1975			31.0						
1980			51.2						
1985			60.3						
1990			82.8						
1995			84.4						
2000			110.0						
2010			145.2	152.4	156.6	161.7	173.7		182.5
2020	133.7	154.8	156.7	166.4	176.3	185.4	193.9	199.4	212.3
2030			173.0	183.6	187.7	198.5	235.7		259.6

Kissimmee River Valley (KSV)

Year	usgs-m	sfwmd	usgs-h	em-m	em-h	q-m	pop-m	pop-h	q-h
1970				8.0					
1975				9.0					
1980				11.4					
1985				16.8					
1990				22.6					
1995				29.4					
2000				41.4					
2010				51.9	57.7	58.6	63.6	64.3	65.0
2020	38.4	40.1	54.0	57.0	68.2	68.3	80.2	81.5	83.6
2030				63.6	79.9	82.6	98.4	102.5	102.8

Upper East Coast (UEC)

Year	em-m	usgs-m	sfwmd	em-h	q-m	pop-m	pop-h	usgs-h	q-h
1970	5.9								
1975	11.9								
1980	15.8								
1985	20.2								
1990	28.1								
1995	29.3								
2000	36.4								
2010	45.9			50.0	50.2	54.2	55.7		56.2
2020	47.4	49.2	54.4	54.7	55.8	64.0	71.3	73.5	75.1
2030	50.4			62.3	64.0	79.5	90.5		94.7

South Florida (SF)

Year	em-m	usgs-m	sfwmd	em-h	pop-m	q-med	pop-h	q-h	usgs-h
1970	401.7								
1975	552.7								
1980	703.1								
1985	771.5								
1990	828.7								
1995	939.0								
2000	1070.0								
2010	1284.7			1369.0	1342.9	1391.0	1355.4	1475.7	
2020	1317.9	1360.9	1464.5	1465.4	1507.2	1486.7	1539.6	1659.9	1851.3
2030	1385.5			1615.8	1625.1	1631.8	1695.4	1939.3	

Rest of Florida (ROF)

Year	usgs-m	em-m	q-m	em-h	q-h	usgs-h	pop-m	pop-h
1970		481.7						
1975		590.6						
1980		703.3						
1985		913.9						
1990		1096.5						
1995		1126.3						
2000		1366.8						
2010		1667.1	1759.5	1809.3			1844.2	1856.3
2020	1526.9	1738.1	1785.4	1918.0	1977.7	2044.6	2240.4	2282.6
2030		1852.9	1891.2	2148.4	2243.2		2585.2	2698.8

Florida (FL)

Year	usgs-m	em-m	q-m	em-h	pop-m	q-h	pop-h	usgs-h
1970		883.4						
1975		1143.3						
1980		1406.4						
1985		1685.4						
1990		1925.2						
1995		2065.3						
2000		2436.8						
2010		2951.8	3119.1	3128.5	3187.1		3211.7	
2020	2887.8	3056.0	3272.1	3383.4	3637.6	3747.6	3822.2	3895.9
2030		3238.5	3523.0	3764.2	4182.6	4210.4	4394.2	

Notes:

Water forecasts using model's economic variables: em-m = Employment, medium; em-h = Employment, high; pop-m = Population, medium; pop-h = Population, high; q-m = Output, medium; q-h = Output, high. Benchmark forecasts given by: usgs-m = US Geological Survey, medium; usgs-h = US Geological Survey, high; sfwmd = South Florida Water Management District.

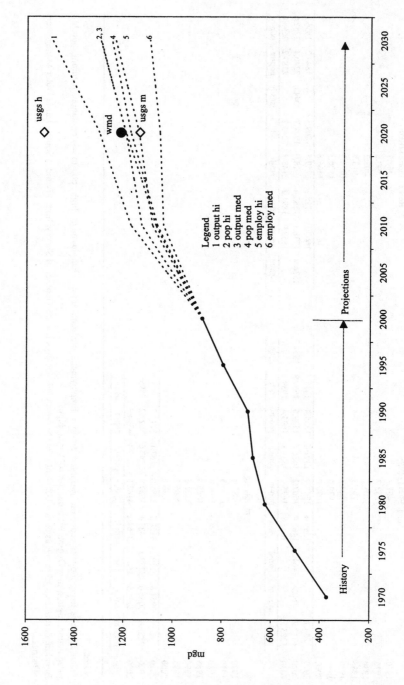

Figure 3.1   Projections of Public Water Supply: Lower East Coast

58

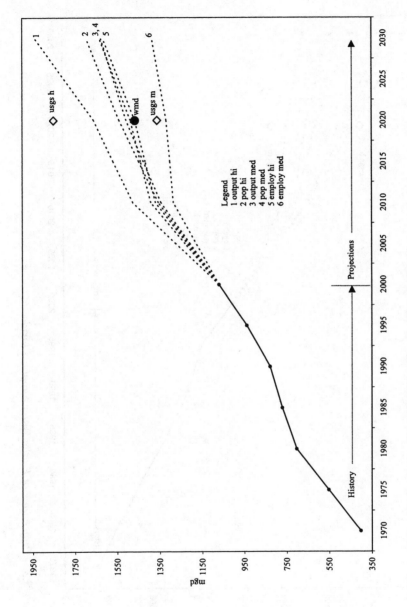

Figure 3.2 Projections of Public Water Supply: South Florida

59

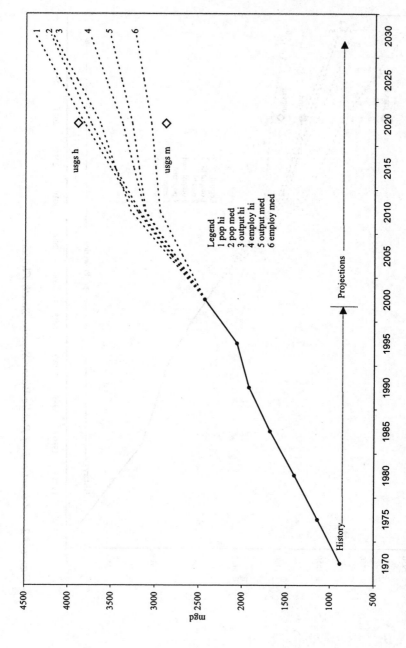

Figure 3.3   Projections of Public Water Supply: Florida

60

diamond. In the LEC, however, the large black circle of the "sfwmd" forecast, labeled "wmd" for "water management district," falls close to the "pop-hi" and above all but one of our forecasts. In SF, the "wmd" marker coincides with "employ-hi" and is below our other four forecasts.

For all of Florida (Figure 3.3), three of our forecasts climb rather steeply and come close to the "usgs-h" benchmark for 2020. Our three slower trajectories, however, are still higher than the "usgs-m" benchmark for 2020. (There is no "sfwmd" benchmark for the all-Florida forecasts.)

TECHNICAL COEFFICIENTS – PUBLIC SUPPLY

The technical coefficient of water, that is, the amount of water required per economic unit, is a key factor in the forecasting methodology. The ratio of the annual regional public water use to each of the three economic indicators for the corresponding region and year, respectively, gives the historical movement of this relationship, the last fifteen years of which were used for predicting future changes in the coefficients themselves. Table 3.2 gives the array of technical coefficients, both historical and projected, for the three economic variables (population, employment, and output) for the regions.

From the historical coefficients for 1970 to 2000 found in the top-most panel of Table 3.2, we note a convergence of values of "water per population served" among the regions, ending with KSV as the highest (0.191 mgd/thou. persons) and UEC the lowest (0.167 mgd/thou. persons) for the year 2000.

The share of the regional population served (the bottom-most panel of Table 3.2) indicates a wide range in the actual and projected coverage for the regions. In the UEC, only 66 percent of the population was served by 2000, in comparison to the 75 percent coverage in the KSV and 97 percent in the LEC in 2000. The continuing upward trend in coverage in the KSV to 85 percent by 2030, together with that region's *increasing* trend in the water coefficients, explain the unexpected increase in demand for PS in the Kissimmee Valley. For the other regions (LEC, LWC, UEC, FL), the coefficients of water/people, water/employment, and water/output either *fell* or have been roughly stable since 1985.

The fact that PS water demands are expected to increase despite the general fall in "water intensity" is due to the pace at which the economy is growing as well as to the increasing share of the population served by the public utilities.

Table 3.2   Coefficients of PS and Economic Variables, 1970–2030

	LEC	LWC	KSV	UEC	FL
Water/population served (mgd per thou. people)					
1980	0.199	0.217	0.186	0.190	0.178
1985	0.193	0.196	0.169	0.246	0.174
1990	0.177	0.193	0.150	0.190	0.170
1995	0.189	0.174	0.176	0.165	0.171
2000	0.183	0.181	0.191	0.167	0.172
2010	0.177	0.166	0.197	0.167	0.171
2020	0.170	0.152	0.202	0.167	0.170
2030	0.164	0.139	0.208	0.167	0.168
Water/employment (mgd per thou. empl.)					
1970	0.345	0.219	0.346	0.177	0.298
1975	0.383	0.300	0.277	0.256	0.310
1980	0.367	0.332	0.255	0.229	0.299
1985	0.340	0.287	0.263	0.231	0.289
1990	0.313	0.302	0.276	0.252	0.282
1995	0.326	0.268	0.313	0.246	0.273
2000	0.323	0.293	0.386	0.263	0.284
2010	0.317	0.300	0.397	0.263	0.282
2020	0.312	0.308	0.408	0.263	0.279
2030	0.307	0.315	0.419	0.263	0.277
Water/output (mgd per bill. 92$)					
1970	5.724	4.323	9.424	3.715	5.633
1975	6.339	6.191	7.218	5.136	5.760
1980	6.032	6.486	6.332	4.341	5.464
1985	5.427	5.601	6.010	4.414	5.043
1990	4.906	5.879	6.358	4.743	4.888
1995	5.014	5.212	6.926	4.652	4.612
2000	4.632	5.309	7.966	4.713	4.489
2010	4.337	5.150	8.191	4.713	4.149
2020	4.060	4.995	8.422	4.713	3.834
2030	3.801	4.844	8.660	4.713	3.543
Percentage of population served					
1980	0.95	0.74	0.51	0.54	0.80
1985	0.94	0.75	0.62	0.42	0.85
1990	0.95	0.81	0.72	0.58	0.87
1995	0.93	0.82	0.71	0.63	0.85
2000	0.97	0.82	0.75	0.66	0.88
2010	0.98	0.83	0.80	0.74	0.89
2020	0.98	0.83	0.83	0.82	0.90
2030	0.98	0.83	0.85	0.90	0.91

Sources and Methods: Coefficients for 1970–2000 were estimated on the basis of water used and population served from USGS files. Employment and output are from REMI model database. Coefficients for 2010–30 are the author's projections, based on the observed trends of most recent 15 years, when plausible.

FORECASTING "REST OF FRESHWATER" WITHDRAWALS

For the sum of the other categories of freshwater withdrawals ("Rest of Freshwater" [RF]), we followed a method similar to that outlined above for estimating PS. The results of the forecasts are given in Table 3.3 and the technical coefficients in Table 3.4. Since the USGS issued no forecasts of water withdrawals other than PS, we have only the "sfwmd" estimates for 2020 for each region to use as benchmarks with our own projections.[4]

We turn now to the forecasts for the "Rest of Freshwater" withdrawals (Table 3.3). For all the regions, the water/employment variable ("em-m") gives the lowest estimate of water demand for the forecasted years 2010 through 2030, and the water/output variable ("q-h") gives the highest, except in the KSV, where population ("p-h") gives the highest estimate of future water needs.

The "sfwmd" benchmark forecasts for 2020, published in the water supply plans, fall generally in the middle or at the high end of our array of forecasts for each region, except in the case of the LWC. In the LWC, the "sfwmd" forecast (1225 mgd) is lower than our low-end moderate employment ("em-m") forecast (1320 mgd) and far short of our upper-end high-output ("q-h") projection of 2111 mgd. The "sfwmd," by basing its forecast primarily on expected acreage increases, might be understating the growing economy's full impact on water demands.

Figures 3.4–3.6 illustrate some of these trends for two of the regions and the whole state. In the LEC (Figure 3.4), the black dot of the "wmd" forecast falls short of the high output forecast for 2020. The five other economic projections are lower than the "wmd" benchmark. In the larger SF region (Figure 3.5), the "wmd" forecast falls in the lower middle range of our economic projections, with the variables of output and population forecasting much higher water use and employment more modest increases. In the case of all Florida, which covers all the water management districts, Figure 3.6 illustrates the wide spread among the forecasts of the economic models that range from 20 700 to 35 300 mgd by 2030, all in contrast to the year 2000 usage of 14 100 mgd.

TECHNICAL COEFFICIENTS – REST OF THE FRESHWATER

The technical coefficients for RF in Table 3.4 show a much wider range of values than those of PS in Table 3.2. This is due to the importance and intensity of agriculture in some regions that are not accurately captured in any of the

Table 3.3 "Rest of Freshwater" (RF), History, 1970–2000, and Forecasts, 2010–2030, All Regions (mgd)

Region: Lower East Coast (LEC)

Year	em-m	pop-m	q-m	em-h	sfwmd	pop-h	q-h
1970	594.8						
1975	758.7						
1980	808.4						
1985	761.4						
1990	1110.8						
1995	1022.4						
2000	1267.5						
2010	1512.2	1577.7	1537.6	1546.6		1819.6	1891.2
2020	1560.8	1688.3	1761.3	1790.8	2155.3	2056.1	2240.2
2030	1650.7	1860.2	1949.1	2021.7		2382.2	2749.6

Region: Lower West Coast (LWC)

Year	em-m	pop-m	q-m	em-h	sfwmd	pop-h	q-h
1970	384.6						
1975	494.8						
1980	521.1						
1985	417.2						
1990	866.9						
1995	914.4						
2000	867.4						
2010	1252.3	1469.1	1497.4	1524.9		1574.6	1759.6
2020	1319.5	1654.2	1678.8	1874.2	1225.1	1971.0	2110.6
2030	1422.0	1923.1	1937.8	2130.8		2304.2	2660.5

Region: Kissimmee River Valley (KSV)

Year	em-m	pop-m	q-m	em-h	sfwmd	pop-h	q-h
1970	231.6						
1975	335.3						
1980	345.3						
1985	288.7						
1990	195.8						
1995	240.0						
2000	212.7						
2010	239.4	252.6	269.9	278.3		270.2	273.0
2020	235.6	254.5	281.6	298.9	286.7	291.3	331.2
2030	235.6	261.9	295.7	325.0		331.9	384.5

Region: Upper East Coast (UEC)

Year	em-m	pop-m	q-m	em-h	sfwmd	pop-h	q-h
1970	281.3						
1975	459.6						
1980	423.0						
1985	401.0						
1990	446.1						
1995	450.6						
2000	442.2						
2010	498.8	525.9	532.9	543.8		530.3	576.2
2020	461.8	546.8	517.9	532.8	590.0	558.8	594.4
2030	439.2	535.4	520.2	542.7		560.5	646.1

South Florida (SF)

Year	em-m	em-h	sfwmd	pop-m	pop-h	q-m	q-h
1970			1596.1				
1975			2058.4				
1980			2041.1				
1985			1775.3				
1990			2663.7				
1995			2600.1				
2000			2925.7				
2010	3502.7	3888.8		3858.6	3924.6	4074.2	4505.4
2020	3577.7	4181.5	4257.1	4473.7	4482.8	4651.7	5244.1
2030	3747.5	4636.5		4947.1	5087.3	5270.9	6381.2

Florida (FL)

Year	em-m	em-h		pop-m	pop-h	q-m	q-h
1970			4728.9				
1975			5524.9				
1980			11822.6				
1985			10883.1				
1990			13138.4				
1995			12364.6				
2000			14075.4				
2010	18506.8	19614.2		19492.5	19642.7	22454.8	23648.8
2020	19333.3	21404.6		22830.0	23284.8	25490.7	28337.5
2030	20672.9	24029.4		25551.3	26666.9	29699.0	35258.7

Rest of Florida (ROF)

Year	em-m	em-h		pop-m	pop-h	q-m	q-h
1970			3132.9				
1975			3466.5				
1980			9781.5				
1985			9107.8				
1990			10474.7				
1995			9764.5				
2000			11149.7				
2010	15004.1	15725.4		15633.9	15718.1	18380.6	19143.4
2020	15755.6	17223.1		18356.3	18633.0	21007.9	23093.4
2030	16925.4	19392.9		20604.2	21396.0	24611.7	28877.4

Notes:

Water forecasts using model's economic variables: em-m = Employment, medium; em-h = Employment, high; pop-m = Population, medium; pop-h = Population, high; q-m = Output, medium; q-h = Output, high.

Benchmark forecasts given by: sfwmd = South Florida Water Management District.

Methods: Public Supply was subtracted from total freshwater withdrawals for each county and summed to get regions for 1970–2000. Weisskoff–REMI projections of pop, employment, and output for medium and high scenarios were then applied to the corresponding coefficients. Coefficients were usually averages of the last three or four historical years for stability.

65

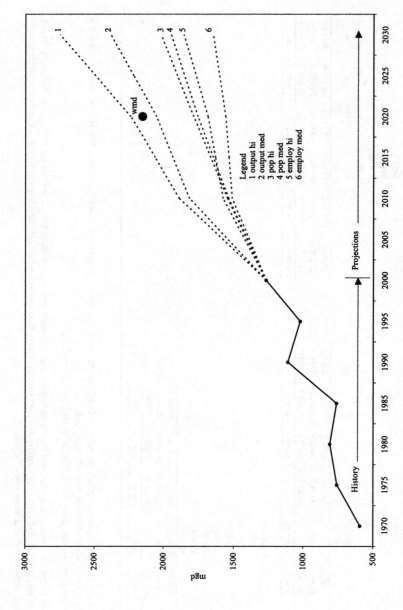

Figure 3.4   Projections of "Rest of Freshwater" Demand: Lower East Coast

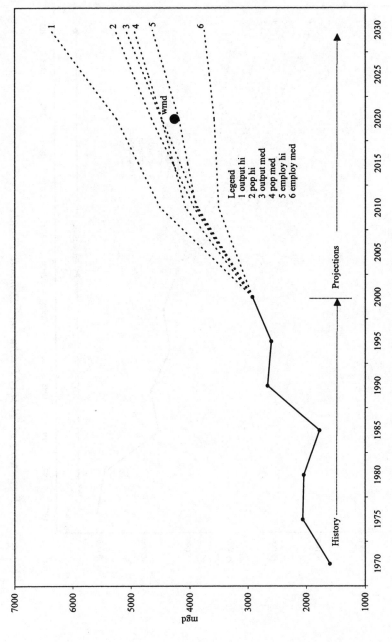

Figure 3.5 Projections of "Rest of Freshwater" Demand: South Florida

67

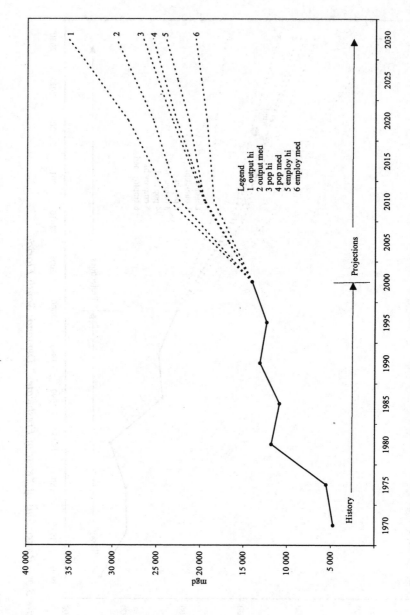

Figure 3.6 Projections of "Rest of Freshwater" Demand: Florida

three economic variables – population, employment, and output – that we are using in this analysis. The coefficient, for example, of water/population served in the LEC in 2000 was 0.255 mgd/thou. persons, which is one-third the technical coefficient of 0.732 for KSV and one-fifth of the value of 1.178 for the LWC.

The extremely high water/population coefficients for the three regions in contrast to LEC do not indicate extreme "water wasting" on the part of their population in contrast to "water efficiency" by the LEC. On the contrary, high water consumption per person reflects rather a relatively small consuming population and other water-intensive users not associated with population, employment, or output. These include intensive use of water for farming and cattle grazing, landscape and recreational demand (golf courses), industry (rock mining, construction), and domestic self-supply (rural or suburban homes using wells).

Similarly, the coefficients of water/employment and water/output are much lower for the LEC than the LWC, KSV, or UEC. For these variables, it is the UEC that appears the most water-intensive region.

The coefficients for all three economic models (Table 3.4) and the forecasts resulting from their projections (Table 3.3) are presented because it is not obvious which model is the most "appropriate" predictor. Is it population, which is defective because it excludes tourists and seasonal residents? Is it employment, which grows more slowly than population but fluctuates with the business cycle? Or is regional output in 1992 dollars the correct economic variable, although output captures the value of all economic activity, water using or not? My instinct is that the high-output and high-population models represent the upper limits of probable demand for the indicated years, and the employment variables capture the conservative end. Growth in these counties has tended toward the high end in the past.

OTHER INFORMATION – RF

The two bottom-most panels of Table 3.4 summarize some other interesting information regarding the RF component of total water withdrawals. The ratio, "ground in RF: (all ground + surface freshwater)," gives the shares of groundwater to total freshwater withdrawals. Note, for example, that in the LEC and UEC in the year 2000, 18.9 and 19.9 percent, respectively, of RF was drawn up from the ground in contrast to the 51.2 percent in the LWC and 84.6 percent in the KSV. (The rest of the water supply comes from the surface.)

The lower-most panel gives the ratio of PS to RF for each year and region. Only in the LEC is the supply by PS equal to 70 percent of the other uses. In the other regions, PS amounts to no more than 8 to 13 percent of RF.

Table 3.4   Coefficients of RF, All Regions, 1970–2030

	LEC	LWC	KSV	UEC	SF	FL
Water: population served (mgd per thou. people)						
1970	0.258	2.375	3.443	3.528	0.610	
1975	0.262	2.068	3.445	2.389	0.614	
1980	0.244	1.626	2.894	1.830	0.522	
1985	0.206	1.013	1.809	1.422	0.397	
1990	0.267	1.648	0.938	1.106	0.518	
1995	0.226	1.536	1.015	0.996	0.462	
2000	0.255	1.178	0.732	0.849	0.462	
2010	0.250	1.344	0.661	1.166	0.473	
2020	0.250	1.344	0.596	1.018	0.472	
2030	0.250	1.344	0.537	0.889	0.469	
Water: employment (mgd per thou. empl.)						
1970	0.551	5.323	10.000	8.451	1.321	
1975	0.580	4.783	10.391	9.939	1.382	
1980	0.475	3.374	7.738	6.124	1.035	
1985	0.384	1.984	4.501	4.600	0.757	
1990	0.500	3.165	2.395	4.003	0.990	
1995	0.419	2.902	2.553	3.788	0.876	
2000	0.464	2.313	1.984	3.196	0.873	
2010	0.461	2.591	1.829	2.861	0.861	
2020	0.461	2.591	1.685	2.560	0.849	
2030	0.461	2.591	1.553	2.292	0.838	
Water: output (mgd per bill. 92$)						
1970	9.153	105.228	272.435	177.166	22.456	
1975	9.602	98.824	270.403	199.047	23.507	
1980	7.806	65.959	192.475	115.917	17.460	
1985	6.128	38.766	103.016	87.795	12.469	
1990	7.838	61.519	55.111	75.424	16.117	
1995	6.442	56.447	56.479	71.511	14.020	
2000	6.656	41.848	40.967	57.254	13.056	
2010	6.979	49.645	35.849	50.061	13.227	
2020	6.979	49.645	31.371	43.772	12.885	
2030	6.979	49.645	27.452	38.273	12.617	
Ratio: ground in RF: (all ground + surface freshwater)						
1970	0.400	0.285	0.187	0.167	0.286	0.430
1975	0.238	0.424	0.493	0.138	0.303	0.408
1980	0.290	0.515	0.561	0.219	0.371	0.518
1985	0.298	0.437	0.836	0.235	0.376	0.607
1990	0.277	0.505	0.880	0.272	0.405	0.581
1995	0.270	0.436	0.887	0.225	0.371	0.551
2000	0.189	0.512	0.846	0.199	0.364	0.574

(continued)

Table 3.4   Coefficients of RF, All Regions, 1970–2030 (continued)

	LEC	LWC	KSV	UEC	SF	FL
Ratio: public supply (PS) to "rest of freshwater" (RF)						
1970	0.625	0.041	0.024	0.021	0.252	0.187
1975	0.660	0.063	0.026	0.026	0.268	0.207
1980	0.773	0.098	0.039	0.037	0.344	0.119
1985	0.886	0.144	0.086	0.050	0.435	0.155
1990	0.626	0.096	0.094	0.063	0.311	0.147
1995	0.778	0.092	0.138	0.065	0.361	0.167
2000	0.696	0.127	0.119	0.082	0.366	0.173

Method: Coefficients were computed by dividing the mgd flows for each region by the relevant economic variable for that year. Values for 1970–2000 are historical; values of the coefficients for 2010–30 are averages of the latest three or four observations, or they are estimated by projecting the rate of growth of latest three observations. Coefficients of 2010–30 were used to compute forecast mgd, with the exception of SF forecasts, which are the sums of sub-regions divided by each forecast economic variable. Ratios for the 1970–2000 series (bottom two panels) were computed from USGS water files.

The importance of this observation is that the PS water withdrawals are actual recorded numbers reported by the public utilities. The historical RF series are numbers "constructed" by computer models. In the case of agriculture, for example, "water withdrawals" are derived from data regarding crop acreage, type of irrigation system, the weather, and soil characteristics. In Florida, the nationally calibrated models favored by the USDA are now being replaced by a University of Florida model that has been extensively field tested in only one major north central county.[5] The accuracy of these water-use models in South Florida has yet to be verified, as well as the degree to which water use depends on different management practices specific to each crop.

If the supply of water was truly unlimited, then the estimates of future demand and the technical coefficients on which they are based, as well as the basic historical record of usage, would all be of little concern. But the national debate now has turned to assuring farmers, the cities, and the advocates of the natural system that no one will be prejudiced by the Everglades restoration. Therefore, it has become essential to know the actual record of measured usage rather than continue to rely on estimates made by computer simulations calibrated with national rather than local data.

The incentives and charges associated with introducing "best management practices" in the Everglades Agricultural Area (EAA) have dramatically changed the quantity and quality of the water discharges.[6] One wonders how much "give" there is in actual practice with farm operators in our regions and how much water could be saved by agriculture, construction, and golf courses in response to price and other incentives with very modest changes in technologies.

FORECASTING TOTAL FRESHWATER WITHDRAWALS

The total freshwater withdrawals, which are the sum of PS and RF, are given in Table 3.5 for all the regions. Again, we shall rely on the "sfwmd" benchmarks, shown in Figures 3.7–3.12 by the location of the black circle labeled "wmd" for the water management district. Note that in the cases of the LEC and UEC (Figures 3.7 and 3.10) the black "wmd" spot is on the high end of our projections. In the KSV (Figure 3.9), the "wmd" spot falls in the lower range of our forecasts. In the LWC (Figure 3.8), the "wmd" spot for 2020 falls below all of our economic forecasts of water demand. For all of South Florida (Figure 3.11), the "wmd" benchmark falls close to the middle of all our forecasts. For all of Florida (Figure 3.12), there is no benchmark, but a majority of our forecasts indicate a high growth of total freshwater demand.

In all of South Florida (Table 3.5), total freshwater demand was 4000 mgd in the year 2000, and this could reach as high as 6900 mgd by 2020 (as opposed to the "sfwmd" forecast of 5722 mgd), and 8321 mgd by 2030. This implies a percentage increase in water demand for SF ranging from 68.2 percent for the medium output ("q-med") forecast to 108.2 percent for the high output ("q-h") forecast. These percentages are lower than the percentages of growth found in the medium and high forecasts of output alone, which are 108.0 and 124.1 percent, respectively, as computed in Table 2.4. Taken together, the rate of change in water use relative to the rate of change in output implies a long-run elasticity between 0.631 and 0.872 with respect to output for SF.

For the LWC, the percentage increase in water demand is 116.0 percent in the medium output model and 198.7 percent for the high model. The regional output itself is forecast to rise 147.4 and 184.2 percent, respectively, for the medium and high output models. The long-run elasticity of demand for water with respect to output, therefore, ranges from 0.787 to 1.079 in the LWC, higher than the general SF elasticities.

These elasticities may be viewed as "fixed" only in the sense that they represent the consequences of unfettered growth continuing "full steam ahead" with no interruption and no change in policy. The introduction of "pricing" water as a scarce commodity, monitoring, charging for withdrawals above certain levels, or encouraging water-saving practices through incentives could lead to radically different forecasts.

Note that all this addresses only the demand side of the picture, that is, how much water the regional and state *economy* would *need* to continue its forward march at the different historically-observed paces. We have said nothing about the supply side or the ability or desirability of meeting these needs.

Is there enough water? Would certain well-fields collapse before reaching those limits, as has happened in the Tampa Bay area recently? Will saltwater intrusion contaminate the coastal supplies and lead to heavier than expected reliance on wells further inland, closer to the Everglades? None of those issues is explored here.

But if the demand for water is expected to grow by 108 percent in SF, does that not mean that wastewater will also grow by a similar magnitude? Much of the water will be absorbed back into the agricultural fields and eventually "recharge" the ground supplies. Much of it will be discharged into the canals and flow downstream and eventually reach the Everglades or exit into the coastal waters, the estuaries, or Biscayne Bay. Here we are addressing only the total *quantity* of water, all of which will be compromised in some way by the usual contaminants that characterize both urban and rural water use today.

By measuring the range of future demands for freshwater, we are implicitly measuring the derived demand for services to treat, clean, and dispose of the increasing levels of wastewater in the context of a fragile environment. Indeed the current reliance on massive injections of partially-treated wastewater into deep wells[7] under such conditions of rapid urban growth may no longer be possible. So, too, the public cost of correctly treating wastewater, if factored into the basic price of water supply, might lead the public to seek a reduction of freshwater consumption in the first place, not only because of supply and environmental considerations, but also to reduce the amount of wastewater that needs to be treated.

It is therefore crucial that the public understand the full dynamics of economic growth and its implications for water supply and water disposal.

Table 3.5   All Water (PS + RF), History, 1970–2000, and Forecasts, 2010–30 (mgd)

Region — Lower East Coast (LEC)

Year	Value
1970	966.8
1975	1259.5
1980	1433.1
1985	1435.6
1990	1806.0
1995	1818.2
2000	2149.7

Year	em-m	em-h	pop-m	pop-h	q-med	sfwmd	q-h
2010	2553.9	2664.4	2603.9	2619.1	2950.3		3066.5
2020	2617.5	2831.4	2937.2	2986.3	3252.3	3370.1	3543.5
2030	2749.2	3098.2	3201.8	3321.1	3679.6		4247.2

Region — Lower West Coast (LWC)

Year	Value
1970	400.4
1975	525.8
1980	572.3
1985	477.4
1990	949.8
1995	998.8
2000	977.4

Year	em-m	em-h	pop-m	pop-h	q-med	sfwmd	q-h
2010	1397.5	1621.5	1671.1	1681.5	1736.3		1942.2
2020	1476.2	1820.6	1878.2	2050.5	2156.3	1380.2	2323.0
2030	1595.0	2110.7	2173.6	2314.4	2502.7		2920.2

Region — Kissimmee River Valley (KSV)

Year	Value
1970	239.6
1975	344.3
1980	356.7
1985	305.5
1990	218.4
1995	269.4
2000	254.1

Year	em-m	em-h	pop-m	pop-h	q-med	sfwmd	q-h
2010	291.3	310.3	328.5	341.9	334.5		338.0
2020	292.7	322.8	349.8	379.1	372.9	329.6	414.8
2030	299.2	344.5	375.6	427.6	430.2		487.3

Region — Upper East Coast (UEC)

Year	Value
1970	287.2
1975	471.5
1980	438.8
1985	421.1
1990	474.1
1995	479.9
2000	478.6

Year	em-m	em-h	pop-m	pop-h	q-med	sfwmd	q-h
2010	583.1	586.5	593.8	581.6	544.6		630.4
2020	573.7	587.6	620.4	633.9	509.2		658.4
2030	584.2	605.0	625.9	655.3	489.6		725.6

South Florida (SF)

	em-m	em-h	sfwmd	pop-m	q-med	pop-h	q-h
1970			1997.7				
1975			2611.0				
1980			2744.2				
1985			2546.8				
1990			3492.4				
1995			3539.1				
2000			3995.7				
2010	4787.4	5257.8		5201.5	5465.2	5279.9	5981.1
2020	4895.6	5646.9	5721.6	5980.9	5969.5	6191.4	6904.0
2030	5133.0	6252.3		6572.3	6719.2	6966.3	8320.5

Rest of Florida (ROF)

	em-m	em-h	pop-m	pop-h	q-med	q-h
1970			3614.6			
1975			4057.1			
1980			10484.8			
1985			10021.8			
1990			11571.2			
1995			10890.8			
2000			12516.5			
2010	16671.2	17484.9	17478.1	17574.5	20108.7	20952.7
2020	17493.7	19141.1	20596.7	20915.6	22793.3	25071.1
2030	18778.4	21541.3	23189.4	24094.8	26502.9	31120.7

Florida (FL)

	em-m	em-h	pop-m	pop-h	q-med	q-h
1970			5612.3			
1975			6668.2			
1980			13229.0			
1985			12568.6			
1990			15063.6			
1995			14429.9			
2000			16512.1			
2010	21458.6	22742.7	22679.6	22854.4	25573.9	26933.8
2020	22389.3	24788.0	26577.6	27107.0	28762.8	31975.1
2030	23911.4	27793.6	29761.7	31061.1	33222.0	39441.2

Methods: Series for Public Supply (Table 3.1) and Rest of Freshwater (Table 3.3) were summed.

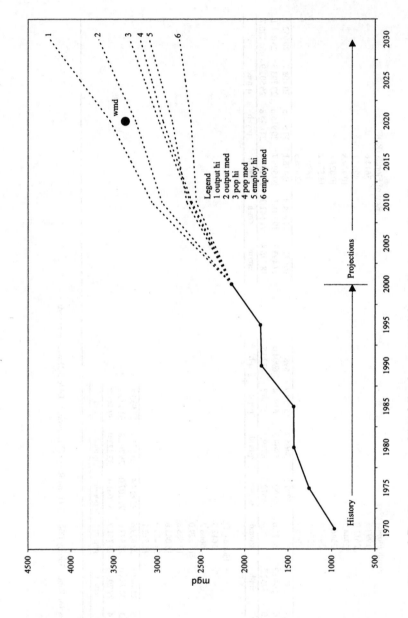

Figure 3.7   Projections of Total Freshwater Withdrawals: Lower East Coast

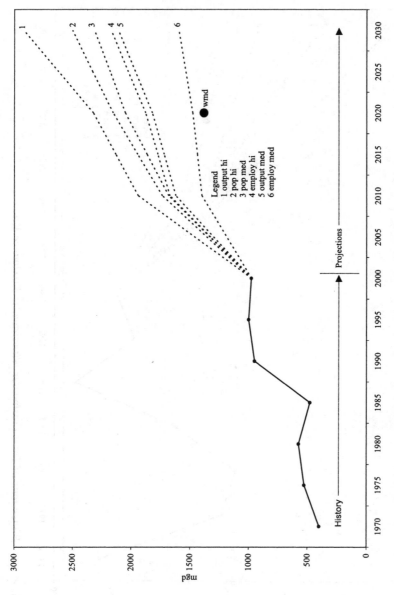

Figure 3.8   Projections of Total Freshwater Withdrawals: Lower West Coast

77

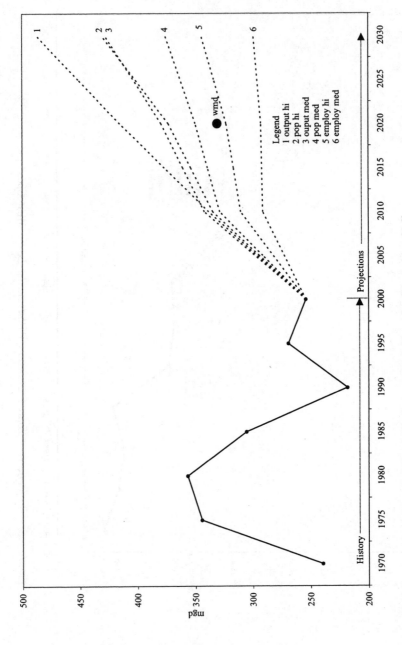

Figure 3.9   Projections of Total Freshwater Withdrawals: Kissimmee Valley

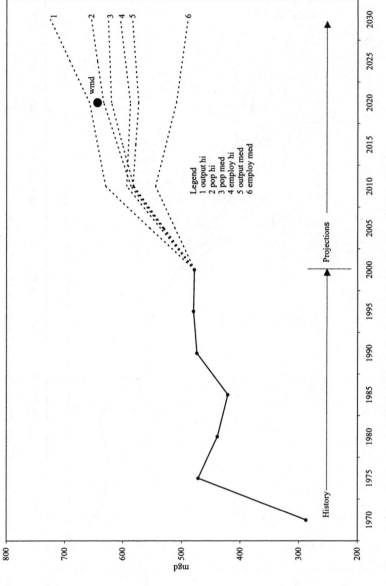

Figure 3.10   Projections of Total Freshwater Withdrawals: Upper East Coast

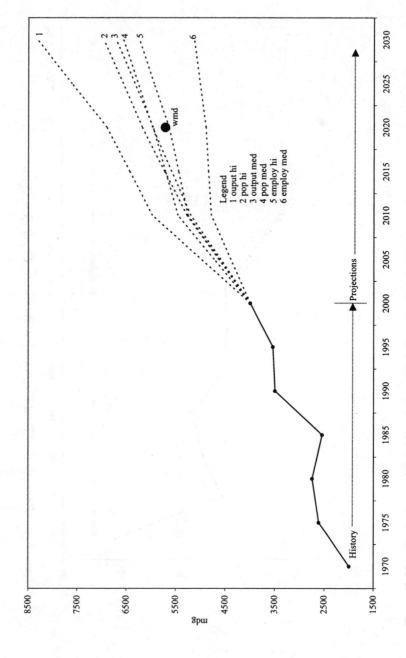

Figure 3.11   Projections of Total Freshwater Withdrawals: South Florida

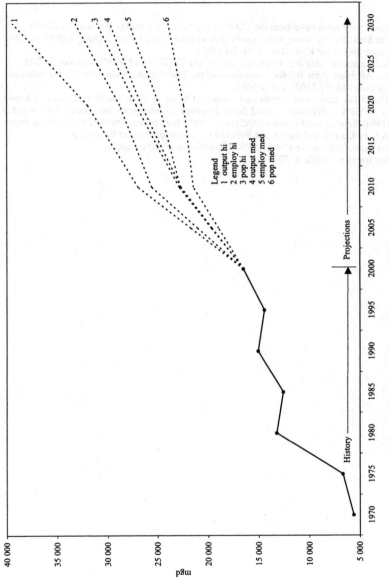

Figure 3.12   Projections of Total Freshwater Withdrawals: Florida

NOTES

1. These were aggregated from the USGS forecasts for each county. See Marella (1992).
2. See South Florida Water Management District (May 2000) for LEC; (April 2000b) for LWC; (April 2000a) for KSV; (Feb. 1998) for UEC.
3. See Appendix Table B.1 for comparisons of the USGS and SFWMD estimates for 2020.
4. See Appendix Table B.2 for comparisons of the 1995 detailed count estimates for both water categories by the USGS and SFWMD.
5. The USDA model was introduced by Blaney-Criddle in 1950. The Florida model is known as AFSIRS – Agricultural Field Scale Irrigation Requirements Simulation. See Smajstrla (1990), Smajstrla and Zazueta (1995) on AFSIRS. See Southern DataStream (2000) for testing in Levy County, and Jacobs and Satti (2001) for comparisons of the models.
6. See Izuno and Capone (1995); SFWMD (1997a) and (2003), ch. 3.
7. See Bacchus (2002), p. 703.

4. Forecasting the Demand for Urban Land

LAND REQUIREMENTS OF GROWTH

What will be the demands for urban land in SF as the economy grows? The problem of habitat destruction is nothing but the flip side of urban sprawl and agricultural expansion: as the economy grows, lands are "developed" and are removed from their natural uses.

In this chapter, we shall connect our economic growth model to the urban land required for the different scenarios and compute the quantity of additional lands that are likely to be absorbed into urban uses.[1] The device for connecting the population forecasts generated by the regional model and the urban land needed is a set of "technical land coefficients" that measures "urban land per person." But these coefficients are themselves changing over time. To measure the "elasticity" or "responsiveness" of changing land as population changes, we need to know the amount of urban land in each county for at least two different years and the population corresponding to those years.

An increasing coefficient over time corresponds to a "sprawling" or expanding need for land per person as the population grows, an indicator of preferred spaciousness. Greater compactness, on the other hand, or "urban compression," the inverse measure of population density, corresponds to a decrease in the ratio of "acres per person" as the economy grows. A region might experience a "sprawling" phase in its early development and a "compression" with rising densities as it reaches the limits of its available land. In the South Florida context, we might expect some counties to be sprawling and others to be compacting.[2]

The urban land in South Florida that we have totaled from the original data recorded in the GIS land use survey for 1995 amounts to some 1.28 million acres. (See Table 4.1, column 2, bottom line.) Fifty six percent of these urban acres (but 80 percent of the urban population) are found in the LEC counties.

The urban land requirements per person (Table 4.1, column 3) vary across the full range of counties. Broward and Miami-Dade are already highly compacted, with measured land requirements between 0.14 and 0.12 acres per person, half the coefficient of Monroe and Palm Beach Counties, which are 0.27 and 0.25, respectively. The urban land requirements in the other counties

Table 4.1   Population and Urban Land Comparisons, 1995

	Population (no.) (1)		Urban land (acres) (2)		Urban land per person (3)
LEC					
Broward	1 438 287		199 307		0.1386
Miami-Dade	2 085 340		247 332		0.1186
Monroe	79 853		21 806		0.2731
Palm Beach	994 936		250 269		0.2515
Region	4 598 416		718 714		0.1563
LWC					
Collier	199 297		78 848		0.3956
Glades	8 871		9 264		1.0443
Hendry	31 580		22 468		0.7115
Lee	384 937		189 249		0.4916
Region	624 685		299 830		0.4800
KSV					
Highlands	79 034		62 591		0.7920
Okeechobee	32 729		21 424		0.6546
Osceola	141 527		52 249		0.3692
Region	253 290		136 264		0.5380
UEC					
Martin	114 221		49 847		0.4364
St Lucie	173 227		72 699		0.4197
Region	287 448		122 546		0.4263
Summary		%		%	
LEC	4 598 416	79.8	718 714	56.3	0.1563
LWC	624 685	10.8	299 830	23.4	0.4800
KSV	253 290	4.4	136 264	10.7	0.5380
UEC	287 448	5.0	122 546	9.6	0.4263
All SF	5 763 839	100.0	1 277 354	100.0	0.2216

Sources:
Population from BEBR fsa 2002, t. 1.20.
Urban land computed from SFWMD 1997b GIS CD-ROM.

range from a middle level of 0.37 for Osceola and 0.40 for Collier to a spacious 0.79 for Highlands and 1.04 for Glades.

Once the counties are aggregated, their regions demonstrate strikingly similar land requirements, ranging from 0.43 for the UEC to 0.54 for KSV, with the LWC in between at 0.48 acres per person. Only the LEC is notably more compact, with 0.16 acres per person. (See Table 4.1, column 3, bottom lines.) The overall urban coefficient for SF is 0.22, a composite of two very different patterns, the LEC and the three other, more spacious regions.

The counties of South Florida are arrayed in Figure 4.1 according to the degree of urban spaciousness/compactness (the vertical axis) and their population (the horizontal axis). Only the three most populous counties, together with Monroe (the Keys), stand apart in their compactness. The four counties with the highest coefficients are all agricultural counties with relatively small urban centers, while the middle-range counties are slightly larger and more urbanized.

How have the land requirements changed over time? Records for only eight counties in SF from the GIS land use surveys of 1988 and 1995 appear to be consistent over time.

In Table 4.2 we note that the ratios of land per person *decline* in all those counties with comparable data for 1988 and 1995, except for Okeechobee, implying urban compacting (see columns 1–4). The *marginal* land requirements (column 5), that is, the *new* land required by the *new* population, are lowest for Broward, St Lucie, Miami-Dade and Palm Beach, and are highest for Okeechobee and Glades. The *average* land requirements (column 6) are lowest for Broward and Miami-Dade. The implicit *elasticity* of urban land with respect to population (column 7) is lowest for St Lucie, Broward, and Palm Beach, and highest for Okeechobee.

The counties with consistent data for the two study years, 1988 and 1995, were then aggregated to represent their entire regions. The resulting regional coefficients for 1995 (bottom panel, Regional totals, Table 4.2) are lowest (columns 1–2) in the LEC (0.15 acres/person) and almost seven times higher in the LWC (1.04 acres/person). The marginal coefficients (column 5) range from 0.11 in the LEC to 0.93 in the LWC, almost 8.5 times higher. The implicit land–people elasticities for the regions (column 7) are lowest for the UEC (0.35), similar for the LEC and KSV (0.66 and 0.67), and highest for the LWC (0.88).

Intuitively, one might expect the elasticity to be *lower* for the more compact or denser regions. That is, the denser the region, the lower the percentage change of new land needed for a given percentage change of new people. The record of our four regions does not strongly support this hypothesis (see Figure 4.2).[3]

In order to calculate the future urban land needs for our regions, we will use the medium and high population projections for 2010 through 2030 from our economic model (Chapter 2) and compute the percentage population changes from the 1995 model base year. We shall apply these population percentages to the 1988–1995 land–people elasticities for each region for each of the three periods, 1995–2010, 2010–2020, and 2020–2030, assuming that the urban land–people elasticity remains constant over time. This will give us

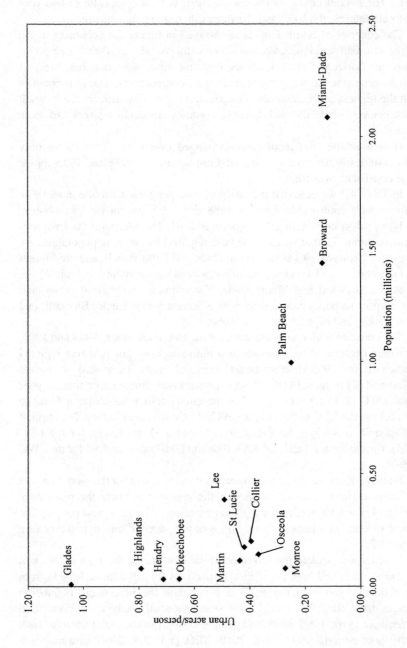

Figure 4.1 Population and Urban Land per Person, South Florida Counties, 1995

Table 4.2 Urban Land Coefficients and Elasticities, 1988–95

Region	Urban land per person				Marginal coefficient change (land)/change (pop) (5)	Average land/person at midpoint (6)	Elasticity column 5/ column 6 (7)
	Absolute coefficients		Absolute change (3)	% change (4)			
	1988 (1)	1995 (2)					
County sample							
Broward (LEC)	0.1504	0.1386	−0.012	−7.8	0.0766	0.1440	0.5320
Miami-Dade (LEC)	0.1198	0.1186	−0.001	−1.0	0.1085	0.1192	0.9102
Palm Beach (LEC)	0.2755	0.2515	−0.024	−8.7	0.1432	0.2623	0.5458
Glades (LWC)	1.0727	1.0443	−0.028	−2.6	0.9286	1.0570	0.8786
Okeechobee (KSV)	0.6143	0.6546	0.040	6.5	0.9031	0.6360	1.4201
Osceola (KSV)	0.4369	0.3692	−0.068	−15.5	0.2384	0.3961	0.6019
Martin (UEC)	0.4576	0.4364	−0.021	−4.6	0.3404	0.4459	0.7634
St Lucie (UEC)	0.5237	0.4197	−0.104	−19.9	0.0636	0.4650	0.1368
Regional totals:							
LEC	0.1619	0.1542	−0.008	−4.7	0.1067	0.1578	0.6765
LWC	1.0727	1.0443	−0.028	−2.6	0.9286	1.0570	0.8786
KSV	0.4781	0.4228	−0.055	−11.6	0.2958	0.4455	0.6639
UEC	0.4965	0.4263	−0.070	−14.1	0.1592	0.4573	0.3481
All SF	0.1904	0.1809	−0.010	−5.0	0.1264	0.1852	0.6822

Sources: Area of polygons of original land sizes for 1988 and 1995 are from SFWMD (1996) and (1997b), respectively. Population from BEBR.

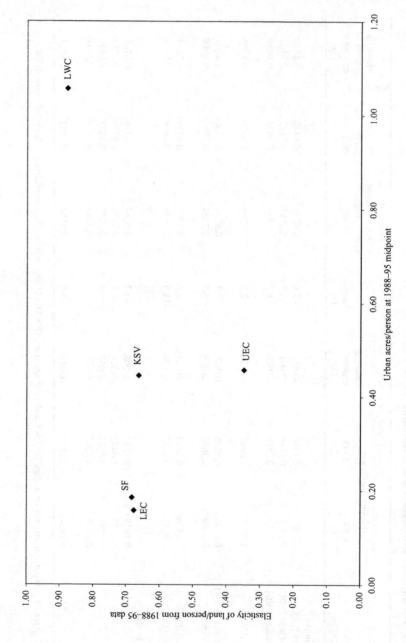

Figure 4.2 South Florida Sub-Regions and their Elasticities, 1988–95

the percentage of new urban land which, when multiplied by the urban land base, yields forecasts for the demand for new urban land in acres.

The detailed computations for all years are presented in Appendix Table C.1. The regional summary is presented in Table 4.3 for urban lands in 1995 (column 2) and for the final year forecasts of 2030 using the medium and high projections (columns 3-6). In the absence of any major zoning changes that would alter the urban "appetite" for land, approximately one million new acres or 1577 square miles of land can be expected to be absorbed by SF cities for all types of uses (see Table 4.3, bottom line, columns 3-4). The smallest gain can be expected in the UEC with only 45 000 new urban acres (with high population growth, column 4) in contrast to the 365 000 and 478 000 acres of new land forecast for the LEC and LWC, respectively. Urban land in the LWC is forecast to increase by 160 percent.

COMPARING URBAN LAND FORECASTS

Are these projections of urban land consistent with other research? Other researchers use very different methodologies to estimate the amount of urban land for different time periods and different geographical units. Reynolds and Dillman (1990) divide the state into MSA and non-MSA counties in the North and South-Central regions. Burchell et al. (1999) study the LEC and UEC counties. Burchell et al. (2002) emphasize the Miami-Ft Lauderdale economic area and its ten counties, and Burchell et al. (2003) use the Regional Planning Districts as units of analysis. Nevertheless, it is possible to compare our results to the elasticities or coefficients implicit in their computations.

Reynolds and Dillman (1990) estimate marginal land coefficients on the basis of aerial photographs for the 1973–1984 period. Their elasticity for South Florida is higher than mine, as are the other comparable coefficients (Table 4.4, column 2), suggesting perhaps that the elasticities fell between the decade of the seventies and the eighties. Moreover, the relationships between their coefficients are remarkably similar to mine, namely, the coefficient for all Florida is higher than that for South Florida (lines 2 and 3) and the coefficient for the more rural regions (lines 6 and 7) is higher than the more urbanized regions (lines 4–5).

The comparison with Burchell et al. (1999) is even more remarkable, for projections of population and employment convert into urban land based on "unit" or "building size" requirements. By dividing their projection of new urban land by their projected increase in population, we find that their implicit coefficient for the four-county LEC (column 3, line 4) is remarkably similar to ours (0.106 to our 0.107) and their estimate for Broward County (0.066) is also close to ours (0.077).

Table 4.3 Summary of Urban Land Forecasts

Region	1988–95 elasticity (1)	Urban acres 1995 (2)	Forecast gain urban acres, 2030, with		Total urban land, 2030		Percent increase urban land, 1995–2030	
			med. pop. (3)	high pop. (4)	med. pop. (5)	high pop. (6)	med. pop. (7)	high pop. (8)
LEC	0.6765	718 714	336 718	364 512	1 055 432	1 083 226	46.9	50.7
LWC	0.8786	299 830	424 902	478 423	724 732	778 253	141.7	159.6
KSV	0.6639	136 264	113 451	121 418	249 715	257 682	83.3	89.1
UEC	0.3481	122 546	41 941	44 964	164 487	167 510	34.2	36.7
SF	—	1 277 354	917 012	1 009 317	2 194 366	2 286 671	71.7	79.0
% change in population:			87.4	95.8				
Long-run elasticity of urban land with respect to population:			0.821	0.825				

Source: See Appendix C.1 for detailed computations.

Table 4.4 Comparison of Parameters of Urban Land per Person

	This study Weisskoff 1988–95 data (1)	1990 Reynolds and Dillman 1973–84 data (2)	1999 Burchell et al. 1995–2020 estim. (3)	2002 Burchell et al. 2000–2025 estim. (4)	2003 Burchell et al. 2000–2025 estim. (5)
Elasticities:					
1. South Florida	0.682	1.545			
Marginal coefficients:					
2. All Florida	0.222	0.535			0.205
3. SF	0.126	0.436			0.179
4. LEC	0.107	} 0.347	0.106	0.141	} 0.175
5. UEC	0.159		0.44	—	
6. LWC	0.929	} 0.682			} 0.185
7. KSV	0.296				
8. Broward County	0.077			0.066	
9. Palm Beach County	0.109			0.056	

Notes and Methods:

Elasticity: the percentage change in urban land divided by the percentage change in population.

Marginal coefficients: change in land divided by the change in popoulation.

Column (2): Reynolds and Dillman 1990, line 3, SF, refers to all MSA counties, most of which fall in the center or south; lines 4–5 refer to South and Central MSAs; lines 6–7 refer to South and Central non-MSA only.

Column (4): Burchell et al. 2002, line 4 refers to Miami–Ft Lauderdale Economic Area (EA), 10 counties.

Column (5): Burchell et al. 2003, line 3 refers to 24 county Greater Everglades Ecosystem Region (GEER); lines 4–5 refers to central GEER, 12 counties; lines 6–7 refer to peripheral GEER, 12 counties.

See Appendix C.2 for detailed computations.

The implicit coefficients for Burchell et al. (2003) are also remarkably similar. Their All Florida coefficient is 0.205, compared to our 0.222, and their South Florida coefficient is 0.179 compared to our 0.125 (see Table 4.4, column 5, lines 2–3). (The line-by-line computations for each source are given in Appendix Table C.2.)

The confirmation of our otherwise ominous forecasts of urban land requirements by these four studies lends support to what every environmentalist and practicing developer knows from experience: a growing society has a tremendous appetite for land. We have here attached stark figures to that appetite.

NOTES

1. Additional land required by agriculture will not be considered here as this calls for another type of economic model that must measure the impacts of changing technology, crop yields, commodity prices, national farm policy, and international trade on each county's agriculture.
2. Population density, the usual measure of the people–land relationship, is generally expressed as "persons per acre." Therefore, a rising density (that is, more people/acre) corresponds to a greater compactness or fewer acres of urban land per person, as people create a more vertical rather than a horizontal habitat for themselves.
3. The structure of inflexible zoning codes and minimum land requirements for different uses – residential, commercial, industrial, recreational, and so on – may prolong the "sprawl" phase, especially if undeveloped lands are thought to be still available.

PART II

The Economy of the South Florida Ecosystem

The Economy of the South Florida Ecosystem

5. Fundamental Issues and Conceptual Models

Why is South Florida so different? Miami is not Florida. South Florida is not like the rest of America. Visitors from elsewhere in the US and from abroad find South Florida equally exotic. Why is that?[1]

I propose that it is the very connection between economy and ecology that makes South Florida so different and difficult to understand. In the case of South Florida, the connection is even more crucial due to the dynamism of the economy and the fragility of the ecosystem.

Economy and ecology are almost polar disciplines. Economy is about production and consumption in the human sphere, using resources to create new products and services designed to satisfy our needs. Economy is also about human welfare – poverty, wealth, and the public spending needed to keep our society together and whole.

Ecology, on the other hand, is about the natural system and the laws that keep all its elements together: animals, plants, land, water, and air. Economy deals with values, money, and jobs; ecology, with natural materials, living matter, and energy of all forms.

Without economy, there would be no environmental crisis.

In another sense, economy and ecology play identical roles in the two parallel spheres. Economy is actually the "vessel" in which human society operates: money, jobs, homes, banks, offices, and farms. These are the support structures that permit humans to carry out the higher mission of living, although the amount of human activity required to keep the vessel intact and expanding at times seems to occupy almost all our personal energy and time.

Ecology is the natural setting, the primeval stage with its own inherent laws that were set in motion long before commercial traders and real estate developers ever set foot in the region. Just as economic laws seem to govern the flow of values in the material world, so the natural laws seem to govern the natural flows.

South Florida illustrates both approaches: the conflict between economy and ecology and their mutual complementarities. The simple view of conflict appears often enough in the feuds over land development, cutting channels, and draining swamps. The view of complementarity is less apparent but far more important, for it is this direction that we must recognize and move towards, namely, that ecology provides the *basis*, the platform for the economy to act on. The stage must support the actors and not collapse under their weight as they strut and fret about. The economy itself then allows all human activity to move forward. Ecology, in this sense, is the larger vessel within which the economic vessel must operate.

This is true even more so in South Florida where the very rationale for settling the coastal ridges was first undertaken with an appreciation for the climate and the natural beauty of the place. Unfortunately, most of the rest – the soggy swamps, the meandering rivers and shallow lakes, the limitless flocks of birds, and other teeming wildlife – became regarded, after the initial explorers sense of awe wore thin, as obstacles to be conquered: the swamps drained, the rivers channeled, the lakes diked, the birds slaughtered for exotic hat plumage, and the alligator hunted for handbag, belt, and shoe leather.

After this process was all finished and the formerly hunted species, the remaining waters, wetlands, and forests were duly protected by new laws, an even stranger battle of the survivors began. Can the endangered, now "protected" Florida panther live in a much-reduced habitat without sufficient lands to roam and wildlife to hunt? Can the snail kite survive if the eggs of its unique food source, the apple snail, are drowned by a change in water levels that were raised to follow new drainage regulations? Can the phosphorous levels indeed be lowered – in our lifetime – to the level thought necessary to restore the low-nutrient environment that lies downstream from the agricultural areas?

In one sense, the modern restoration process began as the result of the lawsuit brought by a lone US attorney in Miami against the state governor and the governor-appointed administration of the South Florida Water Management District (SFWMD) for failing to enforce the state's own environmental codes and naming the sugar growers as the primary polluters of the Everglades. In the seminal 1988 case, *US v. South Florida Water Management District, et al.*, in the Southern District of Florida, Judge Hoeveler found the State of Florida in violation of its own water pollution laws.[2] The legal actions, themselves based on ecological findings, gave rise to a long and complicated series of suits and countersuits, and was concluded in part with a remedy designed by the state legislature and modestly named The Everglades Forever Act (1994).[3]

An amended act, hurriedly passed by the Florida legislature and signed by Governor Jeb Bush in May of 2003, extended the cleanup deadline from 2006 to 2016 and added the words, "to the maximum extent practicable" numerous times to qualify the goal of attaining the 10-parts-per-billion phosphorus limit. The new legislation also averages the phosphorous standard over dozens of monitoring stations over a five-year period and blunts the "polluter pays" amendment to the state constitution, removing the prospect of new taxes for the sugar growers.[4]

However, due to his outspoken criticism of the legislation cited in the interviews he gave various newspapers including the *Miami Herald*, Federal Judge Hoeveler was removed from the case on September 23, 2003 – after fifteen years of his oversight![5] A new federal judge was randomly selected to replace Judge Hoeveler. Judge Federico Moreno moved quickly to appoint an expert to monitor the Everglades cleanup. In April of 2004, Judge Moreno issued a one-page order giving the "special master broad authority to monitor compliance," taking the issue temporarily off the public stage.[6]

The challenge of the present era of restoration is to design and implement a plan that will improve the natural system to the same extent that it devours state and federal funding.[7]

Even during the restoration process, the competitive and complementary characters of economy and ecology persist. The "productive" or profit-making sectors – agriculture, urban development, construction, tourism, and services, for example – all need land and water, and they create pollution that affects the natural system. The current economy, using present technologies and producing for our patterned needs, may be incompatible with the natural system as we would like to see it. But a restored environment creates a setting for an expanded eco-tourist industry and organic marsh farming that, by requiring less drainage, sprays, and fertilizer, may allow agriculture and nature to thrive side by side.

The interwovenness between economy and ecology in South Florida were first made painfully clear in Marjorie Stoneman Douglas' *The Everglades: River of Grass* in 1947. Widely quoted today for its lyrical descriptions of the dying marsh and its battle cry to action, the book is actually an interesting economic treatise about the South Florida scene. Douglas brings a journalistic and poetic flavor to her understanding of the dynamic economy and all the hustle and bustle of the new enterprise. For her, it is the rise of farming, new cities, and tourism that spells the death of the Everglades. Even her earlier short stories about the real estate boom, drainage of the swamps, plume hunters, and the murder of a game warden are graphic contributions to our understanding of how economy and ecology are interconnected.[8]

The literature since 1947 takes two separate streams. The first contains narratives and exposés of environmental disasters and their associated causes. Cleo and Mesouf's *Florida: Polluted Paradise* (1964), McCluney's *Environmental Destruction of South Florida* (1969), and Mines' *The Last Days of Mankind: Ecological Survival or Extinction* (1971), are among the early titles.[9]

Parallel to this was a national awareness of the plight of the migrant worker. As the nation sat down to Thanksgiving dinner in 1960, it was shocked by Edward R. Murrow's TV documentary, *Harvest of Shame*,[10] which traced the migrant stream north from the fields of Belle Glade on the southeastern shore of Florida's Lake Okeechobee. Thirty years later, PBS Frontline reporter

David Marash revisited the migrant camps and found little change, except perhaps the nationality of the farm worker. Today, the casual traveler might want to visit Centro Campesino in Homestead or other migrant projects in Immokalee in Collier County or in Belle Glade itself. From South Dade to Palm Beach, a portion of the migrant stream has "settled out" into year-round jobs in the nurseries that raise tropical ornamentals for the rest of the nation.

The formal industrial and agricultural history and the struggle for the land are captured in such books as Tebeau's *Florida's Last Frontier: The History of Collier County* (1966), Will's *Swamp to Sugar Bowl: Pioneer Days in Belle Glade* (1968), Derr's *Some Kind of Paradise: A Chronicle of Man and Land in Florida* (1989), and Watercourse and SFWMD, *Discover a Watershed: The Everglades* (1996).

A second stream of literature consists of ecological studies of the watershed, the piecemeal impacts of change, and a fascinating array of professional investigations. Fernald and Patton (1984) and Fernald and Purdum's *Water Resources Atlas of Florida* (1998) are encyclopedic in their overview of the state's water situation and current issues, and they provide detail on all the regional water management districts. Fernald and Purdum's *Atlas of Florida* (1996) adds the county-level geographical dimension to the economic and natural systems. Especially interesting are the sections on history, population, infrastructure, and tourism. Randazzo and Jones' *The Geology of Florida* (1997) gives the epochal history of the local landmasses as well as information on economic minerals and environmental geology.

Regarding South Florida ecology in particular, two great collections are now available – Davis and Ogden, *The Everglades: The Ecosystem and its Restoration* (1994) and Porter and Porter, *The Everglades, Florida Bay and Coral Reefs of the Florida Keys: An Ecosystem Sourcebook* (2002). Lodge's *The Everglades Handbook: Understanding the Ecosystem* (1998) provides useful detail on the region's habitats and biology with an insightful summary of human impacts on the environment. McCally's *The Everglades: An Environmental History* (1999) emphasizes the interactions of human society and ecology.

For the most part, the ecological literature treats nature as micro-scientific puzzles. Except for certain exceptions in the above-cited collections and a general discussion of pollution, there are no analytic economic or social studies to be found. The exceptions are the two historical narratives, one by Light and Dineen (1994) on the water control system and the other by Snyder and Davidson (1994) on Everglades agriculture, both in the Davis and Ogden collection (1994), and Sydney Bacchus' (2002) distressing warning on the "Ostrich" component of multiple stressors in the Porter and Porter volume (2002).

In a 1981 "popular" social geography, journalist Joel Garreau argued that the North American continent should be considered as if it were peopled by "nine nations" corresponding to the unique caricature that could be ascribed to each region. The Florida peninsula south of Lake Okeechobee is severed from the rest of "Dixie" and belongs rather to "The Islands." Garreau focused on the cultural and trade connections between South Florida and the Caribbean, the technology of smuggling, and the financial flows that result from illicit trade. While impressionistic and journalistic, he provides an illuminating working hypothesis about what makes South Florida grow in its special way (see Figure 5.1).

Odum, Odum, and Brown's *Environment and Society in Florida* (1998) is an antidote to Garreau and a complement to Scoggins and Pierce's *The Economy of Florida* (1995). The latter is a collection of vignettes with some statistics describing the state's important economic activities. The Odum volume is a refreshing analysis of energy systems applied first to each of Florida's environmental systems, and then to each major economic sector – the cities, tourism, agriculture, mining, forestry, fisheries, and industry in general. Included is also a remarkable series of mazes, diagrams, maps, and sketches that emphasize the changes in the South Florida landscape (see esp. the maps on pp. 219 and 232). The book's only drawback is its conciseness, for here is a one-volume introduction to a worldview, which first dissects each piece of society in terms of its energy flows and then reconstructs the society by putting the pieces back together.

The new field of ecological economics also attempts to reconnect human activity with its natural setting. In a series of remarkable papers, Solecki (2001) links South Florida's growth to national and global changes, Walker (2001) models fifty years of land cover change, Sklar et al. (2001) summarize how six landscape models are applied to test the "applied science strategy" for Everglades restoration, and Gunderson (2001) tracks management policies in what he calls a "surprising" ecosystem.[11] All of these papers contain helpful historical data regarding growth of population, land use changes, and the hydraulic works of South Florida.

Novelists exhibit much less regard for proper disciplinary or geographical boundaries, for their job is to put a story together. Peter Matthiessen's *Killing Mister Watson* (1991) takes us into frontier disputes, farming, and a hurricane on South Florida's west coast at the turn of the century. Each of Patrick Smith's novels draws us into the human side of South Florida's different worlds. *Forever Island* (1973) deals with large-scale development and its impact on local people. *Angel City* (1978) treats the migrant worker, his family, and the labor camps needed for vegetable farming in Homestead. *Allapatah* (1987) is a heartbreaking story of a Miccosukee Indian's life in the Everglades and his irresolvable clash with the "white man's" economy. John Keasler's *Surrounded on Three Sides* (1958), an early novel on Florida real estate promotion, anticipates what was to come in John Sayles' feature film, *Sunshine State* (2002).

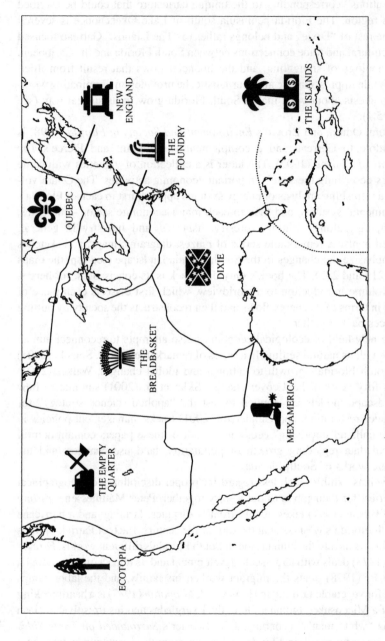

Source: Reproduced from Joel Garreau (1981), *The Nine Nations of North America* by kind permission of the author.

Figure 5.1   The Nine Nations of North America

In her juvenile novels, *The Talking Earth* (1983) and the eco-mystery, *The Missing 'Gator of Gumbo Limbo* (1992), Jean Craighead George places her characters into the specific Everglades setting. In doing so, she introduces the reader to such issues as homelessness, condo developments, pollution, and saltwater intrusion, in short, many of the social, political, and scientific themes being played out in South Florida today.

Judith Bauer Stamper's *Save the Everglades* (1993), a short, non-fictionalized history also written for the young reader, describes the successful campaign in the early 1970s to block the construction of the world's largest jetport to be located in the Big Cypress Swamp.[12]

Despite all the descriptive and circumstantial evidence, a direct quantitative connection between local economy and Everglades ecology eluded me until one day at the SFWMD District Headquarters when I mistakenly walked into a meeting of the Science Working Group of the Restudy. Committees of scientists for years had been collaborating to construct "conceptual" or schematic models of eight prototypical habitats which, together with their narratives, provide flowchart-like guides to the functioning of the major ecosystems within the Greater Everglades Region: Florida Bay, marl prairie and rocky glades, the Everglades sloughs, the St Lucie estuary, the Caloosahatchee estuary, Lake Okeechobee, and the areas in mangrove/estuarine transition. Biscayne Bay, a ninth, has recently been added. These nine major wetland physiographic regions of South Florida are located in Figure 5.2.

The conceptual models are non-quantitative "idea plans" that detail for each habitat the interconnectedness within the natural system. In Figure 5.3, we reproduce the conceptual model for one of the habitats, Florida Bay, only because it is visually the clearest.[13] The top-most rectangles represents the major sources of ecosystem stress such as the Flagler Railway, water management, development, and agriculture. The next row of ovals represent the ecosystem stressors themselves, such as altered salinity regimes and fishing pressure. The diamond shapes below these trace the ecological and biological responses and their interactions. The octagons toward the bottom of the page give the general endpoints or indicators of ecological integrity, such as water quality, seagrass community, and fish populations. The parallelograms at the bottom of the figure are the specific measurable features of the endpoints, such as the salinity of the water and the diversity of the fish population.

Most striking about the top row of rectangles, which are the sources or "external driving forces,"[14] is that they are almost all economic in origin. Even sea level rise in the case of the Florida Bay conceptual model, the effect of which may truly "swamp" all the other economic factors in the long run, is accelerated by the levels of global economic activity.

The major stressors (the top rectangles) of all nine conceptual models are summarized in Table 5.1. The models identify similar economic stressors

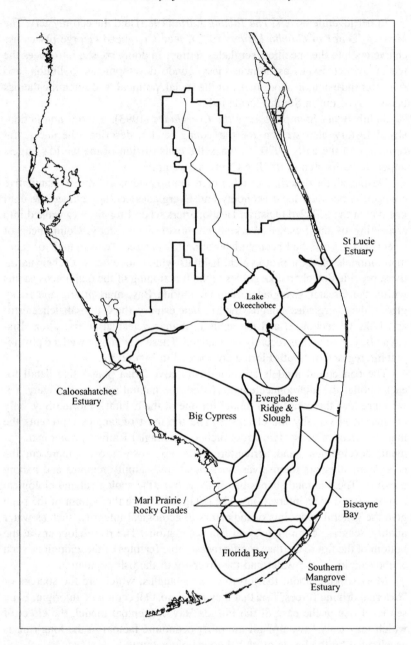

Source: US Army Corps of Engineers (2001).

Figure 5.2   Major Wetlands Physiographic Regions of South Florida

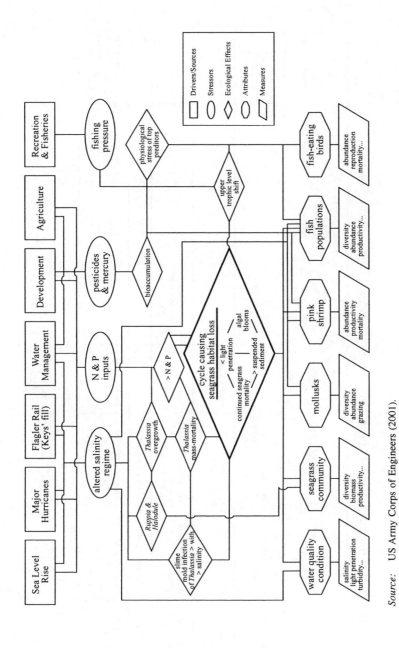

Source: US Army Corps of Engineers (2001).

Figure 5.3 Florida Bay Conceptual Model (6/6/97)

Table 5.1 Summary of Principal External Driving Forces on Major Wetland Physiographic Regions

Drivers / Region	C&SF Project water management practices (1)	Agriculture and urban development (2)	Natural forces (3)	Introduction of exotic flora and fauna* (4)	Other economy navigation recreation fisheries (5)	Input of mercury and toxins (6)	Fire management (7)
1 Lake Okeechobee	Increase nutrient inputs	Waste water discharge from agriculture, urban, and residential lands		Exotic and nuisance plants animals			
2 St Lucie and Indian River Lagoon	Water management	Land use and development	Sea level rise				
3 Everglades ridge and slough	Water management practices	Urban and agriculture expansion Industrial practices		Society's value system for plants, animals			
4 Biscayne Bay	Water management	Watershed development					
5 Marl prarie and rocky glades**	C&SF Project/ South Dade conveyance system	Agriculture and urban development	Sea level rise			Input of mercury and toxins	Fire management exacerbated by compartmental-ization

104

	Water management	Agriculture, Development, Flagler (Keys' fill), Railroad	Sea level rise, Major hurricanes	Exotic fishes, plants	Recreation Fisheries	Input of mercury and toxins
6 Florida Bay	C&SF Project		Sea level rise			
7 Mangrove estuarine transition**						
8 Big Cypress	Canal system and drainage ditches	Agriculture and urban enroachment Land use changes Urban and agriculture wellfield withdrawals Pesticide use and other contaminant sources		Melaleuca Feral hogs Exotic fish		Altered fire regime
9 Caloosahatchee Estuary	Water management	Land use and development	Sea level rise		Navigation	
Number regions	9	8	5	4	2	2

Notes:

* Escaped, abandoned, or purposeful.

** From draft of 6/5/97. Draft of 2001 omits all drivers.

Source: Extracted from the nine conceptual models given in US Army Corps of Engineers (2001).

across habitats. All nine models cite water management practices (or the C&SF Project) and eight regions cite agricultural or urban development as major stressors. The introduction of exotic plants and fishes threatens four of the habitats. Even this stressor is economic in origin, as exotics were introduced intentionally to dry up marshland, as in the cases of melaleuca and torpedo grass, or inadvertently, as in the cases of water hyacinth, Brazilian pepper, and nearly twenty species of fishes, mollusks, and micro invertebrates that escaped from nurseries or that were abandoned to the natural environment. Moreover, the measures of ecological integrity, the parallelograms in the bottom row of Figure 5.3, also have important economic implications, especially for fishing, tourism, recreation, and boating.

In conclusion, it seems that the restoration scientists working on all of the Everglades habitats agreed relatively early in the planning process that economics lies at the beginning and the end of the ecological story. But once this recognition was made, the economic connection drops out of sight, for none of the hydrology, biology, geological, or landscape modeling ever references the economy again, with the exception perhaps of the crop-mix module tagged onto the water delivery model used by the Water Management District. Once mentioned, the list of stressors – all aspects of the flourishing economy – disappears.

NOTES

1. See Rieff (1987); Portes and Stepick (1993) and Nijman (1996, 1997). Many sources emphasize politics, race, history, and geography.
2. Case No. 88-1886-Civ-Hoeveler. A complete collection of Everglades litigation can be viewed at www.law.miami.edu/library/everglades.
3. See Hazen and Sawyer (1993) for a review of the economic impacts of implementing the Settlement Agreement and the new legislation.
4. See the following articles in the *Miami Herald*: "Bush: Sugar Bill is No Glades Threat," April 8, 2003, p. 5B, "Easing of Pressure on Everglades Polluters Passes a Test," April 10, 2003, p. 5B; "Phosphorous Threat at Center of Debate on Glades Renewal," May 12, 2003, p. 1B; "Criticized Glades Bill Signed by Bush," May 21, 2003, p. 1A, and "Glades Fight Far From Over Despite Revised Water Law," July 21, 2003, p. 1B.
5. The narrative of events can be traced in the following articles that appeared in the *Miami Herald* on September 24, 2003: "Big Sugar Wins Bid to Oust Judge from Case," p. 1A; "The Everglades Lawsuit," p. 20A; "William J. Zloch, the Mercurial Chief Judge, A Former Notre Dame Quarterback, Plays It by the Book," p. 3B; "William Hoeveler Has a Long-Standing Reputation for Being One of Florida's Fairest Federal Judges," p. 3B. Also in the *Miami Herald*: "A Respected Judge Crosses a Line," Sept. 25, 2003, p. 28A; "Hoeveler Will Be Remembered as Glades Hero," Sept. 28, 2003, p. 1L; and "Judge Says He Wanted Best for Glades," Nov. 28, 2003, p. 1A.
6. See the *Miami Herald*: "Cleanup Suit Passes Into Hands of 'Quick, Fair' Judge," Oct. 5, 2003, p. 1B; "Expert to Monitor Cleanup," Oct. 30, 2003, p. 12B; "Judge Sets Up Review of Water-Cleanup Work," March 4, 2004.
7. See www.evergladesplan.gov.

8. See especially ch. 14, "Boom, Blow, Bust, and Recovery," in Douglas ([1947], rev. edn. 1988). Her stories "A Bird in the Hand" (1925) and "Plumes" (1930), are republished in Douglas (1990). Compare Rachel Carson's remarks on her explorations and appreciation of the Everglades delivered in a 1954 address entitled, "The Real World Around Us," in Carson (1998: 154–9).

9. On the last mentioned, see ch. 3 on the Everglades.

10. CBS News documentary (1960), now available as videotape. See comments by Lawrence Will (1968), ch. 29, "Harvest of Shame, " pp. 197–202.

11. Compare this to the "turbulent" Everglades ecosystem in the Light, Gunderson, and Holling (1995) article in the earlier *Barriers and Bridges* volume.

12. The original jet runway, now called the Dade-Collier Training and Transition Airport, is still used for training flights. It is located on the north side of US 41, Tamiami Trail, east of the Visitor Center of the Big Cypress National Preserve. Compare Stamper's account to Marjory Stoneman Douglas' own narrative of how Joe Browder got her started as an activist, as she says, "in her 80th year." See Douglas (1987 p. 224ff). Her organization, Friends of the Everglades, still plays an important and independent role in monitoring Everglades restoration. The so-called "S-9" lawsuit, sponsored by the Friends of the Everglades and the Miccosukee Tribe of Indians, was argued before the Supreme Court in February 2003. The Supreme Court, however, sent the case back to District Court to be reargued in the fall of 2004. See the series of articles in the *Everglades Reporter* posted on the Friends of the Everglades website, www.everglades.org.

13. These have all been released as part of CERP's "Monitoring and Assessment Plan" (MAP) (March 29, 2001). See US Army Corps (2001). The early drafts are dated June 1997, and for Biscayne Bay, October 2000. The recent drafts of the conceptual models may be accessed through the CERP website at http://www.evergladesplan.org/pm/recover/recover_cerp_monitor_plan_1.cfm.

14. See US Army Corps (2001, Section II, p. 2).

6. Overview of the Region's Economy

GENERAL CHARACTERISTICS

In this section, we shall review the overall economy of the region and its past and projected growth.

For the purpose of this study, the boundaries of the Greater Everglades Ecosystem coincide with the limits of the South Florida Water Management District, which itself comprises the majority of thirteen Florida counties and parts of three others. The boundaries of the South Florida Water Management District were drawn to include all the related Everglades water basins, but since these cut across various counties, we include in this socio-economic analysis only those thirteen South Florida counties with more than a majority of their land or people falling within the ecosystem.[1] The included counties cover more than 15 000 square miles or the size of Connecticut and Massachusetts together. The South Florida region in our analysis accounts for 28 percent of Florida's land area, but its 6.5 million people account for 40.4 percent of Florida's population (see Table 6.1, lines 1–2, columns 1 and 4). The personal income of the region totaled $193 billion in 2000 (line 3), with a per capita income of almost $30 000 (line 4), which is 7 percent over the state's average (cf. line 4, column 2). This "premium" disappears, however, once the higher cost of living for South Florida is considered.[2]

Thirteen percent of the region's population, or 849 000 people in 1999 (line 5), were considered poor. Bank deposits totaled $110.5 billion in 2001 (line 6). In summary, the region accounts for 40 percent of the people, 43 percent of the personal income, 44 percent of the state's poor, and almost half of the state's bank deposits (lines 2, 3, 5, 6, column 4).

The number of new housing starts in 2001 (line 7) was 63 600, nearly 39 percent of the state's total during a year when the construction boom affected all parts of Florida. The region's 124 000 mobile homes (line 8) accounted for only a quarter of the state's total, which is much less than the share of all housing due to the tightening of the building codes in the more hurricane-prone southern counties.

Table 6.1 Economic Characteristics of the Greater Everglades (South Florida) Ecosystem, 2000–2001

	South Florida (1)	State (2)	US (3)	% SF in FL (4)	% FL in US (5)	% SF in US (6)
A. General						
1. Land area (thou. sq. mi.)	15.1	53.9	3 537.4	28.0	1.5	0.43
2. Resident population (2000) (mill.)	6.5	16.0	281.4	40.4	5.7	2.29
3. Personal income (2000) (curr. $ bill.)	192.7	445.7	8 314.0	43.2	5.4	2.32
4. Personal income per cap (2000) ($ curr.)	29 876	27 894	29 545	—	—	—
5. Poverty population (1999) (thou.)	849.3	1 939.5	32 791	43.8	5.9	2.59
Poverty as % of region	13.3	12.4	11.9	—	—	—
6. Bank deposits (2001) ($ bill.)	110.5	222.8	4 326.3	49.6	5.1	2.55
7. New housing starts (2001) (thou.)	63.6	163.8	1 602.7	38.8	10.2	3.97
8. Mobile homes licensed (2001) (thou.)	124.0	495.1	n.c.	25.0	n.a.	n.a
9. Freshwater use (2000) (mgd)	3 995.5	8 256.1	n.a.	48.4	n.a.	n.a.
10. Solid waste, municipal (1999) (mill. t.)	10.1	25.0	229.9	40.4	10.9	4.39
11. Commercial fish caught (1996) (mill. lbs.)	32.0	101.7	9 491.9	31.5	1.1	0.34
12. Motor vehicle tags sold (2001) (mill.)	7.5	20.6	230.4	36.4	8.9	3.26
13. Passenger car tags sold (2001) (mill.)	4.2	9.2	137.6	45.7	6.7	3.05
14. Visitors (air and auto) (2001) (mill.)	24.8	62.3	n.c.	39.8	n.a.	n.a
15. Visitor-years (2001) (thou.)	360.1	904.8	n.c.	39.8	n.a.	n.a
16. Visitor-years as % of residents	5.5	4.9	n.c.	112.2	n.a.	n.a
17. National park visitors (2001) (mill.)	5.7	8.9	279.9	64.0	3.2	2.04
18. State park visitors (2001-2) (mill.)	5.8	17.7	766.0	32.8	2.3	0.76
19. Municipalities (1997) (number)	117	394	36 001	29.7	1.1	0.32
20. Special districts (1997) (number)	196	526	34 683	37.3	1.5	0.57

B. Agricultural 1997 Ag Census

1. No. farms (thou.)	6.6	34.8	1912.0	19.0	1.8	0.35
2. Farm land (mill. acres)	4.0	10.4	931.8	38.5	1.1	0.43
3. Aver. farm size (acres)	604	300	487	201.2	61.6	124.0
4. Share of land in farms (%)	41.2	30.1	48.0	—	—	—
5. Irrigated farm land (thou. acr.)	1149	1862	55 058	61.7	3.4	2.09

6. Size distribution of farms

	% no.	% area	% no.	% area	% no.	% area			
1–49 ac.	65.0	1.6	57.8	3.9	29.5	1.4	112.5	195.9	220.3
50–999 ac.	26.5	15.2	37.5	37.3	61.3	36.1	70.7	61.2	43.2
1000 ac.<	8.4	83.2	4.7	58.8	9.2	62.5	178.7	51.1	91.30
Kuznets ratio	1.50		1.08		1.07				

7. Value of all farm produce sold (mill. $)	2862	6005	196 865	47.7	3.1	1.45
8. Cattle and calves inventory (thou.)	626	1809	98 989	34.6	1.8	0.63
9. Sugarcane (thou. acr.)	436	436	919	100.0	47.4	47.4
10. Vegetables (thou. acr.)	124	251	3 733	49.6	6.7	3.33
11. Citrus trees (mill.)	56.8	107.2	151.5	53.0	70.8	37.5
12. Nursery, greenhouse sales (mill. $)	609	1450	10 943	42.0	13.3	5.6

C. Environment and climate

1. Threat. and endang. animals, Fed. list (no.)	35	57	517	61.4	11.0	6.8
2. Threat. and endang. plants, Fed. list (no.)	34	54	745	63.0	7.2	4.6
3. Elevation, max (ft.)	50	345	20 320	14.5	1.7	0.25
4. Water area (thou. sq. mi.)	2.5	5.99	181.3	41.1	3.3	1.36
5. Climate						
Aver. max. temp. (2000) degr. F	83.4	81.6	65.7	102.2	124.2	126.9
Aver. min. temp. (2000) degr. F	65.8	62.5	48.9	105.3	127.8	134.6
Precipitation (1996–2000) inches	56.3	53.0	37.3	106.2	142.1	150.9

Method: For each of the sources listed below, data are given on a county basis. The county data in the South Florida region (and its subregions: LEC, LWC, KSV, and UEC) were summed, and the regional totals compared to the state and US totals, when available.

Sources: fsa = Florida Statistical Abstract 2002, unless other year specified; saus = Statistical Abstract of US 2001.

(continued)

Table 6.1   Economic Characteristics of the Greater Everglades (South Florida) Ecosystem, 2000–2001 (continued)

General:

Line 1: from t. 8.01 fsa; line 2: t. 1.01 and 1.12 fsa. April 1 est.; line 3: IMPLAN database, 2000; also t. 5.08 fsa.

Line 4 = 1. 3 divid 1. 2; line 5: from US Census Bureau, March 2000 CPS model for 1999, T. A99-12. US totals from t. A99-00.

The range of poverty rates in the CPS model covers the rates observed in the US census for the same year, 1999. See www.census.gov.

Line 6: t. 17.09 fsa; US from FDIC www.fdic.gov; line 7: sum single and multi-family construction starts from t. 11.05, fsa; US totals from US Census site: New privately owned housing units started.

Line 8: t. 2.36 fsa; line 9: USGS unpublished data; line 10: Municipal collected, t. 8.16, US from T. 359 saus.

Line 11: t. 10.40 fsa, US from NOAA "Fisheries of the US" (2001 edn) website. Line 12.

Lines 12–13: t.13.32 fsa, US from US Federal Highway Admin website, which gives state and national totals;

Lines 14–16: Number of visitors and length of stay from t. 19.20 fsa. Regional distrib. from lodging and food spending by county, t. 19.05 fsa from 1997 Economic Census. Total visitor days were converted to visitor years and compared to resident pop. In 2001 given in t. 1.14 fsa.

Line 17: t. 19.53 fsa. US totals from National Park Service www.nps.gov; line 18: t. 19.52 fsa, summed by counties.

US totals from website National Assoc. of State Park Directors; lines 19–20: US Census of Governments, Vol 1, T. 13, Local Govt. summed by county for columns 5 and 8.

Agriculture:

All data from U.S. Department of Agriculture Census of Agriculture (1999). Each subregion is summed from county data given in the state files.

Line 4, share of US in farms, from saus, from T. 346, total surface area, divided by total land in farms, T. 796.

The size distribution of land (line 6) is constructed by multiplying the midpoints of all the detailed closed intervals of land sizes by the number of farms in each interval. The number of acres in the open-ended interval was computed as a residual. The shares of the numbers of farms and their corresponding area were then computed and aggregated to three intervals. The Kuznets ratio of inequality is computed by summing the absolute differences of the percentage of the number of farms in each interval and the percentage of the corresponding area occupied by those farms. The Kuznets ratio ranges from zero (extreme equality) to 2 (extreme inequality).

Line 9 includes land in sugarcane for both seed and sugar production; line 10 refers to land in vegetables harvested for sale.

Environment:

Lines 1–2: Species on the national list are from the county files, summed for our regions, from EnviroTools, Inc (1998) CD-ROM, compared to the state and national listings TESS, posted by the US Fish & Wildlife Service, www.fws.gov accessed 23 Jan 2003.

Subregional totals do not add to South Florida region, as there are repetitions and unique species in each subregion.

Line 3: from *Atlas of Florida* (1992), p. 15.

Line 4: t. 8.03 fsa, includes inland and coastal waters, excluding territorial waters.

Line 5: SF temperatures are annual averages of monthly averages from the various US weather stations: Miami and WPB (LEC); Orlando (KSV); Naples (LWC).

All Florida is the average of all 12 stations, t. 8.70 fsa. US is from t. 8.74, averaging LA, Atlanta, Chicago, NYC for 1961–1990, while the Florida data are for the single year indicated. Precipitation (rainfall) was averaged for 1996–2000 due to drought cycles for Florida and its subregions taken from t. 8.70, annual yearbooks. US refers to 1961–1990 average from t. 8.74.

Freshwater use of nearly 4 billion gallons per day (line 9) represents more than 48 percent of the state's total consumption, higher than the region's 40 percent share of population, due to the importance of irrigated agriculture in the region. The region generated 10.1 million tons of solid waste in 1999 (line 10) and landed 32 million pounds of fish, or 31.5 percent of the state's total in 1996.

A total of 7.5 million motor vehicle tags were sold in the region in 2001 (line 12). This figure includes 4.2 million passenger cars or 46 percent of the state's total but excludes cars driven by "snow birds" not licensed within the state.

In 2001, almost 25 million visitors came to South Florida by auto and air, almost 40 percent of the state's total (line 14). When this number is multiplied by the average number of days per visitor, this visitation represents a total of 360 000 visitor-years, an increase of 5.5 percent over the region's resident population (lines 15–16). This presumes that the visitors were distributed evenly throughout the year. If the 360 000 visitor-year equivalents (line 15) are concentrated in a four-month period, then the "effective population" (residents plus visitors) may represent as much as a 15 percent increase over the "estimated" resident population, expanding the "peak" demand for water, transport, and medical services over the "average" loads based on year-round resident population.

Because of the concentration of national sites – Everglades Park, Biscayne Park, and Big Cypress Preserve – the South Florida region attracted 5.7 million visitors, or almost two thirds the state's total national park visitation (line 17). The state parks, however, are distributed more widely around the state. Therefore, the 5.8 million visitors to South Florida's state parks (line 18) represent but a third of all visitors to the entire state park system.

In 1997, there were 117 municipalities in South Florida, nearly 30 percent of the total in the state (line 19), and 196 "special districts" (or 37 percent of the total) that serve a variety of transit, health, welfare, and environmental purposes (line 20).

In summary, the South Florida area, while representing 0.4 of one percent of America's land area (line 1, column 6), contains 2.3 percent if the country's population and personal income (lines 2–3) and 2.6 percent of both the country's poor and bank deposits (lines 5–6). But the region accounted for 4 percent of all housing starts in the nation in 2001,[3] 4.4 of the nation's solid waste, 3 percent of all new passenger car tags, and 2 percent of all national park visitors (see lines 7, 10, 13, 17, column 6).

The region is even more varied if we consider its agricultural character. Its 6600 farms, which comprise 19 percent of the state's total number but occupy 39 percent of the state's total farmland, average 604 acres each or more than twice the average for the state (lines B. 1–3, columns 1, 2, 4).

Forty-one percent of the land area of South Florida is in farms, compared to 30 percent for the entire state and 48 percent for the US (line 4). More than 1.1 million of South Florida's 4 million farm acres are irrigated (compare line B.5 to line B.2), which is 62 percent of all irrigated land in the state.

The size distribution of farms suggests a wider dispersion in the region than for the state and nation as a whole (line B.6, columns 1–3). In South Florida, almost two thirds, or 65 percent, of the farms are small, ranging from 1 to 49 acres. These small farms account for 1.6 percent of the farm area, in contrast to the 8.4 percent of the category of farms that are 1000 acres or more and that occupy 83.2 percent of the land area. For the state as a whole, the small farms accounted for a lower share, 58 percent, of the number, and a higher share, 4 percent, of the land, than in South Florida. The large farms in the state account for 5 percent of the number and 59 percent of the land. In South Florida, the category of middle-size farms, which range from 50 to 999 acres, accounts for 15.2 percent of the farmland compared to 37.3 percent of farmland for the state.

South Florida agriculture is thus characterized by extremes: a relatively large share of the number of both very small and very large farms and a weak representation of middle-size farms. In this respect, the South Florida region and the state *both* differ from the overall US profile (line B.6, column 3), in which only 29.5 percent of all farms are small (less than 50 acres). Sixty-one percent are middle-sized (50–999 acres), and the almost 10 percent of the number which are the very large farms (1000 acres or bigger) account for 62.5 percent of the total farm area, a lower share of land than in South Florida, but higher than in the state. The Kuznets ratio, which is a measure of inequality, indicates the highest value (1.50) for South Florida compared to 1.08 for Florida and 1.07 for the US.

The value of South Florida's agricultural produce in 1997 was $2.9 billion, 48 percent of the state total (line B.7). Thus, South Florida, with but 0.43 percent of the nation's farm acres and 2 percent of the nation's irrigated areas, produced 1.5 percent of the value of US farm output in 1997.

The great inequality in the size distribution of South Florida farms – a great many small farms, fewer middle-sized farms, and a few very large farms – is due to the range of crops and agricultural activities. In 1997, the Agricultural Census for this region recorded 626 000 cows and calves, 436 000 acres of sugar cane, 124 000 acres of vegetables, 56.8 million citrus trees, and $609 million in nursery and green house sales (lines B.8–12). Of the state's total agricultural activities, South Florida represented 35 percent of the cattle inventory, 100 percent of all cane lands, half of all vegetable land, 53 percent of all citrus trees, and 42 percent of all nursery sales (column 4).

In terms of national ranking, South Florida agriculture is significant. It accounts for 47 percent of the nation's sugarcane land, 37.5 percent of citrus trees, 6 percent of all nursery sales, and 3.37 percent of all vegetable acreage.

In terms of its environmental importance, the region is home to 35 animal and 34 plant species that are listed as threatened or endangered (TESS) by the US Fish and Wildlife Service. These represent 61 percent and 63 percent, respectively, of the total number of threatened and endangered species found in the entire state (lines C.1–2, columns 1, 4). It is important to note that South Florida, which represents 0.43 percent of the total US land area and 1.36 percent of US water area, provides a habitat for 6.8 percent of the animal and 4.6 percent of the plant species on the federal threatened and endangered lists (lines A.1, C.1–2, 4, column 6).

Compared to the rest of the state and the nation, the maximum elevation of the region is considerably lower, the water area more extensive, and the climate warmer and wetter (see lines C.3–5, columns 1–6).

THE GROWTH OF THE REGION, 1970–2000, AND PROJECTIONS

South Florida has been growing at sustained and breakneck speeds throughout the past four decades. The population of 2.6 million in 1970 doubled by 1990 and rose another 20 percent by 2000. The area's population could surpass 10.5 million by 2030 (see Table 6.2, line 1). Employment and output in real terms (lines 2 and 3) grew at faster rates than population from 1970 to 2000 and, as a result, real output per person rose by almost 17 percent during the period (line 4). (Annual growth rates for the indicators are given in the furthest right columns of Table 6.2.)

During the thirty-year housing boom (line 5), the greatest average annual number of multi-family starts occurred in the decade of the 1970s, but the number of single-family starts doubled from the 1970s to the 1990s. The result has been almost a constant average number of all housing starts ranging from 65 000 to 69 000 units per *year* for the three decades!

The number of starts forecast for the decades 2000–2010 shows a marked increase in multi-family and a decline in single-family starts.[4]

The age distribution for South Florida (line 6) shows stability for the period 1980 to 2000 with a quarter of the people under 25 years, 56 percent between 25 and 65 years, and 19 percent over 65 years. The projections to 2020 indicate a decline in the two younger groups and an increase in the over-65 group to 28 percent of the total.

Table 6.2 *South Florida Growth, Historical 1970–2000, and Projections, 2010–2030**

| | Historical | | | | Projections | | | Annual growth rates for period | | | | | |
| | | | | | | | | Historical | | | | Projections | |
	1970	1980	1990	2000	2010	2020	2030	1970–1979	1980–1989	1990–1999	2000–2009	2010–2019	2020–2030
1. Population (thou.)	2 593	3 868	5 112	6 444	8 156	9 482	10 559	4.08	2.83	2.34	2.38	1.52	1.08
2. Employment (thou.)	1 208	1 971	2 689	3 473	4 289	4 548	4 919	5.02	3.16	2.59	2.13	0.59	0.79
3. Real output ($92 bill.)	71.1	116.9	165.3	231.3	322.6	373.2	441.3	5.10	3.53	3.42	3.38	1.47	1.69
4. Real output/cap ($92)	27 420	30 222	32 336	35 894	39 554	39 359	41 794	0.98	0.68	1.05	0.98	−0.05	0.60
5. Private housing starts (thou.) (av. annu. per decade)		1970–79	1980–89	1990–99	2000–09								
a. Multi-family		40.3	33.4	16.1	29.2	na	na	—	−1.86	−7.04	6.13	na	na
b. Single-family		24.8	32.6	53.1	42.0	na	na	—	2.77	5.00	−2.32	na	na
c. All		65.1	66.0	69.2	71.0	na	na	—	0.14	0.47	0.26	na	na
6. Population distrib. (%)													
a. 0–24 yrs.	29.1	25.3	24.8	25.2	23.7	20.4	—						
b. 25–65 yrs.	53.3	55.6	56.3	56.2	57.4	51.3	—						
c. 65+ yrs.	17.5	19.1	19.0	18.6	18.9	28.3	—						
7. Employment shares (%)													
a. Farm and ag services	3.8	3.9	3.2	3.0	2.7	2.9	3.0						
b. Mining and const	8.0	7.4	6.6	5.6	5.6	5.5	5.8						
c. Manufacturing	10.6	9.4	7.0	5.4	4.6	3.8	3.2						
d. Trans./public util.	6.8	6.1	5.3	5.5	5.0	4.3	3.7						

116

c. Fin/Ins/real est	9.2	11.4	10.2	8.8	8.3	8.0	7.8
f. Commerce	23.2	23.9	24.1	23.9	23.5	21.5	19.9
g. Services, pers. and business	25.6	26.5	31.8	36.5	39.2	42.2	45.0
h. Government	12.8	11.4	11.8	11.2	11.1	11.6	11.7
Sum	100.0	100.0	100.0	100.0	100.0	100.0	100.0
8. Emp. shares summary (%)							
A+	3.8	3.9	3.2	3.0	2.7	2.9	3.0
M+	25.5	22.9	18.9	16.5	15.3	13.7	12.6
S+	70.7	73.2	77.9	80.5	82.0	83.4	84.4
Totals	100.0	100.0	100.0	100.0	100.0	100.0	100.0
9. So. Fl in state (%)							
a. Population	38.2	39.7	39.5	40.3	38.8	38.5	38.4
b. Employment	40.7	41.9	39.4	39.2	39.0	38.7	38.4
c. Output	45.3	45.4	42.0	41.3	41.1	40.8	40.5
d. Housing starts:	1970–79	1980–89	1990–99	2000–09			
1) Multi-fam.	53.5	49.0	50.3	69.5	na	na	na
2) Single-fam.	36.8	34.3	32.3	38.2	na	na	na
3) All	45.6	40.4	35.2	46.7	na	na	na

Note: * Projections are from REMI runs of Weisskoff, medium projections, 2000–2030.

Sources and Methods:

Historical data: Lines 1 and 9a are from Census 1970–2000. Lines 2–3, 6–9 b, c are from REMI historical database, obtained by summing the four subregions for South Florida and the "rest of Florida" to obtain Florida state estimates for line 9. Data for line 5 are from BEBR, Long-term Economic Forecast (1997) which gives historical series back to 1970. BEBR (Aug. 2002) updates the series.

Projections: Lines 1 and 9a are from REMI model for 2010–2030; Lines 2–3 and 9b,c for 2000–2030 are based on Weisskoff medium projections with all missing pieces. Lines 5 and 9d are from BEBR (Aug. 2002) summed from the counties. Lines 6–8 are from REMI control corrected for "employment update."

Employment shares summary (line 8): A+ is agriculture and ag. services (line 7a); M+ is manufacturing plus construction and public utilities (lines 7 b–d); S+ includes all services (lines 7 e–h).

These distributions contrast with the US profiles (not shown) in which the youngest group, which comprised 35.3 percent of the total in 2000, is projected to *decline* to 32.9 percent by 2020. The middle group of the 25–65 working years comprised 52.2 percent of the US in 2000, and is projected to decline to 50.6 percent by 2020.[5] Thus, South Florida has a smaller share of young people and a slightly greater share of working age people. But the greatest difference lies in the shares of retirees who comprised 12.4 percent of the US total in 2000 with a projected increase to 16.5 percent in 2020. This highlights the role of South Florida as a preferred retirement destination but still with a significant working-age and under 24 population.

The employment distribution (line 7) traces the declining shares of many of the basic economic sectors through the three decades. The shares of workers in agriculture, construction, manufacturing, transport, public utilities, finance, and real estate all declined over the years and are projected to continue to fall. The shares of commerce (line 7f) and government (line 7h) have remained constant. Only the share of personal and business services (line 7g), which grew from 26.5 to 36.5 percent between 1980 and 2000, is projected to increase by 2030.

The summary shares of employment (line 8) indicate agriculture will persist at around 3 percent of the total. The M+ sector, which declined from 25.5 to 16.5 percent between 1970 and 2000, is projected to fall to 12.6 percent by 2030. The S+ sector, which grew from 70.7 to 80.5 percent between 1970 and 2000, is projected to grow to 84.4 percent by 2030. The future South Florida will be truly a "service economy," but with significant if reduced traces of the agriculture and manufacturing sectors.

The share of South Florida's population in the state (line 9a) is projected to fall from 40.3 percent in 2000 to 38.4 percent by 2030. As a fraction of the entire state, employment will remain around 39 or falling to 38 percent and output at 41 percent of the state totals (line 9b–c). The region's multi-family housing starts, which have accounted for 49–50 percent of the state's total in the past twenty years, is expected to rise to 70 percent of the state's total and the share of single-family starts, which has accounted for a third of the state's total, is expected to rise to 38 percent by the end of the present decade. In conclusion, South Florida, with 39 percent of the region's population in 2010, will account for 41 percent of the state's output and 47 percent of housing starts of all types (lines 9a, c, and d-3).

NOTES

1. The counties we include in this analysis are given in Table 4.1.
2. The indices of the cost of living for the region's three biggest counties – Miami-Dade, Broward, and Palm Beach – average almost 7 percent higher than the statewide index. See BEBR fsa (2002b), Table 24.80.
3. The whole of Florida accounted for 10.2 percent! See line 7, columns 5–6.
4. The data available so far for 2000–2002 reveal an annual average issuing of 40 000 single-family and 25 000 multi-family housing permits, which is consistent with the targeted projections. See BEBR (2003).
5. US Census Bureau (2001, Tables 11 and 13).

7. History: Carving up South Florida

How did it all get started? How did we get to where we are today? The history of the drainage works and the transportation system is the history of the region. Ecologists view history as the interaction of the natural phenomena, such as floods, hurricanes, and droughts, with the impulse to build and manage the drainage system. The goal of this chapter is to highlight those economic events that have played an important role and to trace the major changes through a series of maps.

The historic Everglades (Figure 7.1) includes the Kissimmee River Basin in the north, the Big Cypress Swamp to the west, the historic Everglades south of Lake Okeechobee, and Florida Bay and the Keys in the south.

The first large-scale development attempt in South Florida began in 1881 with Hamilton Disston's $1 million purchase of 4 million acres west of Lake Okeechobee to be drained for sugar and rice farming. The "Panic" of 1893 and the depression that followed put an end to this speculative project.[1]

Miami was connected to Flagler's East Coast Railway in 1896[2] and work began on its extension south to Key West.

The 1905 gubernatorial election was a "referendum on the fate of the Everglades,"[3] and once elected, Napoleon Bonaparte Broward took immediate responsibility for Everglades drainage.[4] By 1917, the four major canals for draining Lake Okeechobee – the West Palm Beach Canal, the Hillsboro Canal, the North New River Canal, and the Miami Canal – were operating[5] (see Figure 7.2). (These were to become the backbone of the C&SF Project thirty years later.) Flagler reached Key West in 1912, and the great east–west "dig" across the lower Florida peninsula began in 1915 (to be finished by 1928) as US 41, the *Tam*pa–*Miami* Trail, now known as the Tamiami Trail. This project integrated the entire south coast for the first time, and it also effectively dammed up the sheet flow moving into the southern Everglades.

Major hurricanes in 1926 and 1928 put an end to Florida land speculation when it became recognized that the lands that were sold and resold were submerged and unreachable. Professor Galbraith reminds us of a more important effect of those hurricanes. Once the Florida land frenzy ceased, the nation's speculative millions moved north from the real estate offices to Wall Street and became involved in another uncontrollable frenzy that would ultimately result

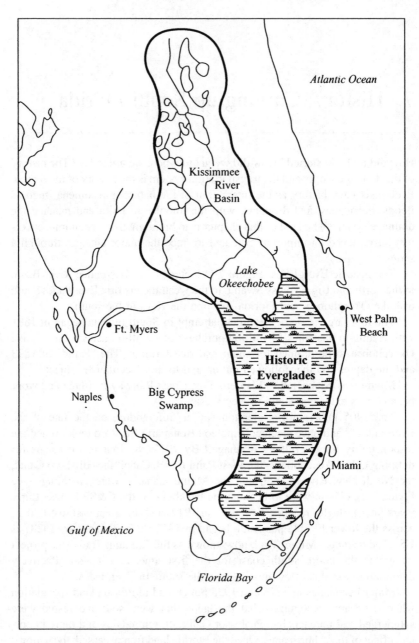

Source: Light and Dineen (1994, p. 52).

Figure 7.1 Historic Everglades: Kissimmee–Okeechobee–Everglades Watershed

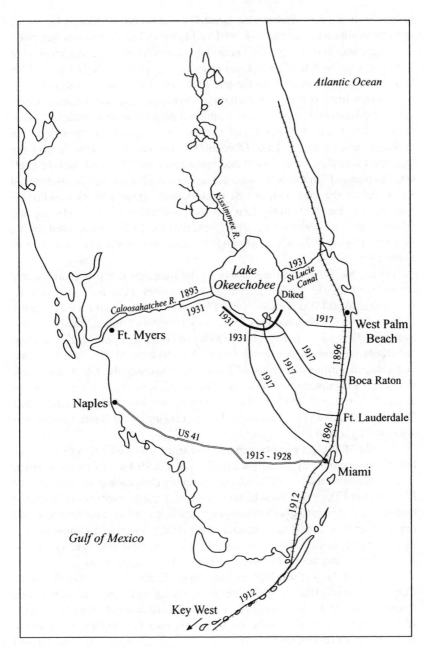

Figure 7.2 The First Cuts

in the Crash of 1929.[6] Perhaps the Great Depression can be seen as having its roots in the drainage schemes of the Everglades and the hurricanes that put a temporary stop to them.[7] Seventy years later, a similar reversal is again playing itself out, with the fate of Everglades restoration, especially the Homestead Air Base controversy, determining the fate of the presidency of the nation.[8]

Another irony is that even during the Depression era, when South Florida suffered considerable neglect, four important projects were nevertheless completed. The Bolles & Cross Canal cut east–west across the three southern drainage canals south of Lake Okeechobee. The entire southern face of the lake itself was diked with a sand and muck levee by 1931, and the lake itself was "unplugged" to the west with a canal connection to the Caloosahatchee River and to the east with the St Lucie Canal. These provided additional controls over the levels in the lake. All told, 440 miles of canal were dug and 47 miles of levee constructed.[9] This, then, was the basic infrastructure of the first cuts (Figure 7.2), which allowed the basic expansion and settlement of South Florida.

During the Depression era, a more solid dike was completed around the entire lake by 1938, named after President Hoover. Four major events then occurred as World War II ended. In 1947, Everglades National Park was finally dedicated into the National Park System by President Truman,[10] and Marjorie Stoneman Douglas' *The Everglades: River of Grass* was published. The great hurricanes and subsequent flooding of 1946–48 brought 106 inches of rain and deluged millions of acres of land.[11] In response, the US Army Corps developed a Comprehensive Plan in 1948, which was authorized by Congress as the "Central and Southern Florida Project for Flood Control and Other Purposes" (PL80-858).[12] The second great carving up of South Florida was about to begin (see Figure 7.3).

The C&SF Project was planned and constructed by the Corps of Engineers, but it was operated by a civilian district, the C&SF Flood Control District, which succeeded the older Everglades Drainage District and the Okeechobee Flood Control District.[13] Four technologies were used: levees for establishing boundaries and blocking water flows; large surface reservoirs for storing water; improvements in canals and channels for moving water; and pumps – some of the largest in the world – for moving water around the system's canals, storage areas, and out to the ocean or toward the Gulf of Mexico.

The C&SF Project was built in four stages. From 1952 to 1954, the Army Corps constructed 100 miles of levees from 9 to 18 feet high from Palm Beach County to South Dade. "Borrow" canals were constructed along the levees, so-called because the fill for the levee was excavated or "borrowed" from the canal (never to be replaced, or, in some cases, to be repaid 50 years later in "Everglades Restoration"). This series of levees interrupted the east–west surface or sheet flow.

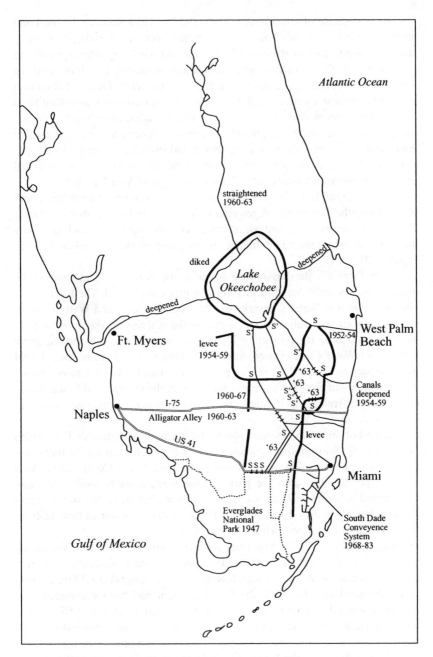

Figure 7.3   Carving up South Florida

The next phase of construction, from 1954 to 1959, secured the west and north boundaries of the Water Conservation Areas by installing pumping stations ("water control structures"), carving out the Everglades Agricultural Area (EAA) with a series of seven levees and deepening the three southern drainage canals (Hillsboro, North New River, and Miami). Three water control structures, modestly called the S-1 A, B, and C, moved water westward from Water Conservation Area No. 2 to Water Conservation Area No. 3. The S-9 pump station, according to Light and Dineen, was "one of few examples where back-pumping from suburbs was designed and installed in the project," specifically to move water from east to west, from the South New River Canal in Western Broward County into Water Conservation Area No. 3.[14]

What emerged from the muck was 700 000 acres of prime farm land south of the lake (the Everglades Agricultural Area), three large bath tubs (Water Conservation Areas 1, 2, and 3), or levee-enclosed sumps for holding waters that could be manipulated or shunted by the pumping stations (labeled "S" in Figure 7.3).

From 1960–63, the Kissimmee River to the north was straightened, its meandering stream reduced from 103 to 56 miles of channel. The levees were completed around Water Conservation Areas 1, 2, and 3, and Water Conservation Area 2B was sub-partitioned due to the inability of the area "to hold water as needed by the project."[15] The S-141 structure was designed to move water from Water Conservation Area 2B to Water Conservation Area 3, and the S-38 structure was designed to pump water eastward to recharge coastal ground water and slow the saltwater intrusion of the coastal well fields. Water Conservation Area 3 was divided into two segments by a diagonal levee and a borrow canal.

At the bottom of the system and at the northern boundary of Everglades National Park, four control structures were built, each with six 25-foot-wide vertical lift gates to allow water to discharge from Water Conservation Area 3A through the levee into the park. To the west, a north–south levee was constructed separating Water Conservation Area 3A from the Big Cypress Swamp, but a gap of 7.5 miles was left open to allow water to flow in from the west rather than flood privately held lands.

Alligator Alley, or I-75, a second east–west highway across the Everglades, was constructed in the early 1960s from Ft Lauderdale to Naples, but this highway incorporated many design features to allow water and wildlife to cross under the roadbed. By 1973, the C&SF System had been completed, and minimum water deliveries to the park had been negotiated. From 1968 to 1983, the South Dade Conveyance System was created, a series of complicated canals and structures to improve water supply to the park and protect the South Dade farmlands.[16] By the early 1980s, South Florida's basic infrastructure was in place.

All this is to say that one of the most complicated water management systems in the world is at work daily and unobtrusively. The famous "levees" are rather modest-looking structures, barely bumps to those from more mountainous regions, marked by simple signs, such as "L-30" or "L-40."

The water control structures so critical to the system may not even be noticed by the casual passerby. They sit, like perpetual watchdogs ready to spring into action when the floats that mark the water levels in their feeder canals signal headquarters that action needs to be taken. Then by remote control, the pumps are turned on and water begins to move around the system in anticipation of coming rainfall or in response to weather events. The main control center in West Palm Beach, attended around the clock by a team of applied weather forecaster-practitioners, is also a truly impressive operation.

Back on the road, the casual driver heading north from Alligator Alley along US 27 will miss the three S-11s (A, B, C) in the blink of an eye. Yet, it is those three pumping stations that move water between Water Conservation Areas 2 and 3. Further north, on US 441 between Belle Glade and Palm Beach at the very top of Water Conservation Area 1, also known as Loxahatchee National Wildlife Refuge, the four S-5s (A, AW, AE, AS), pump vast quantities of water from agricultural canals. Their frothy foam is ringed by the periscope-like eyes of countless alligators awaiting the fish discharged through the churning waters.

To the south, along Tamiami Trail west of Miami toward Buffalo Tiger's Airboat Ride and the Shark Valley entrance of Everglades National Park, the four S-12s (A–D), sit like primeval pyramids fitted with sluice-gates that control the life waters of all that would flow south.

None of these structures has a "welcome" sign. Some have modest parking lots for repair or operators' vehicles. Others warn "keep out." But each structure, levee, and canal is critically important to the system, since these are the artificial kidneys, hearts, livers and by-passes that have been inserted all around to keep the waters contained or in their course and, above all, to keep the cities dry.

What is the next stage? What was once crooked and then straightened – the Kissimmee River – was "restored" to some of its original crookedness by the year 2000[17] and holds out a model of what restoration can accomplish. The Comprehensive Everglades Restoration Plan (CERP) is intended to adjust the flows, and an overly simplified caricature of the Plan is reproduced in Figure 7.4. Some of the EAA will be dedicated to water storage; the levees between the Water Conservation Areas will be dismantled and the borrow canals filled. More water, of better quality, and in a more natural timing should be directed to Everglades National Park. These are the objectives.

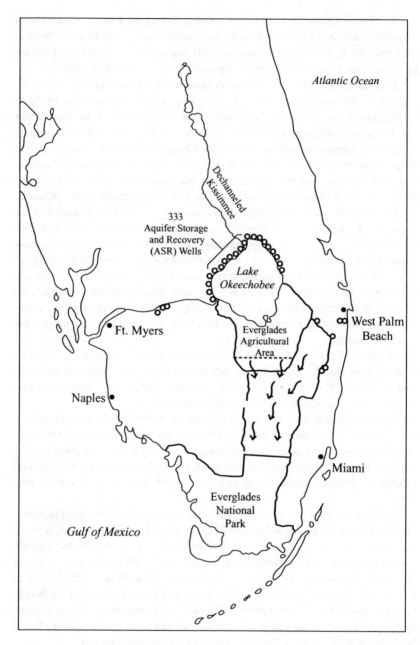

Source: National Research Council (2001, Figure 2).

Figure 7.4   Restoration Plans

Let us turn now to the historical record of how the first C&SF Project and its antecedents allowed society to grow and to construct a vibrant economy on otherwise inhospitable terrain.

NOTES

1. See Douglas (1947: pp. 282–6). Disston dug one short drainage canal in the lower Caloosa-hatchee. McCally (1999: p. 89), adds that Disston also had a contract by which he could claim half of all the other lands that his companies drained. Light and Dineen (1994: p. 53) write that Disston drained 50 000 acres, and that he demonstrated the productiveness of the upper Kissimmee River, opened the Kissimmee River to navigation, and linked the Caloosa-hatchee River to Lake Okeechobee. See Blake, *Land into Water* (1980: pp. 77–83).
2. See Fernald and Purdum, *Atlas of Florida* (1996: p. 104). For a narrative, see Muir, *Miami USA* (1953), "The Word is Railroad," pp. 46–53.
3. Light and Dineen (1994: p. 54).
4. See Douglas (1947: pp. 312–14).
5. Sklar et al. (2001) gives the following dates for the "opening" of the canals, stating that the dates themselves are not "well defined:" West Palm Beach, 1920; Hillsboro, 1915; North New River, 1912; Miami, 1913. My dates are from Fernald and Purdum (1996: p. 106), and Light and Dineen (1994: p. 55).
6. See J.K. Galbraith (1954, 2nd edn 1961: pp. 8–28).
7. Solecki (2001: Fig. 2, p. 347) points out that much of Florida history reflects national and international changes on its land patterns.
8. See Michael Grunwald, "From Homestead to the White House, by Way of the Everglades," *Washington Post*, June 23, 2002, p. A16.
9. Sklar et al. (2001) have the Caloosahatchee Canal begun in 1915 and opened in 1925; the St Lucie initiated in 1916 and opened in 1926; the muck levee on the south shore of Lake Okeechobee, initiated in 1921 and opened in 1926. The year 1931 used in my Figure 7.2 is from Light and Dineen (1994: p. 55).
10. See Douglas (1947: pp. 380–81), for a narrative of the struggle to make the Everglades into a national park.
11. See Light and Dineen (1994: Fig. 4.7) for a map of the flood areas.
12. See the US 80th Congress, 2nd Session, "Comprehensive Report on Central and Southern Florida…" (1949), House Document No. 643.
13. Today the agency is known as the South Florida Water Management District, as reorganized under Florida's Water Resources Act of 1972. See Fernald and Purdum (1998: p. 161), and the insights of Light, Gunderson, and Holling (1995: pp. 133–4). The Florida Comprehensive Planning Act was passed in the same year.
14. Light and Dineen (1994: p. 63), quoting R.M. Cooper and J. Roy, "Atlas of Surface Water Management Basics", SFWMD, West Palm Beach, 1991.
15. Light and Dineen (1994: p. 65).
16. Light and Dineen (1994: pp. 66–71).
17. See Michael Grunwald, "An Environmental Reversal of Fortune: The Kissimmee's Revival Could Provide Lessons for Restoring the Everglades," *Washington Post*, June 26, 2002; p. A01.

8. Population and the Regions

In this chapter, our goal is to reconstruct the numerical record of South Florida's growth. Various historical accounts give narratives of the trials and happenings, political histories, and histories of public works and drainage. Missing from these has been a solid statistical record, pieced together from the long series of population and agricultural censuses, the latter giving us a continuous recording of the dramatic changes in farmland use.

We shall divide South Florida into four sub-regions: the Lower East Coast (LEC), consisting of Broward, Dade (changed to Miami-Dade in 1996), Monroe, and Palm Beach counties; the Lower West Coast (LWC), consisting of Collier, Glades, Henry, and Lee; the Kissimmee River Valley (KSV), consisting of Highlands, Okeechobee, and Osceola; and finally, the Upper East Coast (UEC), consisting of Martin and St Lucie.

These regions correspond roughly to different sub-watersheds within the Greater Everglades Area and, to some extent, parallel the four "Planning Areas" used by the South Florida Water Management District. Later in this study we shall also examine detailed economic models of these four regions and the role they play in Everglades restoration.

POPULATION SERIES

The South Florida population of 24 224 in 1890 doubled to 55 000 by 1910 and then doubled again in every ten-year census until 1960 when it reached 1.7 million people. By 1980, twenty years later, South Florida more than doubled to 3.9 million. The next doubling is expected by 2010, with the middle level forecast of 7.7 million. By 2030, the South Florida population is expected to exceed 10 million (Table 8.1, column 2).

In absolute numbers, South Florida has gained more in the last three decades than in earlier decades, adding more than 1.2 to 1.3 million new people per decade. Thus the "slowing" growth *rate* (Table 8.2, column 4) is really a mirage due to the larger base on which the "percentage increases" are based.

Until 1920, South Florida was a relatively insignificant fraction of the state, accounting for less than 12 percent of the state's population (see Table 8.3, column 2). By 1930, the share of South Florida in the state had grown to

Table 8.1   Time Series of Population by Region, 1890–2030

	Florida (1)	SF (2)	LEC (3)	LWC (4)	KSV (5)	UEC (6)
1890	391 400	24 224	19 677	1 414	3 133	
1900	528 500	29 476	22 961	3 071	3 444	
1910	752 600	54 949	39 073	6 294	5 507	4 075
1920	968 500	112 845	86 092	9 540	9 327	7 886
1930	1 468 200	288 769	228 454	24 127	24 020	12 168
1940	1 897 414	472 703	401 600	30 572	22 365	18 166
1950	2 771 305	818 287	723 662	38 142	28 496	27 987
1960	4 951 560	1 729 398	1 545 020	81 361	46 791	56 226
1970	6 791 418	2 593 133	2 289 471	158 784	66 007	78 871
1980	9 746 961	3 867 813	3 283 712	315 828	117 077	151 196
1990	12 938 071	5 111 686	4 134 252	520 576	205 787	251 071
2000	15 982 378	6 444 399	5 090 153	739 051	295 769	319 426
2010	18 866 700	7 654 000	5 939 300	953 900	375 300	385 500
2020	21 792 600	8 908 600	6 825 600	1 172 200	458 600	452 200
2030	24 528 600	10 089 100	7 656 000	1 380 500	537 900	514 700

Note: Data from 1890 to 2000 are census estimates, 2010–2030 are BEBR medium projections.

Source: US Census aggregated counties into sub-regions. Projections from BEBR fsa 2002, t. 1.41, aggregating counties.

20 percent, by 1950 to 30 percent, and by 1980 to 40 percent, where it has remained since.

Within South Florida, the population of the Lower East Coast increased more rapidly than the other regions until 1960, when the four counties with 1.5 million accounted for 89 percent of South Florida's people. This share fell to 79 percent in 2000, as the LWC developed from 81,000 to almost three quarters of a million between 1960 and 2000. The LWC is expected to reach 1.4 million by 2030, with the remaining regions – Kissimmee and the UEC – growing to around half a million by 2030 or to 5 percent of South Florida's population. Although the UEC is currently larger in population than the Kissimmee Valley, the KSV is expected to be slightly more populated by 2030.

Note that the high rates of population growth do not necessarily mean high absolute gains in population. The smaller regions, KSV and UEC and even LWC, grew fastest in the decades of the 1950s and 1970s, with the ROG (rate of growth) of population of LWC and KSV falling to around 40 percent for the decades of the 1990s and the 2000s. LEC grew fastest in the 1920s, 1930s, and 1950s, when its population too was less than a million. The 1990–2000 ROG fell to 23 percent, but the region added nearly a million people, more than in any decade except for 1970–80. This word of caution is directed to

Table 8.2 Time Series of Absolute and Percentage Population Change by Decade and Region, 1890–2030

	Florida		South Florida		LEC		LWC		KSV		UEC	
	Abs. chg. (1)	% chg. (2)	Abs. chg. (3)	% chg. (4)	Abs. chg. (5)	% chg. (6)	Abs. chg. (7)	% chg. (8)	Abs. chg. (9)	% chg. (10)	Abs. chg. (11)	% chg. (12)
1890–1900	137 100	35.0	5 252	21.7	3 284	16.7	1 657	117.2	311	9.9		
1900–1910	224 100	42.4	25 473	86.4	16 112	70.2	3 223	104.9	2 063	59.9	4 075	93.5
1910–1920	215 900	28.7	57 896	105.4	47 019	120.3	3 246	51.6	3 820	69.4	3 811	54.3
1920–1930	499 700	51.6	175 924	155.9	142 362	165.4	14 587	152.9	14 693	157.5	4 282	54.3
1930–1940	429 214	29.2	183 934	63.7	173 146	75.8	6 445	26.7	−1 655	−6.9	5 998	49.3
1940–1950	873 891	46.1	345 584	73.1	322 062	80.2	7 570	24.8	6 131	27.4	9 821	54.1
1950–1960	2 180 255	78.7	911 111	111.3	821 358	113.5	43 219	113.3	18 295	64.2	28 239	100.9
1960–1970	1 839 858	37.2	863 735	49.9	744 451	48.2	77 423	95.2	19 216	41.1	22 645	40.3
1970–1980	2 955 543	43.5	1 274 680	49.2	994 241	43.4	157 044	98.9	51 070	77.4	72 325	91.7
1980–1990	3 191 110	32.7	1 243 873	32.2	850 540	25.9	204 748	64.8	88 710	75.8	99 875	66.1
1990–2000	3 044 307	23.5	1 332 713	26.1	955 901	23.1	218 475	42.0	89 982	43.7	68 355	27.2
2000–2010	2 884 322	22.3	1 209 601	23.7	849 147	20.5	214 849	41.3	79 531	38.6	66 074	26.3
2010–2020	2 925 900	15.5	1 254 600	16.4	886 300	14.9	218 300	22.9	83 300	22.2	66 700	17.3
2020–2030	2 736 000	12.6	1 180 500	13.3	830 400	12.2	208 300	17.8	79 300	17.3	62 500	13.8

Source: Computed from Table 8.1 above.

133

Table 8.3   Population Shares of South Florida and its Sub-Regions,
             1890–2030

	Florida (1)	% SF/state (2)	% region in SF			
			LEC (3)	LWC (4)	KSV (5)	UEC (6)
1890	100.0	6.2	81.2	5.8	12.9	0.0
1900	100.0	5.6	77.9	10.4	11.7	0.0
1910	100.0	7.3	71.1	11.5	10.0	7.4
1920	100.0	11.7	76.3	8.5	8.3	7.0
1930	100.0	19.7	79.1	8.4	8.3	4.2
1940	100.0	24.9	85.0	6.5	4.7	3.8
1950	100.0	29.5	88.4	4.7	3.5	3.4
1960	100.0	34.9	89.3	4.7	2.7	3.3
1970	100.0	38.2	88.3	6.1	2.5	3.0
1980	100.0	39.7	84.9	8.2	3.0	3.9
1990	100.0	39.5	80.9	10.2	4.0	4.9
2000	100.0	40.3	79.0	11.5	4.6	5.0
2010	100.0	40.6	77.6	12.5	4.9	5.0
2020	100.0	40.9	76.6	13.2	5.1	5.1
2030	100.0	41.1	75.9	13.7	5.3	5.1

Source: Computed from Table 8.1 above.

those who are alarmed solely by high growth rates of population, when it is
the absolute increase in population that measures the true additional burden
of growth.

Figure 8.1 gives us an idea of the phenomenal growth of the state in the
past century. Note the marked inflection upward in the state's growth since
1950 as compared to the more gradual upward tilt in South Florida's growth
since 1970. The slower growth of South Florida's other sub-regions contrasts
with the steeper growth path of the LEC in the lower lines in Figure 8.1.

The straight line growth paths of the actual census counts and the state's
medium forecasts to the year 2020 are actually of little consolation, as the
forecast population, especially BEBR's medium projections of population,
have traditionally understated actual performance for South Florida counties
for at least two reasons. First, the annual population figures themselves, with
the exception of the census years, are estimates projected from the previous
census. Thus, the estimate made in the year 1999 for a certain county, for
example, is itself projected from the 1990 census, and it is this "projection"
that is then used to make further projections to 2020 and 2030. But the 1999
population will itself be revised once the results of the 2000 census become
known, and the entire annual series from 1990 to 1999 will be changed
retrospectively to show gradual and "smooth" annual increases between the

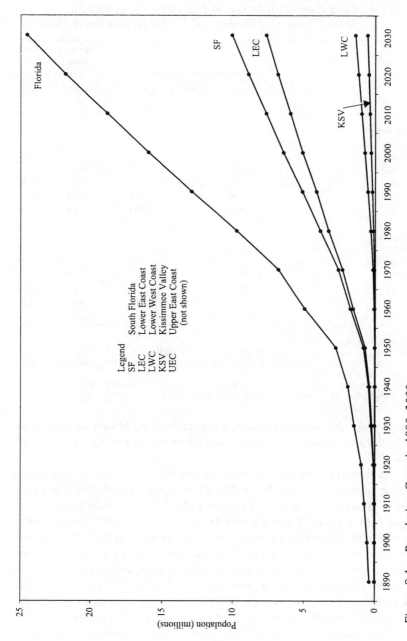

Figure 8.1   Population Growth, 1890–2030

Table 8.4 Comparing Early to Recent Population Projections for South Florida and Florida, 1982–2004 (Population in Millions)

	Census	Projections, made in			Percent error from census or latest projection	
		1982	1995	2004	1982	1995
	(1)	(2)	(3)	(4)	(5)	(6)
South Florida:						
1970	2.593					
1980	3.868					
1990	5.112	4.905			−4.2	
2000	6.444	5.600	6.090		−15.1	−5.8
2010		6.208	7.038	7.804	−25.7	−10.9
2020		6.883	7.972	9.164	−33.1	−15.0
Florida:						
1970	6.791					
1980	9.747					
1990	12.938	12.304			−5.2	
2000	15.982	14.593	15.528		−9.5	−2.9
2010		16.124	17.985	19.285	−19.6	−7.2
2020		17.815	20.350	22.588	−26.8	−11.0

Source and Method:
Projections are from BEBR, fsa 1982 and 1995, t. 1.84, BEBR, fsa 2002 t. 1.41. Percent error (columns 5–6) are comparisons of projections to actual censuses (1990, 2000) or to latest projections (2010, 2020).
Projection for 2010 made in 1982 is an exponential interpolation between 2000–2020.
Latest projection from Stanley K. Smith and Rayer (2004).

census years. Just as the past annual estimates of population are revised on the basis of the latest census, so too will the projections to 2020 and 2030 be revised!

The second reason for the under-forecasting lies in the standard demographic methodology used by BEBR, which relies on birth and death rates plus an allowance for in and out migration. In Table 8.4, I have compared the actual census figures for South Florida and Florida for 1970 through 2000, together with three different BEBR long-term projections for 2020. The first was made in 1982, the second in 1995, and the most recent in 2004. Note that the 1982 projections for the year 2000 (column 5) understated the true population by 15.1 percent and its projection for 2020 by 33.1 percent less than the most recent projections made in 2002! The projections made in 1995 for 2020 (column 6) differ from the latest projections by 15.0 percent.

The forecasts for all Florida fail equally to win our confidence. The statewide medium forecast in 1982 for 2020 differs by 26.8 percent from the projection made in 2004, and the forecast made in 1995 differs by 11.0 percent from the most recent one (see Table 8.4, columns 5 and 6, lower panel).

The three projections for South Florida are plotted in Figure 8.2 and for all Florida in Figure 8.3, "How Projections Fail." In these sketches, the distance between the different projections is a measure of the under-forecasting built into the methodology, and that distance increases the further into the future the year of the target forecast is.

This consistent under-forecasting in the South Florida context is important for a number of reasons. First, large infrastructure projects – water works, sewage lines, roads, schools – require long lead times to build. Second, consistently underestimating the fast-growing population leads us to be consistently under-prepared to face the true magnitude of our future responsibilities. The result is consistent under-investment in social capital and needed infrastructure. We are left periodically wondering "where are all these people coming from" and how are we to provide them with the level of public services they need?

Third, one might think that after several decades of consistently under-estimating future population, the methodology for forecasting – at least for these counties – might have been redesigned in some way to anticipate or monitor the faster growth! For the majority of the state's counties, BEBR's methods provide acceptable estimates.[1] But we are not interested in the major-ity of Florida counties, but in a subset of our 13 counties whose growth has consistently exceeded all statistical and demographic expectations.

The problem, I maintain, lies not with the demographers but with the economists, for population in these Florida counties is *not* solely a demo-graphic variable. People move in and out for economic reasons. Caribbean and Latin American countries collapse economically and their people seek opportunity in South Florida. Retirees are attracted by low taxes and low utility rates, young working people by the apparent low cost of housing, and tourists by the relatively low plane fares. People come, visit, and remain, and the population continues rising.

So it remains a challenge to the economist to relate the economic engines of South Florida to the population explosion by integrating demography with economy, especially because it relates to the need for water, space, and public services.

ECONOMIC PROFILES OF THE REGION

The profile of our four sub-regions is given in Table 8.5. In terms of relative size, the LEC occupies 40 percent of the land surface but has 79 percent of the people of South Florida (lines 1 and 2, column 6). The other regions have much more space relative to their populations. The LWC holds 11.5 percent

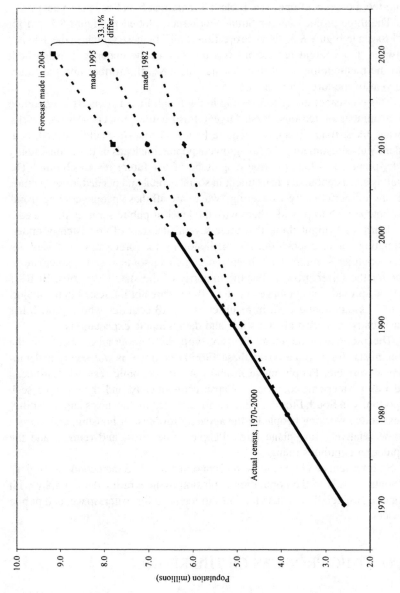

Figure 8.2   How Projections Fail: Various Population Projections for South Florida

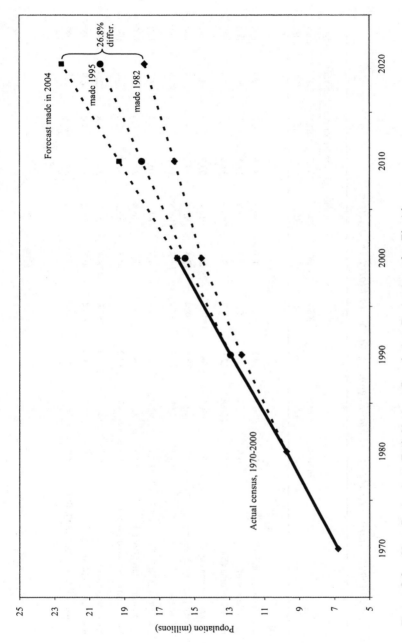

Figure 8.3   How Projections Fail: Various Population Projections for Florida

Table 8.5 *Economic Characteristics of the Sub-Regions of the South Florida Ecosystem*

	South Florida (1)	LEC (2)	LWC (3)	KSV (4)	UEC (5)	% sub-region in SF or ratio sub-region to SF*				
						LEC (6)	LWC (7)	KSV (8)	UEC (9)	Sum (10)
A. General										
1. Land (thou. sq. miles)	15.1	6.1	4.8	3.1	1.1	40.4	31.5	20.6	7.5	100
2. Population (mill.)	6.5	5.1	0.7	0.3	0.3	78.9	11.5	4.7	5.0	100
3. Personal income (bill. $)	192.7	154.8	22.9	5.7	9.4	80.3	11.9	3.0	4.9	100
4. Personal inc per cap ($)	29 876	30 405	30 986	18 967	29 281	101.8	103.7	63.5	98.0	*ratio
5. Poverty population (thou.)	849.3	699.7	73.8	38.4	37.5	82.4	8.7	4.5	4.4	100
% poverty	13.3	13.9	10.1	13.2	11.9	104.5	75.9	99.2	89.5	*ratio
6. Bank deposits (bill. $)	110.5	92.8	11.8	1.6	4.3	84.0	10.7	1.4	3.9	100
7. New housing starts (thou.)	63.6	35.9	18.6	5.4	3.7	56.4	29.2	8.5	5.8	100
8. Mobile homes licensed (thou.)	124.0	43.7	39.2	20.8	20.3	35.2	31.6	16.8	16.4	100
9. Freshwater (mgd)	3 995.5	2 149.6	977.4	389.9	478.6	53.8	24.5	9.8	12.0	100
10. Solid waste (mill. tons)	10.1	7.7	1.3	0.4	0.7	76.2	12.9	4.0	6.9	100
11. Commercial fish caught (mill. lb.)	32.0	16.5	10.6	0.0	4.9	51.6	33.1	0.0	15.3	100

	C1	C2	C3	C4	C5	C6	C7	C8	C9	C10
12. Motor vehicle tags (mill.)	7.5	5.7	1.0		0.4	76.0	13.3	5.3	5.3	100
13. Passenger car tags (mill.)	4.2	3.3	0.5	0.2	0.2	78.6	11.9	4.8	4.8	100
14. Visitors (mill.)	24.8	19.0	3.0	2.0	0.8	76.6	12.1	8.1	3.2	100
15. Visitor-years (thou.)	360.1	275.5	43.9	29.5	11.2	76.5	12.2	8.2	3.1	100
16. Visitor-years (% res. pop.)	5.5	5.3	5.7	8.7	3.4					
17. National park visitors (mill.)	5.7	5.3	0.4	0.0	0.0	93.0	7.0	0.0	0.0	100
18. State park visitors (mill.)	5.8	4.0	1.3	0.0	0.5	69.0	22.4	0.0	8.6	100
19. Municipalities (no.)	117	96	8	6	7	82.1	6.8	5.1	6.0	100
20. Special districts (no.)	196	88	75	16	17	44.9	38.3	8.2	8.7	100
B. Environmental										
1. Threat. and endang. animals (no.)	35	29	21	13	21	82.9	60.0	37.1	60.0	*ratio
2. Threat. and endang. plants (no.)	34	9	3	22	7	26.5	8.8	64.7	20.6	*ratio
3. Water area (thou. sq. miles)	2.5	1.49	0.58	0.38	0.01	60.6	23.6	15.4	0.4	100
4. Climate										
Aver. max. temp. F	83.4	83.3	83.8	83.3	n.a.	99.9	100.5	99.9	n.a.	*ratio
Aver. min. temp. F	65.8	68.6	65.1	61.2	n.a.	104.3	98.9	93.0	n.a.	*ratio
Precipitation (inches)	56.3	60.5	50.1	50.0	n.a.	107.5	89.0	88.8	n.a.	*ratio

Note: * indicates ratio of subregion to South Florida.

For sources, methods, and full titles, see Table 6.1 above.

of the region's people and 31.5 percent of the region's land. The KSV has 5 percent of the region's population and 21 percent of the land. Only in the UEC are the people–land shares comparable, with 5 percent of the region's population living on 7.5 percent of the region's land. (See lines 1 and 2, columns 7 through 9.)

The LEC is the region's urban powerhouse. Along with the lion's share of the population, it also accounts for around 80 percent of the region's personal income, poverty population, bank deposits, solid waste, passenger cars, out-of-state visitors, and number of municipalities. (See lines 2, 3, 5, 6, 10, 13, 14, 19; column 6.)

The LWC, with 11.5 percent of the population, accounted for 29 percent of the new housing starts in 2001, which reflects the great housing boom on the West Coast, and also 32 percent of mobile home licenses, which characterizes the sub-region as a seasonal and vacation destination (lines 7, 8; column 7). The Kissimmee Valley with 4.7 percent and the UEC with 5.0 percent of South Florida's population, each accounts for 16 percent of the mobile homes in the region, a measure of vulnerability when hurricanes strike the area. Three regions – the LEC, LWC, and UEC – have significant coastlines and major commercial fishing industries (line 11).

In short, what distinguishes the LEC from the other regions is its greater population, the concentration of purchasing power, and its more intense urban life with all its attributes and drawbacks. The LWC has a higher per capita income, a lower poverty rate, and much more land for a smaller population. The KSV appears to have the lowest per capita income of all the sub-regions, but its poverty rate is no higher than that of the LEC. The high freshwater consumption of the three less populated regions – together they consume 46 percent of South Florida's total fresh water – reflects the predominance of irrigated agriculture in these regions.

We turn now to examine the growth of farming and its economic characteristics.

NOTE

1. See the series of papers by Stanley K. Smith (1987), (1991) and Smith and Sincich (1988) reviewing the forecast record for all the Florida counties.

9. The Agricultural Emporium

To the reader more accustomed to the urban scene, South Florida's agricultural prominence may come as a surprise. But in terms of land use, water use, and pollution runoff, the agricultural story is of great importance.

The goal of this chapter is to examine the agricultural profiles of the region and its sub-regions with three questions in mind: (1) What is grown and where? (2) When did it get there? (3) Are there any obvious trends that influence the demand for water and the need to restore the environment? Again, the overriding objective is to gain an understanding of the dynamic of the agricultural sector and how it affects the growth of the entire region.

THE CURRENT PICTURE

The current picture (Table 9.1) contrasts the single most heavily populated region (LEC) with the three other predominantly agrarian regions. The Lower East Coast (LEC) has 79 percent of the people (5 out of 6.4 million), 40.5 percent of the total land area, and 42 percent of the number of farms which account for 18 percent of the SF farmland (lines 1–4, columns 2, 4, 8). LEC farms are therefore smaller in size than the other regions, averaging 259 acres compared to the much larger 1042- and 867-acre ranches of the LWC and KSV, respectively, and the 511-acre farms for the UEC (line 5, columns 4–7). Two thirds of the LEC farmland is irrigated in contrast to almost half in the UEC, 21 percent of the LWC, and 12 percent of the KSV (lines 6a, b, columns 4–7).

The LEC farms produce 46.8 percent of the market value of SF (line 7), due mainly to the high proportion (41.5 percent) of the SF's irrigated land. The LEC leads the region in the acreage of sugarcane and vegetables, and the number of nurseries and value of nursery sales (lines 9, 10, 12a, b).

The Lower West Coast (LWC) has 11.5 percent of the population and about a third of the land area and farm area of South Florida (lines 1, 2, 3a, column 9). The average farm size (1042 acres) is a reflection of its large-scale cattle raising, vegetable, citrus, and sugar plantations. Almost 42 percent of SF's citrus trees, 30 percent of the cattle inventory, 26 percent of the vegetable

Table 9.1 The Agricultural Picture: South Florida and its Sub-Regions

	% Florida (1)	SF (2)	SF/FL (3)	Sub-region in South Florida				Percent sub-region in SF				
				LEC (4)	LWC (5)	KSV (6)	UEC (7)	LEC (8)	LWC (9)	KSV (10)	UEC (11)	Sum (12)
1. Population (thou.) 2000	15982.4	6444.4	40.3	5090.2	739.1	295.8	319.4	79.0	11.5	4.6	5.0	100
Land and farms (1997):												
2. All land area (thou. ac.)	34728	9740	28.0	3946	3047	2013	734	40.5	31.3	20.7	7.5	100
3a. Farmland (thou. ac.)	10454	4017	38.4	722	1391	1493	411	18.0	34.6	37.2	10.2	100
3b. Share farmland/all land (%):	30.1	41.2	—	18.3	45.7	74.2	56.0	—	—	—	—	—
4. Number farms	34799	6654	19.1	2791	1335	1723	805	41.9	20.1	25.9	12.1	100
5. Aver. farm size (ac./farm)	300.4	603.7	—	258.7	1041.9	866.5	510.6	41.9	—	—	—	—
6a. Irrigated land (thou. ac.)	1862.4	1149.2	61.7	477.1	289.7	181.3	201	41.5	25.2	15.8	17.5	100
6b. Share irrig./farmland (%):	17.8	28.6	—	66.1	20.8	12.1	48.9	—	—	—	—	—
Farm characteristics:												
7. Market value produce 1997 (mill.$)	6004.6	2861.5	47.7	1338.4	775.3	429.7	318.1	46.8	27.1	15.0	11.1	100
8a. Total cattle and calves 2002 (thou.)	1780	628.0	35.3	23.0	190.0	353.0	62.0	3.7	30.3	56.2	9.9	100
8b. Milk cows 2002 (thou.)	152.0	39.0	25.7	—	—	39.0	—	—	—	100.0	—	100
9. Sugarcane 1997 (thou. ac.)	421.4	421.0	99.9	350.9	56.8	1.7	12.0	83.3	13.5	0.4	2.9	100
10. Vegetables 1997 (thou. ac.)	250.6	133.1	53.1	99.2	33.9	—	—	74.5	25.5	—	—	100
11a. Citrus 2000 (mill. boxes)	297.7	142.8	48.0	3.4	53.0	40.6	45.9	2.4	37.1	28.4	32.1	100
11b. Citrus acreage 2000 (thou.)	832.2	417.1	50.1	11.1	156.8	105.6	143.6	2.7	37.6	25.3	34.4	100
11c. Citrus trees 2000 (mill.)	106.7	57.0	53.4	1.5	23.9	13.5	18.0	2.6	41.9	23.7	31.6	100
12a. Nurseries 1997 (no.)	5121	1698	33.2	1224	237	131	106	72.1	14.0	7.7	6.2	100
12b. Nursery sales 1997 (mill. $)	1500.0	609.0	40.6	454.9	72.8	52.9	28.3	74.7	12.0	8.7	4.6	100

Method and Sources:

Data sources give county-level statistics which were summed for each sub-region.
Line 1: BEBR fsa 2002, table 1.20, US Census totals.
Lines 2–7, 9, 10, 12: 1997 US Agricultural Census.
Line 8: USDA, NASS, State Statistical Report 01LDP23.
Line 11: Florida Agricultural Statistics Service (FASS) Citrus Summary 2000–2001, County Tables, pp. 28–30.

acreage, and 13.5 percent of the sugarcane acreage are found in this region (lines 5, 8a, 9, 10, 11c, column 9).

The Kissimmee Valley (KSV) has about 5 percent of South Florida's population, but 21 percent of the total land and 37 percent of all farmland. Its 1723 farms are second in number to the LEC, but its farms are on average more than three times larger and have the lowest proportion in SF of irrigated land (12.1 percent). The KSV has virtually all of SF's dairy herds and a majority of the cow-and-calf inventory (lines 1–6, 8a, b, columns 6, 10).

The UEC is the smallest of the regions, with 7.5 percent of the land area and 5 percent of the population. However, almost half of its farmland is irrigated (line 6b, column 7), and this enables the UEC to produce 32 percent of the region's citrus (line 11a).

What's striking about these activities is their apparently unobtrusive environmental impacts. The whole area north of the lake is one vast cattle holding area, washed down by the Kissimmee River and other creeks and canals into Lake Okeechobee. The intensive irrigation required for vegetables, and the farm runoff that flows downstream to Biscayne Bay, the Everglades, or to the estuaries are all the consequences of this most successful agricultural development, and perhaps the least examined.

The spectacular agricultural growth is a relatively new development. In the next section, we shall trace the economic history of these changes as they occurred and relate them to the drainage infrastructure.

CHANGE IN FARM CHARACTERISTICS OVER TIME

In tracing the growth of the farm sector in South Florida, we will review three major dimensions available from the Agricultural Census during the course of the century. First, we shall trace changes in acreage of farmland and in number and size of farms for our regions (Tables 9.2 and 9.3). Then we will review the changes in drainage and irrigation, value of farm produce and number of hired personnel (Tables 9.4–9.7). Finally, we will examine cropping patterns and their changes (Table 9.8).

Why do all this? The agricultural censuses are invaluable documentation and quantification of man's encroachment on the land. While the history of settlement in the region has been chronicled and told in anecdotal fashion,[1] there is, to my knowledge, no statistical chronology of the agricultural activity involved in settling and developing these lands.

In Table 9.2, I have traced the quantity and share of farmland from 1910 to 1997 and in Table 9.3, the number of farms and their average size from 1930 to 1997 for the sub-regions. These are also sketched in Figure 9.1 for all of South Florida and Figure 9.2 for the four sub-regions.

Table 9.2 Land in Farms: Acreage and Percentage by Sub-Region, 1910–1997 (farmland in thou. acres)

	LEC		LWC		KSV		UEC		SF		FL	
	farmland	% f/t	farmland	% f/t	farmland	% f/t	farmland	% f/t	farmland	% f/t	farmland	% f/t
1910	65	1.5	54	1.5	93	4.7	18	2.6	230	2.3	5 254	15.0
1920	198	4.5	44	1.4	280	14.0	40	5.8	562	5.5	6 047	17.2
1925	196	4.5	106	13.2	534	26.7	75	10.9	911	11.9	5 865	16.7
1930	113	2.8	141	4.6	151	7.6	27	3.6	432	4.4	5 027	14.3
1935	194	4.9	253	8.2	336	16.8	24	3.2	807	8.2	6 048	17.2
1940	232	5.9	691	22.7	995	49.4	192	26.2	2 110	21.7	8 338	24.0
1945	466	11.8	879	28.8	1 581	78.5	468	63.8	3 394	34.8	13 084	37.7
1950	626	15.9	1 811	59.4	1 474	73.2	588	80.1	4 499	46.2	16 528	47.6
1954	771	19.5	1 584	52.0	1 839	91.3	573	78.1	4 767	48.9	18 162	52.3
1959	583	14.6	1 432	47.0	1 599	79.4	433	59.0	4 047	41.1	15 237	43.9
1964	653	16.5	1 307	42.9	1 716	85.2	512	69.7	4 188	43.0	15 411	44.4
1969	667	16.9	1 566	51.4	1 835	91.1	537	73.2	4 605	47.3	14 032	40.4
1974	640	16.2	1 607	52.7	1 773	88.1	548	74.7	4 568	46.9	13 191	38.0
1978	908	23.0	1 544	50.7	1 718	85.3	519	70.7	4 689	48.1	13 016	37.5
1982	830	20.8	1 426	46.8	1 694	84.1	569	77.5	4 519	46.2	12 814	36.9
1987	778	19.7	1 232	40.4	1 584	78.7	528	71.9	4 122	42.3	11 194	32.2
1992	749	19.0	1 309	43.0	1 753	87.1	492	67.0	4 303	44.2	10 766	31.0
1997	722	18.3	1 391	45.7	1 493	74.2	411	56.0	4 017	41.2	10 454	30.1

Note: % f/t = percentage of farmland to total land in sub-region.

Source: Censuses of Agriculture 1935–1997; aggregated from county data.

Table 9.3 Number of Farms and Average Farm Size by Sub-Region, 1925–1997

	LEC		LWC		KSV		UEC		SF		FL	
	No. farms	Av. farm (ac.)	No. farms	Av. farm (ac.)	No. farms	Av. farm (ac.)	No. farms	Av. farm (ac.)	No. farms	Av. farm (ac.)	No. farms	Av. farm (ac.)
1925	2 747	71	901	118	2 230	239	1 087	69	6 965	131	59 217	99
1930	3 045	37	684	206	1 139	133	586	46	5 456	79	58 966	85
1935	4 761	41	934	271	1 482	227	596	40	7 773	104	72 857	83
1940	3 303	70	692	999	1 006	989	715	269	5 715	369	62 248	134
1945	3 460	135	666	1 319	1 171	1 350	812	576	6 110	555	61 159	214
1950	2 581	243	820	2 208	922	1 599	720	817	5 042	892	56 921	290
1954	2 825	273	866	1 830	1 352	1 360	921	622	5 964	799	57 543	316
1959	2 082	280	699	2 047	1 125	1 422	741	584	4 645	871	45 100	338
1964	1 937	337	732	1 786	1 252	1 371	640	800	4 560	918	40 542	380
1969	1 675	398	819	1 912	1 183	1 552	683	786	4 360	1 056	35 586	394
1974	1 687	379	845	1 902	1 266	1 400	635	864	4 433	1 031	32 466	406
1978	2 556	355	1 034	1 493	1 292	1 330	663	783	5 544	846	36 109	360
1982	2 752	302	1 014	1 406	1 355	1 251	713	798	5 834	775	36 352	352
1987	3 067	254	1 229	1 002	1 638	967	836	631	6 770	609	36 556	306
1992	3 249	231	1 369	956	1 839	953	845	583	7 301	589	35 204	306
1997	2 791	259	1 335	1 042	1 723	867	805	511	6 654	604	34 799	300

Note: Average farm size is the aggregated land in farms divided by aggregated no. farms for each region.

Source: Census of Agriculture 1935–1997.

147

Table 9.4 Drainage History, South Florida, 1950–1979

	LEC	LWC	KSV	UEC	SF	FL	%SF/FL
Total land drained, census 1978	717 269	872 000	1 033 583	562 243	3 185 095	6 454 445	49.3
Total land drained, census 1969	403 514	454 451	438 543	249 312	1 545 820	2 482 471	62.3
Land drained, 1969–78	313 755	417 549	595 040	312 931	1 639 275	3 971 974	41.3
Land drained, 1950–59	100 607	192 657	172 687	72 716	538 667	828 400	65.0
Land drained, prior 1959	2 044 782	815 803	627 962	689 718	4 178 265	5 520 054	75.7
Percentages of total SF:							
Total land drained, census 1978	22.5	27.4	32.5	17.7	100.0		
Total land drained, census 1969	26.1	29.4	28.4	16.1	100.0		
Land drained, 1970–78	19.1	25.5	36.3	19.1	100.0		
Land drained, 1950–59	18.7	35.8	32.1	13.5	100.0		
Land drained, prior 1959	48.9	19.5	15.0	16.5	100.0		

Source: U.S. Agricultural Censuses, Drainage Reports.

148

Table 9.5 Irrigated Land: Acreage and Percentage Shares by Sub-Region, 1949–1997

	Acres						%		% Sub-region/SF		
	LEC	LWC	KSV	UEC	SF	FL	SF/FL	LEC	LWC	KSV	UEC
1949	79 589	14 866	10 349	41 414	146 218	356 421	41.0	54.4	10.2	7.1	28.3
1954	115 309	50 342	17 015	52 295	234 961	427 807	54.9	49.1	21.4	7.2	22.3
1959	114 306	38 379	31 181	47 587	231 453	413 526	56.0	49.4	16.6	13.5	20.6
1964	294 984	150 187	125 230	100 347	670 748	1 217 192	55.1	44.0	22.4	18.7	15.0
1969	370 144	167 574	99 248	148 553	785 519	1 365 206	57.5	47.1	21.3	12.6	18.9
1974	360 776	326 612	95 914	155 593	938 895	1 558 735	60.2	38.4	34.8	10.2	16.6
1978	553 920	314 248	104 000	187 688	1 159 856	1 979 814	58.6	47.8	27.1	9.0	16.2
1982	345 604	256 279	103 759	166 661	872 303	1 585 080	55.0	39.6	29.4	11.9	19.1
1987	481 935	254 273	116 813	168 474	1 021 495	1 622 750	62.9	47.2	24.9	11.4	16.5
1992	478 727	320 468	125 437	196 875	1 121 507	1 782 680	62.9	42.7	28.6	11.2	17.6
1997	477 119	289 737	181 337	201 027	1 149 220	1 862 404	61.7	41.5	25.2	15.8	17.5

Source: Census of Agriculture 1954–1997.

149

Table 9.6   Sales of Farm Produce: Value and Percentage Shares by Sub-Region, 1940–1992

	Value of farm sales (millions of current $)						% SF/FL	% Sub-region/SF			
	LEC	LWC	KSV	UEC	SF	FL		LEC	LWC	KSV	UEC
1940	16.2	4.5	2.1	1.9	24.7	80.4	30.7	65.6	18.2	8.5	7.7
1945	36.2	7.6	8.2	6.7	58.7	240.2	24.4	61.7	12.9	14.0	11.4
1949	54.4	18.2	8.3	6.1	87.0	338.6	25.7	62.5	20.9	9.5	7.0
1954	82.5	23.4	14.7	14.4	135.0	466.1	29.0	61.1	17.3	10.9	10.7
1959	104.3	35.0	29.5	25.0	193.8	700.5	27.7	53.8	18.1	15.2	12.9
1964	165.3	47.2	52.3	44.0	308.8	954.0	32.4	53.5	15.3	16.9	14.2
1969	198.4	94.0	65.6	45.4	403.4	1 132.1	35.6	49.2	23.3	16.3	11.3
1974	378.	176.2	105.9	73.2	733.3	1 898.7	38.6	51.5	24.0	14.4	10.0
1978	657.5	192.1	167.0	145.2	1 161.8	3 025.6	38.4	56.6	16.5	14.4	12.5
1982	759.6	245.3	216.7	174.5	1 396.1	3 522.1	39.6	54.4	17.6	15.5	12.5
1987	1 149.0	390.6	310.1	295.7	2 145.4	4 351.4	49.3	53.6	18.2	14.5	13.8
1992	1 282.8	672.0	372.3	362.1	2 689.2	5 266.0	51.1	47.7	25.0	13.8	13.5
1997	1 338.4	775.3	429.7	318.1	2 861.5	6 004.6	47.7	46.8	27.1	15.0	11.1

Source: Census of Agriculture, county data aggregated to sub-regions.

Table 9.7 Hired Workers: Number and Percentage Shares by Sub-Region, 1935–1992

	No. hired workers						%	% Sub-region/SF			
	LEC	LWC	KSV	UEC	SF	FL	SF/FL	LEC	LWC	KSV	UEC
1935	15 499	4 940	599	607	21 645	60 627	35.7	71.6	22.8	2.8	2.8
1940	20 966	3 311	852	1 696	26 825	70 599	38.0	78.2	12.3	3.2	6.3
1945	13 464	4 319	313	426	18 522	36 014	51.4	72.7	23.3	1.7	2.3
1949	15 125	3 542	668	1 812	21 147	66 483	31.8	71.5	16.7	3.2	8.6
1954	9 364	2 236	1 082	1 915	14 597	47 935	30.5	64.2	15.3	7.4	13.1
1959	13 794	3 862	1 724	1 669	21 049	56 901	37.0	65.5	18.3	8.2	7.9
1964	12 425	5 608	1 726	2 796	22 555	54 752	41.2	55.1	24.9	7.7	12.4
1969	30 852	12 648	4 553	7 771	55 824	163 745	34.1	55.3	22.7	8.2	13.9
1974	35 378	17 669	6 773	6 477	66 297	172 580	38.4	53.4	26.7	10.2	9.8
1978	46 148	30 168	4 895	8 755	89 966	207 904	43.3	51.3	33.5	5.4	9.7
1992	36 626	31 255	6 223	5 752	79 856	161 047	49.6	45.9	39.1	7.8	7.2
1997	20 524	19 572	5 656	4 812	50 564	124 969	40.5	40.6	38.7	11.2	9.5

Sources:

Census of Agriculture 1935–1997.

For 1945 and 1940 data: persons 14 years old and over working the equivalent of 2 or more days during specific week (first week of January 1945; the last week of March 1940) (1945: p. 32). For years 1959 and 1964, hired workers include those who worked 150 days or more. For the rest of the years, hired workers refers to those that worked both more than 150 days and less than 150 days, including paid family members (1992 Appendix A-7). For years 1969 and 1974, include only workers on farms with sales of $2500 or more.

Table 9.8   *Agriculture Characteristics of the Sub-Regions, 1925, 1954, 1992, 1997*

| | | Sub-regions | | | | | | % |
		LEC (1)	LWC (2)	KSV (3)	UEC (4)	SF (5)	FL (6)	SF/FL (7)
Cattle and calf	1925	12 348	22 261	86 267	8 829	129 705	656 217	19.8
inventory (no.)	1954	138 575	117 899	167 241	51 418	475 133	1 647 348	28.8
	1992	19 683	188 366	358 775	77 565	644 389	1 783 968	36.1
	1997	18 655	181 916	374 044	51 540	626 155	1 808 900	34.6
Sugarcane	1925	3 091	83	57	—	3 231	12 349	26.2
(acres)	1954	402	298	16	3	719	2 745	26.2
	1992	351 440	69 548	—	—	420 988	431 677	97.5
	1997	344 904	68 855	—	7 107	420 866	421 421	99.9
Vegetables	1925	5 341	4 691	658	1 606	12 296	94 000	13.1
(acres)	1954	117 091	23 065	2 645	11 559	154 360	323 909	47.7
	1992	123 417	41 499	1 427	2 803	169 146	299 867	56.4
	1997	99 150	33 944	1 460	—	134 554	250 562	53.7
All citrus trees	1925	893	522	421	885	2 721	17 274	15.8
(thou.)	1954	709	167	1 475	1 745	4 096	35 753	11.5
	1992	2 741	20 219	10 808	16 631	50 398	92 233	54.6
	1997	1 968	22 909	13 298	18 651	56 826	107 256	53.0

Source: Censuses of Agriculture.   Computed by aggregating county data.

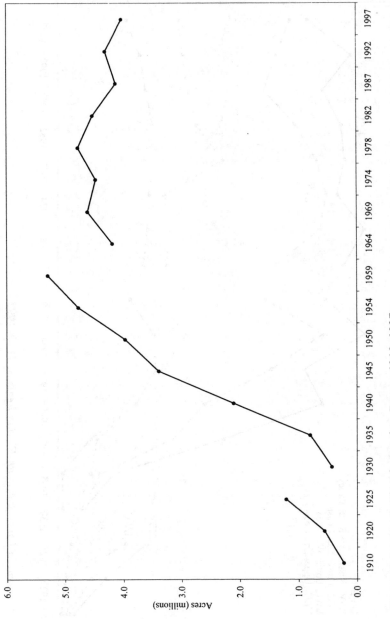

Figure 9.1   South Florida Land in Farms, 1910–1997

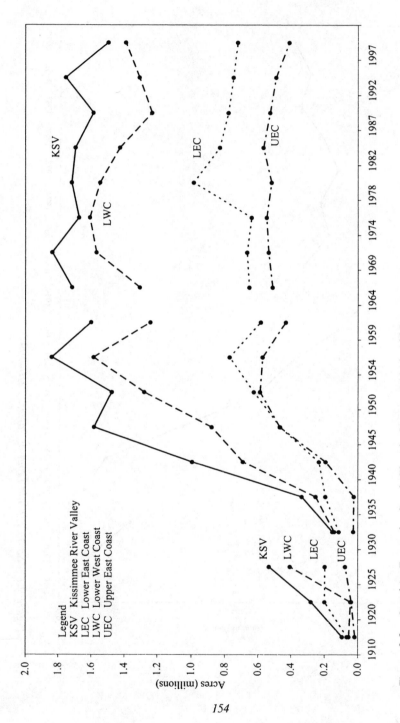

Figure 9.2   Land in Farms for South Florida Regions, 1910–1997

Growth of farmland in South Florida was strong from 1910 to 1925, especially in the LWC and the Kissimmee Valley. Following the collapse recorded in the 1930 and 1935 censuses, the SF region resumed its growth as noted in the censuses of 1940 through 1950. By the 1954 census, 4.8 million acres of land had been put in farms, higher than recorded in all the later censuses for the rest of the century. Almost three quarters of this acreage was found in the LWC and the KSV (see Table 9.2).

Agriculture in the sub-regions, however, expanded during different periods. The Kissimmee Valley grew most rapidly between 1935 and 1945. The LEC and UEC expanded most quickly from 1940 to 1950 and the LWC from 1935 to 1940 and from 1945 to 1950 (see Table 9.2). The average size of farms grew rapidly in all the regions during the 1935–50 period (Table 9.3). By 1954, the basic structure of farmland in South Florida was in place.

According to the agricultural censuses, a large share of drainage had been undertaken prior to 1959 (see Table 9.4). In the LEC, more than 2 million acres had been drained of a total of 4.2 million acres in all of South Florida. Between 1950 and 1959, another 538 000 acres were drained in South Florida as were another 1.6 million acres more between 1969 and 1978. While the pre-1959 drainage represented three-quarters of the state's total at that time, the drainage in the 1970s represented 41.3 percent of all newly-drained lands in the state.

Hand in hand with the drainage went an increase in irrigation (see Table 9.5). In 1949, South Florida accounted for 41 percent of the state's irrigated land. By 1974, that share had risen to 60 percent, with the greatest increases in acreage occurring between 1959 and 1964 with a steady increase to 1978. In the LEC, the great expansion of irrigation occurred between 1959 and 1969, but in the LWC irrigated acreage doubled from 1969 to 1974. In both the Kissimmee Valley and the UEC, the great jump in irrigation took place between 1959 and 1964 with the UEC expanding until 1978 (see Figures 9.3 and 9.4).

These are bare silhouettes of the three-phased "strands" of the agricultural story: the expansion of farmlands and their drainage and subsequent irrigation in order to raise crops in the wintry dry season.

In Table 9.6 we trace the market value of all agricultural produce sold, as reported in the censuses from 1940 to 1997. These data represent only *current values* for each census year; that is, they have not been deflated to constant dollar values. While we cannot compare different years, we can, for any single year, compare production and the relative importance of each region by noting their changing *shares* of total value. Hence, the value of all of SF's agricultural produce, which was only a quarter of the state's production in 1949, reached a maximum of 51 percent of the state's total in 1992 before falling to 48 percent in 1997. Within this growing agricultural pie, the rising share of the LWC from 16.5 to 27.1 percent between 1978 and 1997 is most noticeable.

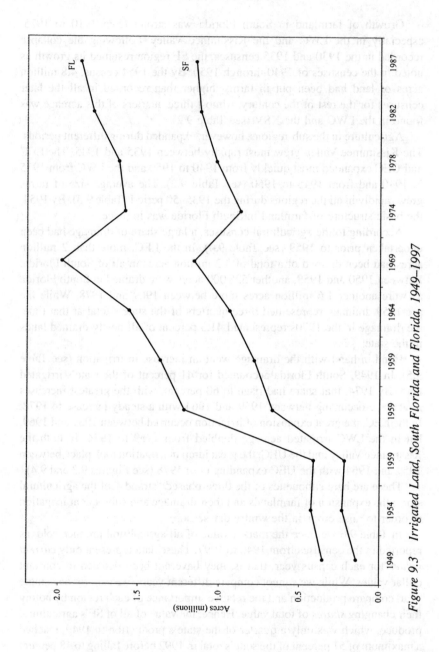

Figure 9.3 Irrigated Land, South Florida and Florida, 1949–1997

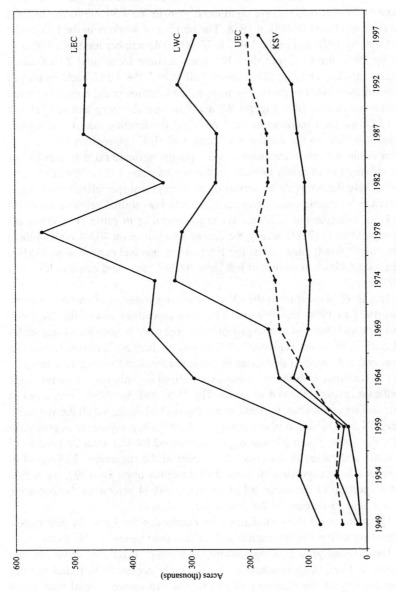

Figure 9.4   Irrigated Land, South Florida Regions, 1949–1997

Likewise, the number of hired workers in SF (Table 9.7, which excludes casual or harvest help) shows continuous growth from 56 000 hands in 1969 to a peak of almost 90 000 in 1978. The number of workers in the LEC grew to 46 000 by 1978 and in the LWC to 30 000. The number has since fallen so that by 1997, the LEC and the LWC each account for around 20 000 hired workers apiece, and the Kissimmee Valley and the UEC each employed approximately 5000 workers. The increase and decline in the number of hired workers are illustrated in Figures 9.5 and 9.6. Note the steep and early rise in the LEC, the later increase in the LWC, and the leveling out of the number of hired workers in the Kissimmee Valley and UEC sub-regions.

In Table 9.8, we trace measures of specific agricultural activities in our four sub-regions of South Florida for the census years 1925, 1954, 1992, and 1997. These data provide footprints of the changes in specialization in cattle, sugarcane, vegetables, and citrus, as these activities shifted between areas. By 1954, for example the LEC had come to specialize in cattle (138 575 head) and vegetables (117 091 acres). Sugarcane was grown on 402 acres and there were only 709 000 citrus trees. By 1997, sugarcane had expanded to 345 000 acres, vegetables had shrunk to less than 100 000 acres and cattle to less than 19 000 head.

This is all in contrast to the LWC, which illustrates an alternative pattern. From 1925 to 1954, the area specialized in vegetables and cattle. By 1992, sugarcane and citrus were also grown on a large scale in addition to vegetables and cattle. The recent census of 1997 shows an increase in citrus, stability in sugar, and only modest decreases in cattle numbers and vegetable acreage.

The Kissimmee Valley has always specialized in cattle with an increasingly significant acreage devoted to citrus. The UEC had, by 1954, specialized in cattle and vegetables but, by 1997, citrus groves had displaced all the vegetable acreage. Cattle raising remains strong, and only token sugarcane is grown. In 1925, the entire South Florida region accounted for less than 20 percent of the cattle and calves in the state, 26 percent of the sugarcane, 13 percent of the vegetable acreage, and 16 percent of the citrus trees. By 1997, the region held 35 percent of the cattle, all of the cane, and 54 percent of the vegetable acreage, and 53 percent of the state's citrus trees.

The point of all these statistics is to emphasize the longevity and importance of agriculture in the region and the dynamic nature of this sector.

The detailed growth of agriculture, a seeming "diversion" from our discussion of Everglades restoration, is absolutely necessary to round out our understanding of the economy of the region. No environmental plan could possibly succeed without full inclusion and treatment of the agricultural component. Certainly the implications of *all* of agriculture's activities for runoff and the drainage requirements of different crops should be part of the

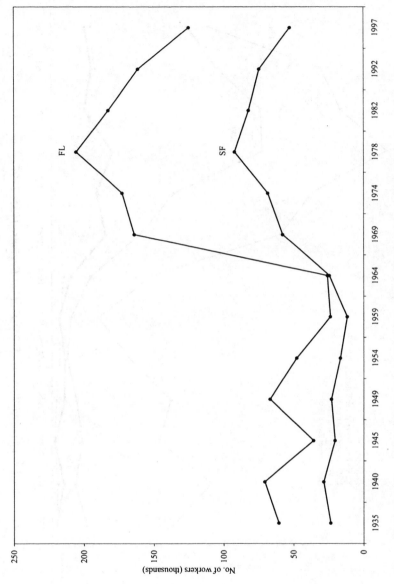

Figure 9.5   Number of Hired Workers, Florida and South Florida, 1935–1997

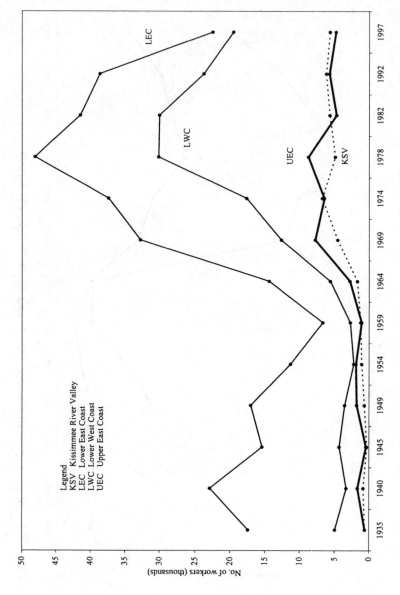

Figure 9.6   Number of Hired Workers, South Florida Regions, 1935–1997

Everglades Plan. Only by understanding the historical profiles presented here can we approach the task of estimating future trends in agriculture and their impacts on the regional economy, tasks that we shall undertake in Chapter 12.

NOTE

1. See Douglas (1947), Tebeau (1966), Will (1968), Derr (1989), and Snyder and Davidson (1994).

10. The Value of Ecosystem Services

METHODOLOGY

In one bold quantitative stroke, Costanza and twelve colleagues (1997) calculated that the economic contribution of the services of the world's ecosystems totaled $33 trillion per year in 1994 US dollars, almost double the global GNP. His team applied an average value per hectare to the land and sea areas for categories of "ecosystem services" listed in Table 10.1. In this chapter, we shall apply a similar methodology to compute the economic contribution of the Everglades ecosystems.[1]

Using the GIS land use/land cover studies of the SFWMD for 1988 and 1995, we shall also measure *changes* in ecosystem services due to changes in land use during this period. We shall apply the international values found in Table 2 of Costanza et al.'s 1997 *Nature* article, as documented in the Supplemental Information, to our measured acreages of different land uses.[2]

The two GIS surveys are not directly comparable. Each survey codes land use categories differently.[3] The level of detail differs due to the different size corresponding to each mapped polygon. The total number of acres mapped differs for a given county between the surveys. The quality of coding varies from year to year and from county to county due to the different contractors. The aerial visibility of certain land uses, for example, land *under* tree foliage or the presence of animals at the time of viewing (to determine grassland or pasture), affects the reliability of certain land categories. Finally, the totals for land, water, and agricultural areas for each county differ from other measured sources, especially from national and agricultural censuses.

I have tried to correct for all the above factors as much as possible. First, a 1988–1995 alignment or "cross-walk" was constructed from the two different land use codebooks (see Table 10.2). Broward County was used as a model county to check the measured totals of the land use categories that correspond to categories in the Comprehensive Plan. Second, since the total areas for both water and land differed between the two surveys and also from published totals for land and water (see BEBR fsa 2002, Table 8.0.3), "true totals" had to be fixed. Total water area was assumed constant between the two years, as the survey differences were assumed to be due to different coverage of lake,

Table 10.1   Ecosystem Services

Ecosystem Goods and Services	Functions and Examples
1. Gas regulation	CO_2/O_2 balance; O_2, SO_4 levels
2. Climate regulation	Temperature, precipitation, greenhouse gases, DMS for cloud formation
3. Disturbance regulation	Storm protection, flood control, drought recovery
4. Water regulation	For agriculture (irrigation), industry (cooling power generators)
5. Water supply	Storage, retention by watersheds, reservoirs, aquifers
6. Erosion control, sediment retention	From wind, runoff, store silt in wetlands
7. Soil formation	Rock weathering, accumulation of organic material
8. Nutrient cycling	Nitrogen fixation, N, P, and other cycles
9. Waste treatment	Nutrient breakdown, pollution control, detoxification
10. Pollination	For reproduction of plant populations
11. Biological control	Regulate animal population; keystone predator control of prey species (Florida panther, alligator)
12. Refugia	For resident and transient populations: nurseries, migratory birds; orchid species
13. Food production	Extractable portion from gross primary production: fish, game, nuts, subsistence farming; Indian tribal activity
14. Raw materials	Extractable portion: lumber, fuel, fodder, peat
15. Genetic resources	Medicines, genes resistant to plant and crop pests, ornamental species
16. Recreation	Eco-tourism: sport fishing, camping, boating, outdoor activities
17. Cultural	Non-commercial: aesthetic, artistic, educational, spiritual, scientific values

Source: Costanza et al. (1997), Table 1.

estuary, and coastal boundaries. Land control totals were taken from the US census sources and held constant for both years. The total of agricultural land for the two land use surveys was taken to be the sum of "grass and scrubland" plus "crop and pastureland" since the distinction between pasture and scrubland may not be clearly visible from the aerial views. The US Agricultural Censuses of 1987 and 1997 supplied the control totals from the categories of "all agricultural land" with woodlands (both pasture and non-pasture) subtracted out, as the area of woodlands in the land use surveys may have been placed in the forest category. This left the "total non-agricultural land" as the control total for both the 1988 and 1995 surveys for each of the 13 counties. This total was then distributed across the nine major use types listed in Table 10.2 below for each county in the same proportion as found in the original surveys. Absolute changes in acreage for each land use type for each county could then be compared for the two years.

No correction was made for inconsistent coding among counties or between the years. When land use categories were ambiguous or not clearly traceable between the years, they were aggregated. These are noted in the 1988–95 alignments, Table 10.2.

All "unit values" of ecosystem services are taken from the *Nature* article (Table 2) and converted to acres. The value per acre of the major land use category "agricultural crop and pastureland" is an average of the values for grassland and agriculture, weighted for the SF counties for both years by the areas of these two categories as found in the 1997 Agriculture Census.

The *change* in the value of ecosystem services is therefore due to the change in observed land use acreages, constrained by a county-specific control total for all non-agricultural land in each of the two years.

RESULTS

The economic contribution of the ecosystem services from the land alone was $31.66 billion in 1995 and thus represents a loss of $2.42 billion from the 1988 total, both computed at 1994 prices (see Table 10.3, lines 14, 15, 17; column 12). If the value of ecosystem services created by the water area is added to each region, then the value of total ecosystem services reaches $58.7 billion in 1995, or $68.2 billion adjusted for the year 2000 prices (Table 10.4, lines 4 and 7, column 5). This amounts to 34.8% or about a third of the total value-added of the "normal" economy (that is, without ecosystem services), estimated by IMPLAN to be $195.8 billion for the year 2000 for the 13 counties.

This value may be conservative. Dr Grace Johns and colleagues[4] calculated that the value of the coral reefs in the four southeastern counties in 2000–2001 for recreation use alone was $8.5 billion. Leeworthy and Vanasse (1999) found visitors to the Florida Keys spent around $1.3 billion per year during the 1996–98 period. In Table 10.5, nine other recreational surveys are evaluated with respect to their per-acre economic contribution or "value." The average of these studies – $331 per freshwater acre and $380 per saltwater acre – are, respectively, 53 percent and 31 percent higher than the corresponding "recreation value" per acre used in the Costanza et al. (1973) study. Further correction for the economic contribution of other ecosystem services, such as water supply, flood control, and food production would probably raise our totals considerably. Hence, the estimates presented here of the contribution of both land and water ecosystem services should be regarded as lower boundaries of the ecosystem's true value.

In Table 10.6, we have adapted Table 2 from the 1997 *Nature* article to correspond to the eight major biomes of the Everglades regions (columns 1–8) for each of the seventeen ecosystem services (rows 1–17). The matrix specifies, for example, that the $8622 per acre contribution of freshwater wetlands

Table 10.2 Land Use FLUCCS Codes for 1988 and 1995 Land Use Studies

Major Category	1988 Code	1995 Name	1995 Code	$/ac.
1. Urban	U	All urban residential, commercial	100	$0
		All transp., commun., utilities	800	
		Canals and locks: send to #7 water	[-816]	
		Swimming beaches	[-181]	
2. Agriculture	A	Crops and pasture	200	$37
3. Rangeland	R		300	Grassland: $94
	RG (grass) Could go to 200 above	Herb	310	
	RS (scrub) Could go to natural areas below	Scrub	320	
		Mixed	330	
4. Agriculture and rangeland	Sum 2 and 3 above			Wtd. av.: 47
5. Upland forest	[F]		[400]	
	FMTH Tropical hammock	Tropical hammock	426	$884
	FEPE Pine flatwoods	Upland pine	410	$133
		Upland pine, hardwoods	420	
		Minus 422, 424, 426		
Exotics:	FOBP Brazilian pepper	Brazilian pepper	422	$0
	WFME Melaleuca	Melaleuca	424	$0

Category	Code	No.	Type	Description	Value
6. Wetlands a. Fresh water	[W]				All: $8 622
	WF	610	Forest	Hardwood	
	WN	620	Non-forest (sawgrass, etc.)	Conifer (could be compared to FEPE above)	
	WX	630	Mixed	Mixed	
		640		Veg.	
		650		Non-veg.	
				Minus 611, 612	
				Minus 642	
				Minus 651, 652, 654	
6. Wetlands b. Salt water	WS	611	Salt (mangroves)	Bay swamp	All: $4 399
	WM	612	Non-forest	Mangrove	
		642		Salt water marsh	
		651		Tidal flat	
		652		Shoreline marsh	
		654		Oyster bar	
7. Water	H	[500]		Lakes and rivers	$3 742
		510		Streams	
		520		Lakes	
		530		Reservoirs	
		550		Springs	
		560		Slough	
		+816		Canals	
		540		Estuaries	$10 054
8. Coastal beaches	bb	710		Beaches, not for swimming	Coastal: $1 784
		+181		Swimming beaches	
9. Barren	B minus bb	700		Minus 710	$0

Sources: 1988 codes from SFWMD (1996); 1995 codes from SFWMD (1997b); $/ac.converted from Costanza et al. (1997), Table 2, in 1994 US dollars.

167

Table 10.3 Land Use 1988 and 1995, South Florida Regions and Values

	Wetlands		Forests			Urban	Beaches	Other	(Control) ag minus wooded ag lands	(Control) all land	% Land acres	Value ecosystem services	
	Fresh (1)	Salt (2)	Temperate (3)	Tropical (4)	Exotics (5)	(6)	(7)	(8)	(9)	(10)	(11)	(mill. $) (12)	(%) (13)
Land use 1995 (thou. ac.)													
1. LEC	1869	430	104	11	62	724	1	24	696	3920	40.5	18057.6	57.0
2. LWC	1063	135	326	1	19	262	1	22	1215	3043	31.4	9860.3	31.1
3. UEC	90	11	80	2	8	134		3	392	722	7.5	861.2	2.7
4. KSV	317	14	170		8	120		10	1360	2000	20.6	2883.9	9.1
5. SF	3342	591	681	14	97	1241	2	59	3666	9693	100.0	31663.0	100.0
Land use 1988 (thou. ac.)													
6. LEC	2106	216	45	6	50	709	2	14	770	3920	40.5	19160.7	56.2
7. LWC	1191	152	326		4	334	3	13	1020	3043	31.4	11023.6	32.3
8. UEC	92	7	51			79	1	2	491	722	7.5	852.9	2.5
9. KSV	344		139			83		6	1427	2000	20.6	3050.7	8.9
10. SF	3733	375	561	6	55	1205	6	36	3709	9685	100.0	34088.0	100.0

											Total	
% Distribution of land												
11. Land use in 1995	34.5	6.1	7.0	0.1	1.0	12.8	0.0	0.6	37.8		100.0	
12. Land use in 1988	38.5	3.9	5.8	0.1	0.6	12.4	0.1	0.4	38.3		100.0	
13. Value /acre ($94)	8 621.8	4 398.9	133.0	883.8	—	—	—	—	46.7			
Total ecosystem services												
14. Value in 1995 (mill. 94$)	28 817.9	2 600.2	90.5	12.1	—	—	—	—	171.1	—	31 663.0	
15. Value in 1988 (mill. 94$)	32 186.2	1 648.6	74.6	5.5	—	—	—	—	173.1	—	34 088.0	
Changes (1995–1988)												
16. Land use (thou. ac.)	−390.7	216.3	120.1	7.4	41.7	36.2	−4.0	23.4	−42.8			
17. Value services (mill. 94$)	−3 368.3	951.5	16.0	6.6	—	—	—	—	−2.0	—	−2 425.0	−7.1

Sources and Methods: Polygons denoting the acreages coded for land use are from the Land Use/Land Cover Studies for 1988 from SFWMD (1996) and for 1995 from SFWMD (1997b). These were summed for each county and then aggregated for the regions. Land use codes were aligned for the two studies according to Table 10.2 above. Control totals for all land (column 10) are from BEBR fsa 2002, Table 8.03, and control totals for ag land are from the US Agricultural Censuses of 1987 and 1997. Land use totals for the categories in columns 1–8 were then adjusted to maintain the distribution computed from the original polygons at the county level. Ecosystem values per acre were converted from $/hectare given in Table 10.2 above, which are from Costanza et al. (1997), Table 2. These were applied to the land use totals in lines 5 and 10 to give the total values in lines 14–15 by land use and in column 12, lines 1–4, 6–9, by region for each year.

Table 10.4   Total Land and Water Area and Total Values, 1995

	LEC (1)	LWC (2)	KSV (3)	UEC (4)	Total SF (5)
Area (thou. acres)					
1. Total land and water	6 319	3 644	2 243	922	13 128
2. Land area	3 920	3 043	2 000	722	9 685
3. Water area*	2 399	600	243	200	3 443
a. Inland	482	369	243	105	1 200
b. Coastal	474	4	—	—	478
c. Territorial	1 443	227	—	95	1 765
Value (bill. 94$)					
4. Total land and water	39 136	13 563	1 771	4 231	**58 702**
5. Land value	18 058	9 860	861	2 884	31 663
6. Water value**	21 079	3 703	910	1 348	27 039
a. Inland	1 802	1 383	910	394	4 489
b. Coastal	4 764	39	—	—	4 803
c. Territorial	14 512	2 281	—	953	17 747
7. Total value land and water (bill. 2000$)***	45 461	15 755	2 057	4 915	**68 188**
Percentage Area					
8a. Land	40.5	31.4	20.6	7.5	100.0
8b. Water	69.7	17.4	7.1	5.8	100.0
Percentage Value					
9a. Land	57.0	31.1	2.7	9.1	100.0
9b. Water	78.0	13.7	3.4	5.0	100.0

Notes and Sources:

* Inland water includes lakes, reservoirs, ponds and rivers, and canals, plus portions of estuaries and bays as defined in BEBR, fsa 2002, T. 8.01, note 3. Coastal water is the area within embayments separated from territorial waters by 1 to 24 nautical miles. Territorial waters are between the 3-mile limit and the shoreline.

** Inland waters (lakes and rivers) valued at $3742/ac. and coastal and territorial waters (estuaries) valued at $10 054/ac. converted from Costanza et al. (1997), T. 2.

*** Consumer price index for 1994–2000 of 1.1616 computed from saus, T. 692.

Land area and value from Table 10.3 above.

(column 1, row 18) accrues from $117 from gas regulation (row 1), $3188 from disturbance regulation (row 3), and so on. Line 19 gives the acreage and line 20 gives the total economic contribution for each biome in the Everglades.

These are contrasted with the global acreages (line 21). The percentage distributions of the world's land–estuarine areas and the Everglades region are compared in lines 22–24. The Everglades region, in percentage terms, exceeds the world profile in the competing categories of freshwater wetlands, urban lands, and inland lakes (columns 1, 4, and 7, line 24), while the world's shares of forestland and farmland are higher (columns 3, 4, 6, line 24).

Turning to the totals of value created by each type of ecosystem service (columns 9–10, lines 1–17), we note that the bulk of the value accrues from disturbance regulation, water supply, and nutrient cycling (lines 3, 5, 8) and lesser amounts from water regulation and waste treatment (lines 4, 9). The difference between the relative importance of these ecosystem services in the Everglades and in the world study (columns 12–13) in which the water supply and disturbance regulation play relatively smaller parts is due to the predominance of a different set of biomes in South Florida and to the possible undervaluation of recreational services.

In conclusion, the exercise highlights several features of the South Florida ecosystem. First, the loss of some $2.4 billion in ecosystem services between 1988 and 1995 corresponds to a rate of decline of 1.05 percent per year mainly due to losses in freshwater wetlands and farmland (Table 10.3, line 16). These were computed at constant per-acre values for both years, with freshwater wetlands making major contributions through the services of water supply and disturbance regulation (Table 10.6, column 1). If, however, the recreational and cultural values we applied are underestimated, then we could be seriously understating the decline in ecosystem services.

Taken alone, the data for 1995 indicate a conservatively estimated contribution of $58.7 billion in 1994 prices or $68.2 billion in 2000 prices. This is roughly a third of the region's value-added for 2000. The value of ecosystem services in SF also represents 0.3 percent of global product ($18 trillion) in 1994 and 0.4 percent of comparable land and water biome acreage of the world.[5]

The computation of ecosystem services puts the values of the South Florida region in global perspective. It also encourages us to systematically track the losses of ecosystem services due to land use changes during "development" and the gains that might come about with ecosystem restoration.

NOTES

1. The original article stimulated a spirited controversy concerning methodological, statistical, conceptual, biological, ethical, and historical questions, among others. Some of these are found in the special issue on "The Value of Ecosystem Services," *Ecological Economics*, Volume 25, No. 1 (April 1998), in which is reproduced the 1997 *Nature* article, 12 different critiques, and a short conclusion by the original *Nature* authors.
2. It may be preferable to use local rather than international values. At the end of this chapter, some comparisons are made to a few recent studies from which "per acre" values for different services could be computed. Letson and Milon (2002: pp. 195–229) list 138 other resource valuation studies done in the region but their Table 16.1 standardizes these on a "per day" value, not per acre.
3. See Florida Department of Transportation (1985) for detailed categories for the earlier study.
4. See Hazen and Sawyer' *Socioeconomic Study of Reefs in Southeast Florida*, 2001.
5. That is, 13 129 thousand acres in SF compared to 32 060 million acres for the global biomes listed in columns 1–8, lines 19, 21. This excludes desert, open ocean, tundra, and ice/rock areas.

Table 10.5 Value of Ecosystem Services from Recent Florida Studies

Study type (1)	Year (1)	Total spending (mill. curr. $) (2)	% Applicable % (3)	% Applicable Source (4)	Acres applicable (thou.) (5)	Acres applicable Source (6)	$ Value/ac (current $) (7)	Deflator (8)	$ Value/ac (1994 $) (9)	Source (10)
Recreational expenditure surveys*										
1. Fishing: fresh water	1996	444.6	31.1	F	448.8	Freshwater	308	1.058	291	K, T.16
2. Fishing: fresh water	1991	548.0 A	31.1	F	448.8		380	1.088	413	L, T.15
3. Fishing: salt water	1996	1 180.8	31.1	F	728.7	Bays, estuaries	504	1.058	476	K, T.16
4. Fishing: salt water	1991	604.7 A 982.8 B	31.1	F	728.7		419	1.088	456	L, T.15
5. Hunting and wildlife assoc. activity	1996	121.0 754.7	43.2	G	4 970.5		76	1.058	72	K, T.15 K, T.35
Sum		875.7								
6. Hunting and wildlife assoc. activity	1991	84.9 556.4	43.2	G	4 970.5		56	1.088	61	L, T.20
Sum		641.3								
7. Boating and hunting	1999/2000	1 566 C	100.0	H	59.5	J	26	1.124	23	M, T.A, p. v.
8a. Ramps and piers: salt water	2000	177.5 D			728.7		243	1.162	209	N
8b. Ramps and piers: fresh water	2000	150.7 E			448.8		336		289	N

172

Willingness to pay:	1996	per HH:	No. HH in FL:		All SF				
9. Full ecosystem restoration	1996	441	$59–70 max	6.3 mill. in 2000	10 511.5	42	1.058	40	O
		595		8.5 mill. in 2015	10 511.5	57	1.058	54	
Average of above studies:									
10. Fishing only, freshwater								331	Lines 1, 2, 8b above
11. Fishing only, saltwater								380	Lines 3, 4, 8a above
12. Other recreation								52	Lines 5, 6, 7 above

Notes:

* Spending on food and lodging, transport, other trip expenses; excl. eqpt.
A. State-residents only.
B. Augmented by the proportion of non-resident to resident spending in 1995, from T. 21, that year.
C. Incl. total sales by visitors, federal, state govt.
D. Most popular uses reported: fishing, sightseeing, swimming, and diving, the last only in the case of saltwater users.
E. Saltwater/freshwater division of expenditure was available only for the aggregate spending on piers and on ramps; these were applied to the county sums.
F. Registered boats, fsa. T. 19.45.
G. All parks and recreation lands (Aug. 2002).
H. Entire study area.
I. All federal, state, county, club, municipal, non-private, commercial recreational lands.
J. Three Lakes Wildlife Mgmt. Area, Osceola County.
K. US Fish and Wildlife Service (1998).
L. US Fish and Wildlife Service (1993).
M. Fl. Fish and Wildlife Conservation Comm. (2000).
N. Thomas and Stratis (2001), County Appendix Tables.
O. Milon et al. (1999).

Table 10.6 Value of Everglades Ecosystem Services by Function and Biome with World Comparisons

Column groups: columns (1)–(8) = Per acre annual value (1994 US $ per acre per year); Wetlands = (1)Fresh, (2)Salt; Forest = (3)Temperate, (4)Tropical; Water = (7)Fresh, (8)Salt**. Columns (10)–(11) = Total annual value; columns (12)–(13) = % Annual value.

Biome / Ecosystem service	Wetlands Fresh (1)	Wetlands Salt (2)	Forest Temperate (3)	Forest Tropical (4)	Urban barren other (5)	Ag* cropland and pasture (6)	Water Fresh (7)	Water Salt** (8)	Sum all biomes (9)	SF (mill. $) (10)	World (bill. $) (11)	SF % (12)	World % (13)	SF minus world (12)–(13) (14)
1. Gas reg.	117								117	390	1341	0.7	4.0	-3.4
2. Climate reg.			39	97					136	28	684	0.0	2.1	-2.0
3. Disturb reg.	3188	810		2				250	3440	11205	1779	19.1	5.3	13.7
4. Water reg.	13			3			2398		3223	3400	1115	5.8	3.4	2.4
5. Water supply	3346						932		4282	12293	1692	20.9	5.1	15.9
6. Erosion control				102					102	1	576	0.0	1.7	-1.7
7. Soil formation			4	4					9	3	53	0.0	0.2	-0.2
8. Nutrient cycl.	730	2949	38	386			293	9291	9677	20846	17075	35.5	51.3	-15.8
9. Waste treat.				36					4047	4560	2277	7.8	6.8	0.9
10. Pollination						7			7		117	0.0	0.4	-0.3
11. Biolog control			2			12	18		48	123	417	0.2	1.3	-1.0
12. Refugia	193	74		13				34	325	819	124	1.4	0.4	1.0
13. Food prod.	21	205	22	132		28		58	536	843	1386	1.4	4.2	-2.7
14. Raw materials	22	71	11	17				229	247	148	721	0.3	2.2	-1.9
15. Genetic resour.								11	17		79	0.0	0.2	-0.2
16. Recreation	216	290	16	47			101	168	838	1402	815	2.4	2.4	-0.1
17. Cultural	775		1	1				13	790	2618	3015	4.5	9.1	-4.6
18. Sum all services ($/acre)	8622	4399	133	844		47	3742	10054	27841	58705	33266	100.0	100.0	0.0
19. SF area (thou. ac.)	3339	591	680	14	1398	3664	1200	2243	13129					
20. SF value (mill. $94)	28789	2600	90	12		172	4490	22551	58705					
21. World area (mill. ac.)	375	375	6711	4315	754	12032	454	7045	32060*** / 117240					
22. World area (%)	1.2	1.2	20.9	13.5	2.4	37.5	1.4	22.0	100.0					
23. SF area (%)	25.4	4.5	5.2	0.1	10.6	27.9	9.1	17.1	100.0					
24. SF minus world (22)–(23)	24.3	3.3	-15.8	-13.4	8.3	-9.6	7.7	-4.9	0.0					

Notes: * Ag cropland includes grass and rangeland. ** Includes coastal and territorial waters. *** World "total" area excludes categories of desert, open ocean, tundra, and ice/rock whereas line immediately below includes all categories of land and ocean.

Sources and Methods:

Per acre values (line 18) for each biome are the average of world unit values, from Costanza et al. (1997: Table 2), weighted by the acreages in sub-categories from Everglades land use study. Line 18 was then redistributed across lines 1–17 in the same proportion as in Table 2 of the original 1997 study.

The entries for the total dollar value for each ecosystem service in SF, given in column 10, are not the simple sums across the columns, but rather are the product of the per acre value for each ecosystem service, given in the matrix of columns 1–8 and lines 1–17, times the corresponding acreage of each biome, given in line 19, summed across the eight biomes (columns 1–8) for each ecosystem service. World totals (column 11) for each ecosystem service are derived in a similar way and are found in the bottom row totals of Table 2 in the 1997 study. SF area (line 19) is derived from Table 10.3 above and is shown in percentages (line 23) for comparison to the 1997 world study (lines 21–22).

PART III

The Economics of the Missing Pieces

11. On Regional Economic Models: Some Introductory Issues

It is not in the research economist's nature to use ready-made or "off-the-shelf" models that fit any size economy. Indeed, the contribution of economic research is usually regarded as the originality and design of the very model itself, created uniquely for the task at hand. What architect wants his building to look like all the others?

The professional economist's approach to "creative" economic model-making thus puts the emphasis on the model apparatus and only secondarily on the data, which are usually appended to give the model the appearance of applicability and relevance. To gather new data and estimate all the parameters afresh, it is said, would delay the project by even more time.[1]

In the early days of regional model-making, both structure and data had to be created from scratch. The models were unique or formulated for a special setting, and the data had to be culled from existing sources for each specific region and fit into the structure.[2]

In the Everglades case, ample resources had been available for the development of hydrological and landscape models,[3] but the minimal resources that were to be spent on economic modeling became available at a late date. There was no time to adapt regional data from truly local sources. As the regional impact evaluator for the Restudy, I was forced to turn to the suppliers of pre-packaged economic models, and I settled on IMPLAN, out of Stillwater, Minn., and REMI, out of Amherst, Mass.

Both modeling systems are based on a standard program for all regions. Only the datasets are unique, and these often involve scaling down the detailed national data to match county control totals.

THE IMPLAN MODEL

IMPLAN is based on a single national input–output model, augmented by local information about consumption, earnings, employment, and transfers of all types. In the days of the custom-made model, the data from the local coal industry, for example, would have been used in all its detail to create the truly unique regional input–output table. In the IMPLAN system, however, the national input–output table takes the "national coal industry" and scales it down to the level indicated by regional control totals. And so it is with "tree crops" (which include citrus), "sugar crops" (which include sugarcane and sugar beets), and so on. If the local sugarcane industry in my region has the same structure as the national "sugar crop" industry, then the coefficients of my IMPLAN model won't be far off the mark. But if the local industry uses a unique technology or operates in a very different way from the national one, then my so-called regional model may not replicate reality on the ground.

Fortunately, the model designers anticipated the need to adjust for specifically regional data or behavioral changes, so the software permits all types of insertions and interventions. Moreover, the IMPLAN user is urged to get "reality checks" from local industry and planning experts regarding the model's results.[4]

In this way, economic models differ from scientific or environmental models in which the data needed to calibrate the computer model must be gathered fresh from the field. In economics, the tax system and national economic censuses have already generated the basic information, and the model-makers can draw from a vast sea of data at the level of the county, zip code, or census tract, which are available for any region in the US and increasingly for regions of other countries.[5]

IMPLAN, in its original form, is a convenient accounting system for a region, as it lays out all the sales and purchases, the wages and income, taxes and imports for a single year for as many as 528 sectors. One key assumption, which allows this accounting scheme to be used to measure the impacts of new activities in the region, is that of proportionality, namely, that $100 million additional sales of a certain product will affect the economic system in a way that is exactly proportional to the existing industry and all its components. Thus, if a current industry is already producing $100 million worth of shoes, then the impact of doubling sales requires the doubling of all material inputs (leather, and so on), wages, rents, and taxes already recorded. The skill of the investigator, therefore, revolves around his or her knowing in considerable detail the nature of the proposed project with all its components and the sectors that are likely to be affected. This kind of information is usually available from the basic engineering studies and cost-estimating programs. This was the approach I used in computing the impact of $8 billion worth of projects in the original Restudy.[6]

A second key assumption of IMPLAN is that the new activities are relatively marginal in nature, so that the additional demand for the new leather or leather workers will not drive up their prices. Even if their prices do rise, the model assumes no substitutions by other, cheaper inputs.[7] Furthermore, IMPLAN impacts are computed to "occur" all in one, non-specified time period. The doubling of inputs, for example, may take one year or ten years to play itself out.

It appears to me that there is also considerable confusion between measuring the impacts of a new project and the impacts of an existing industry: Sector A now sells to B who sells to C. Does that mean that the employment in C "due" to A's activity would disappear if A were to fail?

To answer the question, we performed the following experiment. We took the "top ten" two-digit sectors for Florida from the latest IMPLAN file (see Table 11.1). These ten sectors accounted for 61–67 percent of all direct employment, output, and value-added in the state (line 13, columns 2–4). We then re-entered the current employment of these ten sectors back into the IMPLAN software in order to measure the impacts that would be "caused" by the same set of industries "entering" or "leaving" the state at their current size.[8]

Taken altogether, these ten sectors "cause" direct, indirect, and induced impacts on jobs, output, and value-added that are equal to 108, 69, and 99 percent, respectively, of the current statewide totals (Table 11.1, columns 5–7, line 13)! Does this mean that all the jobs and value-added from the other sectors in the state have already been "accounted for"? Or does it mean that for very large projects (like Everglades restoration) that take place over many years, the "impacts" are likely to be played out in ways more complicated than the IMPLAN method captures?

THE REMI MODEL

REMI is a more complicated modeling software, for it computes how a given project or policy change will affect *all* the relevant regional *markets* as they react and adjust over time.[9] If a $100 million project requires local purchases of concrete, earth-moving equipment, and labor, then REMI will trace out the chain of events as to how this new spending will affect *all* the regional markets and their interactions throughout the first region and spill over into other regions in the model. The increased demand for labor, for example, will bid up wages, and this will lead more workers to move with their families into the region. This, in turn, may cause an increase in school attendance and an increase in housing prices. This induces new home construction and also raises the cost of living in the region, which, over time, discourages further migration into the region.

REMI also asks how the new project will be financed. If it is a public project, will the money come from new taxes or be diverted from existing projects? Thus, every project or policy is played out by simulating every market affected by the project for the next 35 years. The REMI model gives the

Table 11.1 IMPLAN Experiments, Florida Economy, 2000

Top ten direct employment sectors	IMPLAN sector no. (1)	Direct employment (thou.) (2)	Direct output (bill. $) (3)	Direct value-added (bill. $) (4)	Direct, indirect, induced impacts on		
					Employment (thou.) (5)	Output (bill. $) (6)	Value-added (bill. $) (7)
1. Retailing	448–455	1 568.3	69.3	50.8	2 096.0	13.2	78.2
2. Business services	469–476	988.8	44.3	30.5	1 416.9	78.7	52.4
3. Health sevices	490–493	684.8	47.9	31.2	1 154.8	86.1	55.3
4. Construction	48–57	635.0	78.5	25.2	1 378.2	40.4	63.1
5. Education – state and local govt.	522	433.0	15.9	15.9	584.5	27.9	23.5
6. Non-educ. – state and local govt.	510–512, 523	423.8	31.9	26.3	687.5	53.1	39.6
7. Wholesale trade	447	411.6	47.8	33.0	791.3	78.9	52.5
8. Professional services	506–509	336.1	27.1	15.4	654.9	52.0	31.1
9. Real estate	461–462	278.0	93.0	68.0	588.1	79.7	54.2
10. Recreation services	484–489	233.9	11.9	7.7	348.4	21.2	13.5
11. Totals, above industries		5 993.3	467.4	303.9	9 700.7	531.2	463.4
12. State totals		8 983.8	772.7	466.7	8 983.8	772.7	466.7
13. Percent top industries of state		66.7	60.5	65.1	108.0	68.7	99.3

Source: Computed from IMPLAN data for Florida, 2000.

researcher the capability of tracing these impacts on hundreds of economic and demographic variables.[10]

Quite naturally, these models have become the tools of both planners and advocates. In Florida, REMI was routinely used by the Joint Legislative Management Committee to evaluate the long-run rationality of special tax treatment requested of new developments: would such projects earn back for the state the equivalent of the tax relief being solicited?

On a regional level, Tampa Bay, Jacksonville, and Orlando all possess and use REMI as a tool in their planning and promotional evaluations. In addition, REMI is often the tool of choice for large-scale projects and proposals, such as the proposed re-opening by the Homestead Air Force Base or the bullet train to connect Florida cities.[11]

Why was the acquisition of REMI delayed until late 2003 in South Florida when it was finally purchased by the public agencies charged with issuing permits for large projects that have regional or county-wide impacts? My guess is that up to now, no one *really* wanted to know the full consequences of the breakneck paced growth that is underway. Aside from the occasional moralizing or introspection that periodically afflicts public officials and influential citizens alike, there is rather a premium placed on ignorance, on actively *not knowing*. Then, when the final tab is laid on the table, the dinner guests, having eaten their fill, can rightfully claim, "we had no idea," walk away with a clear conscience, and leave with the bill to be paid by future generations.

This is not to say no one is making waves. Journalists both inside and outside the region see the situation close to alarming. The influential *Washington Post* series on the Everglades by Michael Grunwald in June 2002 and the 12-piece series on Florida's water crisis by Debbie Salamone that appeared in the *Orlando Sentinel* between March and November 2002 are but a few of the red flags that have been thrown up to alert the public who will ultimately pay the bill.[12]

On the urban side, a pair of journalists, Neil Pierce and Curtis Johnson, wrote an exhaustive and inspiring four-part series for the Ft Lauderdale *Sun-Sentinel* analyzing the consequences of uncoordinated growth and outlining some remedies. They presented their work at the Urban Land Institute (ULI) and other forums, and the Collins Center for Public Policy republished their findings.[13] This, too, is part of the show that goes on.

When economic models are used to get a more "scientific" estimate of future growth, there is generally – and understandably – a clear motivation as well as a deep-pocketed sponsor willing to foot the bill. IMPLAN, regarded as the "poor man's REMI," is the preferred tool to estimate the new employment that would be created by a proposed race track (usually in an environmentally sensitive area), a new casino, baseball stadium, warehouse development, museum, or even a greenway. None of this is outright wrong or deceptive.

But such studies – and I have done my share of these – are usually incomplete and partial. They exclude the social and economic ramifications of the proposed facility that are *not* pre-programmed or captured in the software. The research economist on his own may find that the modeling process itself reveals the inner workings of both the local economy and of the proposed project. But unfortunately, the sponsor, who pays the piper and may call the tune, is, except on the rarest of occasions, hardly interested in the addictive effects of the gambling casino on the local population or the health effects of truck exhaust on the schools located near the proposed new warehouses. I know of only one case – there may be others – in which a developer willingly collaborated with his investigative-economist, the county government, and the Trust for Public Land to turn a proposed 100-acre warehouse park into a 100-acre recreational park on the basis, in part, of an impact study showing that a recreation–hotel–cultural complex would do as much for the county as the warehouses and the impact fees they would generate.[14]

"Retrospectives" on such studies are rarely done. As the "Big Dig" in Boston nears completion, who will check the forecasts of the REMI models made a decade ago? How accurate was the original 1993 study of the economic impacts of the *US v. SFWMD* settlement agreement?[15] When the baseball teams went on strike and shut down the ballparks, Maryland economist Don Zuchelli asks, did the urban stadiums lose as many jobs as their promoters claimed would be created in normal times? When a freeze hit the Florida orange groves, was the loss of business as great as the positive contribution claimed for the industry in prosperous times?

These rhetorical yet researchable questions are all by way of concluding what must now be obvious to the reader, namely, that the use of economic models is part science and part art. The "scientific" part claims that the results should be published and reproducible. The "art" part requires frequent judgment calls and procedures that are often omitted from the final report. The complicated nature of the models also means that a great many options are available to the researcher, of which only a few may be used. In the section that follows, I shall explore the data sources and the "missing pieces" procedures, the intermediate results, and lessons learned along the way. Hopefully, later researchers may benefit from these trackings.

NOTES

1. A counterexample might be the contribution in Lance Taylor (1990). The goal of this collection was to apply socially relevant models to several different national economies.
2. See, for example, Miernyk et al. (1970) on West Virginia, Karen Polenske (1970) and Polenske et al. (1972, 1974) on the multi-regional model of the US, and the reviews by Nijkamp et al. (1986) of regional models and by Lakshmanan and Bolton (1986) of regional energy and environmental models.

3. The 272-page Appendix B of the Restudy is entitled "Hydrology and Hydraulics Modeling" (US Army Corps, 1999). See DeAngelis et al. (1998) and Institute for Environmental Modeling (1998) on the application of the ATLSS model to forecast the extent of habitats suitable for fish, birds, and other wildlife in the Everglades.
4. See Weisskoff (2000) for an earlier IMPLAN study on the Everglades region. See Hodges and Haydu (1999), Hodges et al. (2000, 2001), and Haydu and Hodges (2002) for IMPLAN-based studies of Florida's horticulture, agriculture, citrus, and golf courses, respectively.
5. See Minnesota IMPLAN Group (1999, Book 3, Database Guide).
6. See US Army Corps of Engineers (1999, Appendix E, pp. 281–310).
7. That is, an infinite elasticity of supply for all factors, with supply instantaneously forthcoming, and a zero elasticity of substitution between factors.
8. These were entered into the model at the 528-sector three-digit level listed in column 1 of Table 11.1 in order to avoid errors due to aggregation.
9. See Treyz (1993), a 500-page book describing the equations and mechanisms. See also Regional Economic Models, Inc. (1995, 1997, 1999, 2000) for documentation. David Reaume wrote in his review of Treyz's book in the *Journal of Economic Literature* 32 (4) (Dec. 1994), p. 1945: "George Treyz has been building big regional economic/econometric models for almost as long as we have had easy access to computers, or so it seems. What he does not know about the subject probably is either not worth knowing or has not been discovered."
10. Each REMI regional model is tied to a national model. Thus, the researcher can also trace the effects of changes in national economic trends or policy on the region. The REMI model for Detroit, operated by George Fulton and colleagues at the Institute of Labor Relations, uses the macro-economic forecasts of the Research Seminar in Quantitative Economics at the University of Michigan, Ann Arbor, to anticipate the effects of national trends on local labor prospects. See Fulton and Grimes (2001) and Hymans, Crary, and Wolfe (2001).
11. The former was undertaken by the Beacon Council and the latter by the Institute of Sciences and Public Affairs of Florida State University. See Lynch et al. (1997).
12. See Grunwald (2002) and Salamone (2002), the latter is available as a reprint. The former can be downloaded from www.washingtonpost.com.
13. Pierce and Johnson (2000), *The CitiStates Project*, Nov. 19, 2000. See also *Sun-Sentinel*, "Getting Nowhere Fast: South Florida's Transportation Crisis," June 2–7, 2002. Published also as a Special Supplement, pp. 1–10.
14. See Weisskoff, "Park Would be Economic Boost, not a Tax Drain," *Miami Herald*, June 12, 2001, and J. Charles, "Cricket, Lovely Cricket: Broward Plans Park to Unite Community," *Miami Herald*, February 9, 2003.
15. See Hazen and Sawyer (1993).

12. The REMI Control and the First Missing Piece: Agriculture

THE REMI STANDARD REGIONAL CONTROL

The REMI Standard Regional Control, or REMI base, as we shall call it, provides the fundamental simulation to which all projects or policy changes are to be compared. Most researchers are interested in the *deviations* from the "control values" generated by a specified project or policy change. However, since we are more interested in the *absolute* values of the control, we shall examine the basic control values as well and the ways in which the control itself is adjusted with newer or locally available information.

In Figure 12.1 we reproduce the five basic "blocks" of the REMI model's structure with only some of the schematic links between the blocks. In Table 12.1, we have listed the principal aggregated variables that appear in each of the blocks of Figure 12.1 along with their values for 1970, 2000, and 2030, which are the beginning, middle, and final years of our model (columns 2–4). The model breaks each of the aggregates into various components for either 14 or 53 industrial sectors, and computes annual values of the detailed occupational categories and the ethnic and age cohorts for the historical and projected years.

The REMI Operator's Manual for the multi-region 14-sector model that we are using lists 667 different regular "translator" and population policy variables which can be manipulated.[1] The model values for 1969–1995 are based on historical data. Values from 1996 to 2035 are the projections, themselves based to some extent on the relative participation of the region in the US "Control Model" that also has been projected to 2035.[2]

We found the most glaring drawback of the REMI Standard Regional Control to be its understatement of the "forecast" population and employment for those years for which "real" or "measured" values had just become available or for the future years for which BEBR had also published its own demographic estimates.

REMI's population estimates for All Florida (Table 12.2, line 1, columns 1–3) miss the census mark for the year 2000 by only 0.5 percent, but its forecast for the SF region as a whole was short by 3.5 percent. REMI's

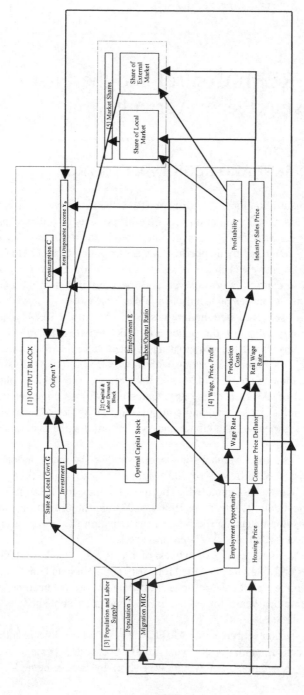

Source: Excerpted from Treyz (1993: p. 291).

Figure 12.1 The Blocks of the REMI Model and Some Connections

Table 12.1 The REMI Model Blocks, Some Totals, 1970–2030

	Symbol	REMI reg. control totals			Employment update (changes in value)	
		1970 (1)	2000 (2)	2030 (3)	2000 (4)	2030 (5)
1. Output (bill. 92$)	Y	71	212	331	12	72
Pers. consumption	C	41	158	241	9	58
Investment	ILp	10	29	42	3	15
State and local govt spending	G	8	20	52		7
Exports	XFG	26	57	92	2	24
Real disposable pers. income	RVD	36	136	204	4	28
2. Labor and capital demand						
Employment (thou.)	E	1 208	3 210	3 840	142	634
Optimal capital stock (bill. 92$)	K*-resid.	20	120	167	4	29
	K*-non-res.	69	153	215	12	48
3. Population and labor supply						
Population (thou.)	N	2 618	6 228	8 391	99	1 299
Migration (thou.)	MIG		91	37	31	–4
4. Wages, prices and profits						
Wage rate (nom. $)	W	5 544	25 827	67 191	490	2 144
Relative industry sales price	SPr	0.994	0.996	0.989	0.007	0.022
Relative wage rate	RWR	0.000	1.001	0.977	0.007	0.002
Consumer price deflator	CP	30	121	246	0.700	4.100
Relative employment opportunity	REO	0.000	0.972	0.937	0.020	–0.005
5. Market share						
Regional purchase coefficient for regional industry	Rr	0.599	0.610	0.613	–0.001	–0.018

estimates of the different SF sub-regions understate the 2000 population by 2.8 to 4.1 percent, depending on the region, except for the UEC, for which REMI gives a population that is 2.4 percent higher than the census (lines 2–6, columns 1–3).

Comparing the REMI population forecasts for 2030 to BEBR's "medium" projections, we find REMI's projections 10.9 percent lower for all of Florida (Table 12.2, line 1, columns 4–6). The shortfall of REMI's regional forecasts for SF and the sub-regions ranges from 15.5 percent in the UEC to 27.8 percent for the LWC. The overall shortfall for SF is 20.2 percent, almost double the shortfall for the statewide estimate (Table 12.2, lines 2–6, columns 4–6).

The deviations between REMI employment forecasts and BEBR's are even greater. The REMI base understates year 2000 employment by 8.8 percent for the state, 7.9 percent for South Florida, and 7.6 to 9.9 percent for the four sub-regions. By 2015, the latest date for which county and state employment forecasts are made, the REMI base underestimates employment by 25.6 percent for the state and by 25 to 37 percent for the other regions (see Table 12.2, columns 10–12).

EMPLOYMENT UPDATE

Due to the discrepancies noted above, the first step to "recalibrate" the REMI base is to force the employment totals for each of the 14 sectors of each sub-region of the model to follow the corresponding *rate of growth* forecast by the state for the years 1997–2007. These are made for the Workforce Development Regions (WDRs) for SIC three-digit-level industries.[3] The 14 REMI sectors are listed in Appendix Table F.1.

In the absence of specific farm sector employment forecasts, the growth rate of REMI sector 10, "agricultural services," was applied to the farm sector (no. 14) as well. These will be corrected later.

The increases in the values in the REMI control due to the "employment update" are given in the last two columns of Table 12.1. In Figure 12.2, we note that employment in SF does indeed grow more steeply for the "corrected" years, 1997–2007. But thereafter, the model generates a pattern of employment similar to the REMI control for 2008 to 2035, only at a higher level.

CORRECTING THE MISSING PIECES: GENERAL

The problem in general is that once the REMI control model is corrected for the employment update (EU), it is still, in our opinion, deficient due to

Table 12.2 *Comparisons of REMI Base to 2000 Census and to BEBR Projections for 2030*

| | Population | | | | | | Employment | | | | | |
| | 2000 | | | 2030 | | | 2000 | | | 2015 | | |
	REMI base (thou.) (1)	US census (thou.) (2)	% diff. (1)–(2)/(1) (3)	REMI base (thou.) (4)	BEBR med. proj. (thou.) (5)	% diff. (4)–(5)/(4) (6)	REMI base (thou.) (7)	REIS (thou.) (8)	% diff. (7)–(8)/(7) (9)	REMI base (thou.) (10)	REIS/ BEBR (thou.) (11)	% diff. (10)–(11)/(10) (12)
1. FL	15 902	15 982	–0.5	22 123	24 529	–10.9	8 225	8 951	–8.8	9 331	11 719	–25.6
2. SF	6 228	6 444	–3.5	8 391	10 089	–20.2	3 210	3 465	–7.9	3 577	4 718	–31.9
3. LEC	4 891	5 090	–4.1	6 420	7 656	–19.3	2 619	2 819	–7.6	2 890	3 801	–31.5
4. LWC	723	739	–2.2	1 081	1 381	–27.8	353	388	–9.9	414	566	–36.7
5. KSV	288	296	–2.8	445	538	–20.9	105	113	–7.6	126	157	–24.6
6. UEC	327	319	2.4	445	514	–15.5	133	145	–9.0	146	193	–32.2

Sources and Methods: Population and employment comparisons are from the REMI base for the various years and the following: column 2 from US Census for 2000; column 5 from BEBR (2002b, Table 1.41) population medium projections for 2030; column 8 from REIS for 2000; and column 11 from BEBR (2002a, Vol. 2, aggregated from data appendix for counties) that gives civilian employment in persons, while REMI and REIS give number of jobs or positions. The rate of growth (ROG) for BEBR employment was applied to REIS 2000 employment to estimate REIS (2015), which is compared to REMI estimates for that year.

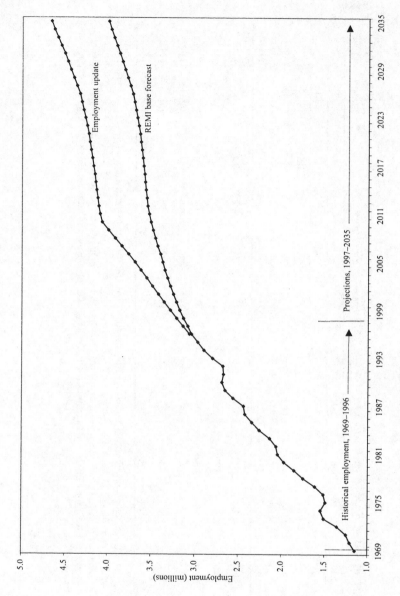

Figure 12.2   South Florida Employment Totals

peculiarities of the region and the importance of agriculture, investment, and tourism, which are largely determined by forces (variables) outside the region. Each of the missing pieces represents a special problem, which must be first researched, and a solution sought based on the available data and measured trends. We therefore begin by reviewing the methodological problems associated with each missing piece in the REMI "EU" model. We shall also compare different sources of historical data and projections for each piece other than those that are currently "built into" the REMI regional control. We shall then design three alternative scenarios (low, medium, high) for each missing piece in each region on the basis of the corrected factors. The sum of the low scenarios for all the missing pieces in each sub-region gives a single low projection for that sub-region. Since the four sub-regions themselves sum to South Florida and the addition of the fifth sub-region, "rest of the Florida counties," yields a statewide model, the "low" scenarios are thus constructed for a total of six models (see Figure 2.1a above for regional composition). Similarly, the medium and high scenarios, respectively, for all the missing pieces in each sub-region will be summed to compute an overall medium and high scenario for each sub-region. We did not create hybrids by mixing, for example, a low scenario for the agricultural missing piece with a medium scenario for the tourism missing piece.

In the rest of this chapter and in the three that follow, we shall review the model's built-in treatment of each missing piece, the historical evidence, alternative data series, and the corrections we have introduced to remedy the deficiencies we have identified.

THE AGRICULTURAL MISSING PIECE

In terms of employment or value-added, farming is a relatively small sector, accounting for around 1 percent of both the recorded work force and the value-added in all South Florida and in the state (see Table 12.3, "Farm" rows for SF and FL, columns 2, 4). In the KSV, farming accounts for 3.2 percent of employment, and in the LWC, KSV, and UEC, farm value-added ranges from 2.4 to 5.7 percent of each region's total. These, of course, understate the true importance of the farm sector, since in these three sub-regions, agriculture is the major user of water. Therefore, any corrections made in modeling agriculture will prove critical to the model's usefulness for forecasting the demand for water.

At the same time, agriculture is one of the least understood sectors and perhaps the most difficult to project for a number of reasons. First, "agriculture" is actually composed of a number of very different crops and activities, the future of each depending on different factors. Forecasts for sugarcane,

Table 12.3   Shares of Employment and Value Added

		Employment (thou.)		Value-added (92$ bill.)	
		2000 (1)	% (2)	2000 (3)	% (4)
1. FL	Private non-farm	7 387.7	86.2	313.4	87.8
	Government	1 102.0	12.9	38.9	10.
	Farm	78.8	0.9	4.7	1.3
	Total	8 568.5	100.0	357.0	100.0
2. SF	Private non-farm	2 946.8	87.9	130.8	90.0
	Government	376.9	11.2	12.9	8.9
	Farm	28.1	0.8	1.7	1.2
	Total	3 351.9	100.0	145.3	100.0
3. LEC	Private non-farm	2 412.0	88.3	111.3	90.8
	Government	306.5	11.2	10.5	8.6
	Farm	12.8	0.5	.8	0.6
	Total	2 731.2	100.0	122.6	100.0
4. LWC	Private non-farm	324.2	86.4	12.0	86.0
	Government	41.0	10.9	1.4	9.8
	Farm	9.9	2.6	.6	4.2
	Total	375.1	100.0	14.0	100.0
5. KSV	Private non-farm	90.3	84.3	3.0	82.2
	Government	13.4	12.5	.4	12.2
	Farm	3.4	3.2	.2	5.7
	Total	107.2	100.0	3.7	100.0
6. UEC	Private non-farm	120.2	86.9	4.5	87.1
	Government	16.1	11.6	.5	10.5
	Farm	2.0	1.5	.1	2.4
	Total	138.4	100.0	5.1	100.0
7. ROF	Private non-farm	4 440.9	85.1	182.6	86.3
	Government	725.1	13.9	26.0	12.3
	Farm	50.6	1.0	3.0	1.4
	Total	5 216.6	100.0	211.7	100.0

citrus, vegetables, sod, nurseries, dairy herds, cow–calf operations would be needed, *each* requiring a specialist's knowledge of factors not found within the REMI modeling framework.[4]

The REMI model, therefore, backs away from modeling the agriculture sector at all, and the user is told upfront that the farming sector (REMI sector 13, SIC 01, 02) is treated differently than the 13 other sectors, including agricultural, forestry, and fishing services (REMI sector 10, SIC 07–09). The REMI model assumes that all agricultural sales are exported and that all material inputs used by agriculture are imported from outside the study area. That is, the value-added generated by sugar farming remains in the region, but the chemicals, seeds, fertilizers, machinery repair, and other purchased inputs needed by growers are all treated as imports. They are "lost" to the local economy.

In other words, REMI treats agriculture as a pure enclave sector, much like a mining operation in the middle of a desert.[5] To correct for this we must estimate the value of the backward and forward linkages of all the major agricultural activities for each of the sub-regions and their trends. Then we must insert these back into the REMI model.

Figure 12.3 gives us a picture of the variety and dominance of the principal crops by region, estimated with IMPLAN data. Sales of vegetables, greenhouse plants, and sugar are most important in the LEC, dairy and livestock in the KSV, and fruit (mainly citrus) in LWC, KSV, and UEC. *Physical measures,* not dollar value, of many agricultural activities *on the county level* are recorded by various agencies: for example, acreage, crates of fruit, and number of citrus trees; number of dairy and meat cattle; acreage of sugarcane. For various vegetable crops, output measures for statewide or reporting districts, not counties, are available on an annual basis. It is ironic, therefore, that we must turn to the IMPLAN database in order to construct a consistent series of *value* of sales of each crop *by county* and then aggregate to our sub-regions for the period 1993–99. (It is the data from the latest year of this series that are plotted in Figure 12.3.)

These are the materials we shall use to change the method by which the REMI model forecasts farm employment and income and how the model treats indirect inputs.

CORRECTING FOR AGRICULTURAL EMPLOYMENT

The REMI control forecasts a steady decline in farm employment due perhaps to the way the model treats this "exogenous sector." But the past 30-year trend as well as the national and regional political commitment to the sector contradict this projection; so, clearly, "farm employment" needs correcting.

The basic problem is illustrated in Figure 12.4. The REMI base for All Florida farm employment gives a number fluctuating around 90 000 workers between 1969 and 1995, which then is projected to fall to around 50 000 by 2035. The Regional Economic Information System (REIS) provides farm employment by county through 2000, and these recent data will be used to estimate the 1995–2000 trend for each region, which we shall use, together with the older series, to estimate our own total agricultural employment for the years 2000–2035. In Figure 12.5, the gap between my projections and the REMI base is indicated by the double-headed arrow. This number is then inserted in the REMI model to correct for the employment deficiency.

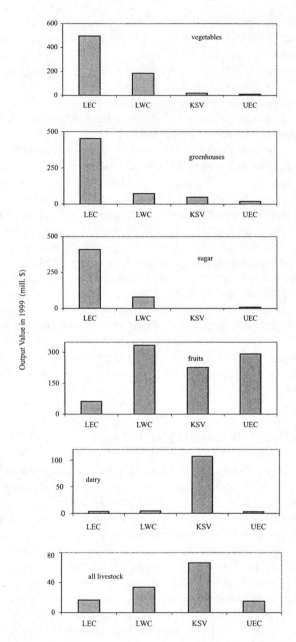

Source: IMPLAN database.

Figure 12.3   Agriculture in the Four Regions (Dollar Sales, 1999)

In Table 12.4, we present the REIS number of agricultural workers in the year 2000 and the average annual rate of growth (AROG) for 1995–2000, which we used to make the projection for each region.

This procedure will be followed for the five sub-regions (the four SF sub-regions and the "Rest of Florida"). Figure 12.6 indicates the declining farm employment for the five sub-regions in the REMI base ("EU"). These contrast with Figure 12.7, our projections of total jobs for each region. The "gap" between the two is illustrated again in Figure 12.8 for the LEC sub-region.

CORRECTING FOR FARM INCOME

Jobs are only part of the story. The income of farm workers and proprietors is, for most regions, under-projected in the REMI base, and the "gap," therefore, between our projections and the REMI base must be corrected in the model in a manner similar to the employment adjustment. Because farm income, unlike employment, has fluctuated widely, even though the overall 30-year trend has been positive, we have selected differing levels of these long-term growth rates to guide our projections.

The selection of the appropriate rate of growth of farm income was guided by the historical series, deflated to constant 1992 dollars. In Table 12.5, the AROGs measured for all the regions from the REMI base ("R-b") for 1970–80 (column 1) and for 1980–95 (column 2) all appear to be quite high. The AROG for later years is measured from the projections of the REMI-EU model for 1996–2001 (column 3) and for 2002–35 (column 4). The measured AROGs for the LWC, KSV, and ROF (rest of Florida) in column 4 are also high, ranging from 3.28 to 5.87 percent.

The REIS data provide a check against which the REMI AROGs may be compared. In columns 5–6 and 7–8, the REMI and REIS AROGs are compared for comparable years, the former for 1991–2000 and the latter for 1995–2000. In the 1991–2000 decade-long series, the REIS AROGs (column 6) are all lower than REMI, but in the shorter 1995–2000 series, the REIS AROGs (column 8) are all higher, except for the KSV. The high absolute values of the REIS AROGs for 1995–2000, ranging from 3 to 10 percent, are not likely to be sustained for the next thirty years. Hence, we selected long-tem AROGs for making our forecasts which reflect more closely the REIS decade-long series (column 6). These were used as the low estimates for the income projections (column 9) or, as in the cases of negative AROGs for the LWC and UEC, they were replaced by a minimum AROG of 1 percent. These modest increases in income, sustainable over the next decades, represent a "minimum" vision of proactive policies that would protect and promote the farm sector.

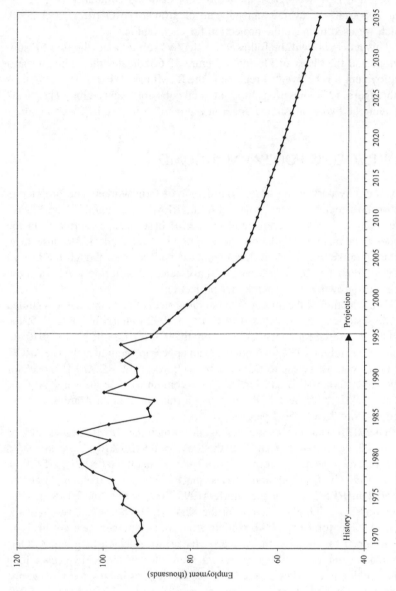

Figure 12.4   REMI Base: All Florida Farm Employment, 1969–2035

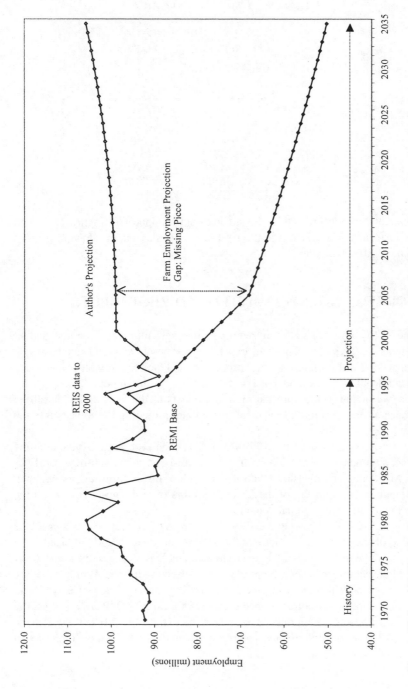

Figure 12.5   All Florida Farm Employment Projections: REMI vs. Missing Pieces

Table 12.4   Employment and AROGs

	For employment projections	
	REIS 2000 2000 no. (1)	AROG used 1995–2000 % (2)
LEC	15 397	0.724
LWC	9 603	0.996
KSV	4 932	0.829
UEC	2 257	0.685
ROF	64 766	0.532
FL	96 955	0.627

The slow-growth projections for all five regions appear in Figure 12.9, with the historical data reflected in the 1991–2000 profiles and the slow projections in the 2001–2035 years.

CORRECTING FOR OMITTED INDIRECT INPUTS

The REMI base treats all required inputs into agriculture as "imports" and all outputs as "exports." Thus, an expanding farm sector would not have any impact on local suppliers or local processors and the "true" effect of a growing sector would thus be understated, or "muffled," in the model. To correct for this, we intend to measure the indirect impacts of the farm sector on all the other non-farm sectors of each sub-region and project these impacts into the future.

To do this, we used the 1999 IMPLAN model, the latest available at the time, aggregated the Florida counties to correspond to the sub-regions of our REMI model, and measured the sales of each of the 23 farm sectors. We then computed the "impact" of the 23 farm sectors in each sub-region on all the sectors of its own regional economy.

IMPLAN distinguishes three types of impacts: "direct" (in this case, the value of the farm sales), "indirect" (the material inputs), and "induced" (the impacts of consumer spending resulting from increased wages due to the direct and indirect impacts). For the purposes of correcting the REMI model, we are interested only in measuring the indirect impacts, which REMI excludes in its treatment of agriculture. Once estimated for all 528 IMPLAN sectors, the indirect impacts are aggregated to correspond to the 14 REMI sectors, deflated to 1992 constant dollars, and entered into the REMI model as "increases in demand" for the impacted sectors.

In this way, we use the IMPLAN model, with its strength in identifying 22 farm sectors, to complement the REMI model with its single "enclave" farm sector. Once the indirect inputs have been added, then the REMI model computes its own "induced impacts" by running the new agricultural sector together with its newly entered indirect inputs through all the "blocks" shown in Figure 12.1. (The IMPLAN–REMI "cross-walk" is given in Appendix Table F.1.)

The rates of growth of these indirect farm impacts should be identical to the rates of growth of the farm sectors causing them. However, the only consistent *sales* data by crop and county from which such rates could be computed are available for a few recent years from the IMPLAN files themselves. We therefore allowed indirect impacts to grow at the same rates as total farm income, as described above. The projection of the sum of the indirect impacts in the ROF for the major REMI sectors for 1999–2035 is given in Figure 12.10.

How realistic are our projections? The National Agricultural Statistical Services of the USDA publishes some "outlook" projections for the coming decade. The "outlook" is generally positive for greenhouse and vegetable sales and stable for citrus for the overall US (Figure 12.11). For sugarcane, prices received by growers are expected to remain low through 2006, rising steadily thereafter (see Figure 12.12). Net farm income for the US as a whole is expected to remain stable (declining in real terms) until 2005 and then increase modestly thereafter (Figure 12.13). No "outlook" projections are made for the state of Florida or for its counties. Nevertheless, the mix of crops in our regions, the overall stability of their progress in the previous decades, the increasing acreages under irrigation, and the success in achieving both national and state intervention would all tend to support our view that the farm sector is likely to continue at least a modest upward trend. This may turn out to be a conservative forecast in view of the likelihood that CERP could bring improvements in the regularity of water supply and greater flood protection and thus more than offset any decline due to a loss of acreage to reservoir construction.

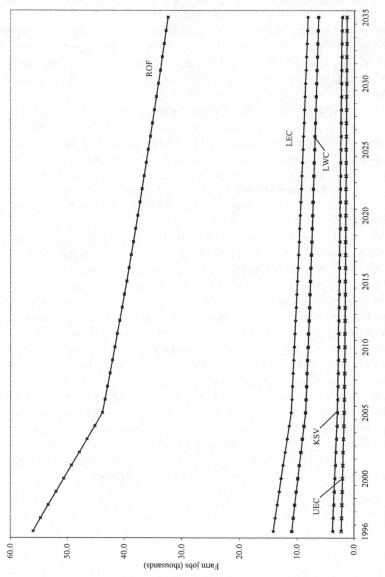

Figure 12.6   Farm Jobs, REMI Base Projections (Employment Update only)

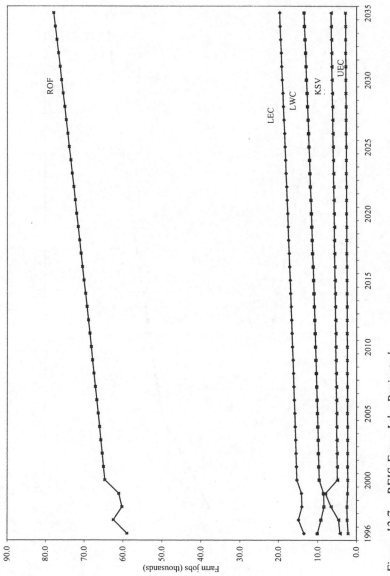

Figure 12.7   REIS Farm Jobs Projected

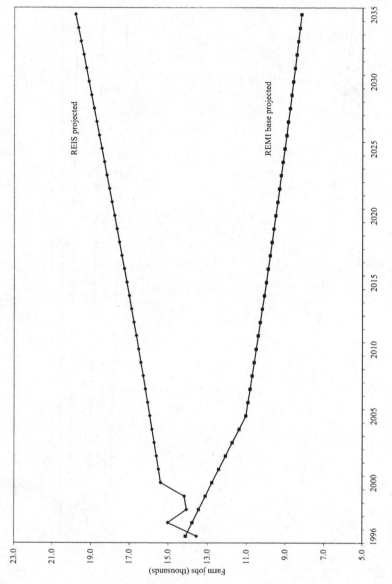

Figure 12.8   Farm Jobs, Lower East Coast, REIS Projected and REMI Base

Table 12.5 Comparison of AROGs for Farm Income, Various Series, and Projected AROGs

| | REMI series | | | | REMI—REIS series | | | | AROGs selected for income projections | | |
	R-b 1970–80 (1)	R-b 1980–95 (2)	R-EU 1996–2001 (3)	R-EU 2002–35 (4)	REMI 1991–2000 (5)	REIS 1991–2000 (6)	REMI 1995–2000 (7)	REIS 1995–2000 (8)	Low (9)	Medium (10)	High (11)
LEC	10.80	9.80	4.55	1.78	4.48	0.47	5.11	5.38	0.47	2.00	4.00
LWC	11.37	7.79	1.60	5.42	-2.03	-1.26	0.84	3.03	1.00	2.00	4.00
KSV	11.75	4.42	11.23	5.87	5.22	3.21	12.40	10.11	3.21	3.21	4.00
UEC	16.55	4.49	2.77	1.55	-0.89	-2.75	2.98	4.66	1.00	2.00	4.00
ROF	9.65	1.48	5.68	3.28	1.29	0.77	6.14	6.58	0.77	2.00	4.00
FL	10.30	3.73	4.78	3.63	1.04	—	5.06	—	—	—	—

Note: R-b = REMI base; R-EU = REMI employment update.

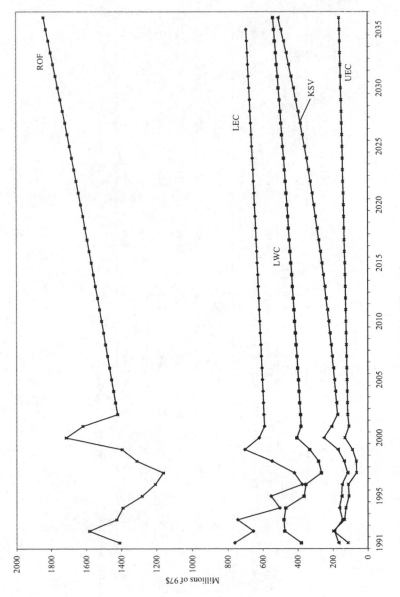

Figure 12.9 Farm Income, Five Regions, Minimal Growth

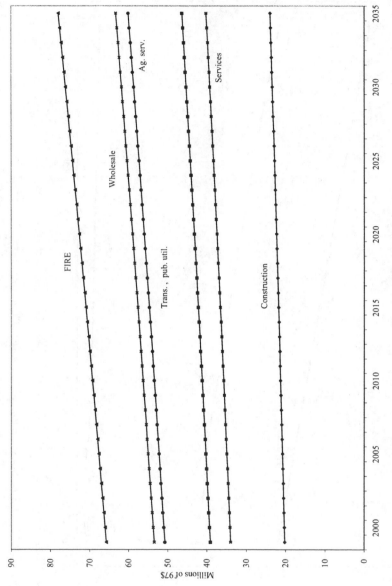

Figure 12.10   Indirect Impacts, Lower East Coast, Major REMI Sectors

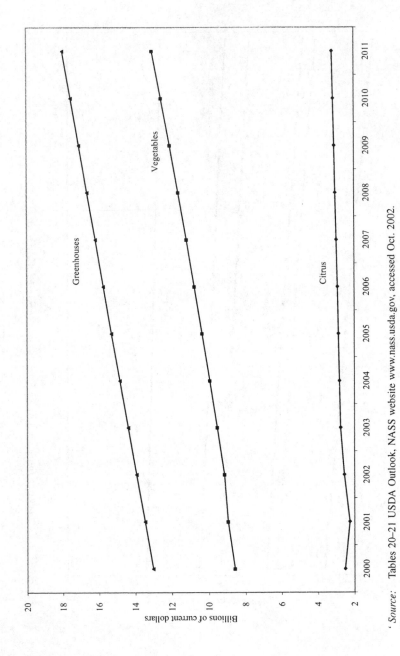

Source: Tables 20–21 USDA Outlook, NASS website www.nass.usda.gov, accessed Oct. 2002.

Figure 12.11   US Outlook for Production Value, Three Crops

206

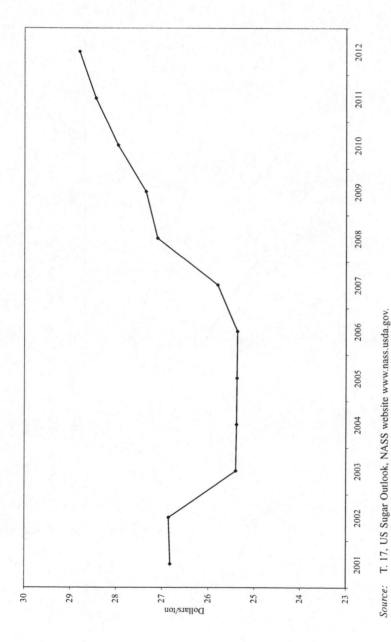

Source: T. 17, US Sugar Outlook, NASS website www.nass.usda.gov.

Figure 12.12   Sugarcane Grower Prices

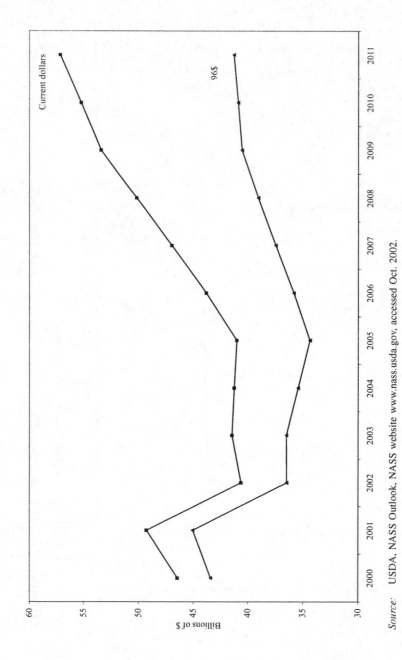

Source: USDA, NASS Outlook, NASS website www.nass.usda.gov, accessed Oct. 2002.

Figure 12.13   Outlook: Net Farm Income

NOTES

1. See Regional Economic Models, Inc (1997, ch. 15).
2. Standard and Poor's monthly publication, *Review of the US Economy*, publishes forecast values of 1400 variables for its quarterly model for six and a half years into the future. Some of these could be applied to the REMI US Control, and the Regional Control would then measure the impact of the *national* changes on the region, for example, a national recession on the local tourist sectors.
3. WDR 21–23 correspond to our LEC; WDR 24 to LWC; and WDR 20 to UEC. Employment growth rates for KSV, consisting of three counties, were taken from the employment projections of BEBR's *Long-Term Economic Forecast* made in 1997 for the major sectors for all the Florida counties through the year 2010.
4. Hazen and Sawyer (1998) preview the future of agriculture in Miami-Dade and Broward Counties by describing two scenarios, "optimistic" and "pessimistic," based on extensive interviewing of farm experts. They attempt no quantitative forecasting.
5. See Weisskoff and Wolff (1977) for a typology of the enclave economy and the different "linkages" and "leakages" that characterize each type of enclave. For an application of the enclave analysis to the western mining regions of the US, see Power (1996).

13. Economics of the Second Missing Piece: Investment

THE ISSUES AND DATA SOURCES

There are three categories of investment in the REMI regional control (the REMI base) that require examining. Residential construction, non-residential construction, and producer durable equipment are all based on internally-generated variables for both the region and the nation. (A fourth investment category, change in business inventories, will not be addressed as a missing piece.)

The REMI model computes investment by adjusting the existing capital stock to an "optimal" capital stock (Equations 3–14 and 7–32 in Treyz, 1993). The optimal capital stock for non-residential structures and for producer equipment is a function of the relative labor and relative capital costs, weighted by the industry's share in the existing stock (Equation 7–39), and the optimal capital stock for residential housing is related to the share of real disposable income in the region (Equation 7–41).

In Florida, however, a significant share of investment in residential and non-residential construction comes from outside the region as speculation unrelated to the "internal" model variables. The speculation may be driven by money fleeing the stock market and by foreign capital looking for a secure location and stable returns. Regardless of the motive, actual investments may differ from the REMI forecast. To measure the extent to which the REMI model understates or overstates residential and non-residential investment, we must compare the REMI series to data from two other sources:

(1) A series known as the "Dodge construction data," as transformed by the State Legislative Economic and Demographic Research Service (LEDRS) to "Value in Place." This series is computed in current dollars for fourteen different categories of construction for the Florida counties for 1968–1999. The categories of "residential construction" (multi-family and single-family, private and public) were aggregated. "Non-residential construction" was computed as a residual from total construction expenditures.

(2) Value of Building Permit Activity. BEBR reports the value of res-
     idential building permits by county. A series was constructed from
     the annual published county data in BEBR fsa, Table 11.15, for
     1964 through 2001. All the data through June 2002 were used for
     estimating the full 2002 year by assuming a continuation of the
     growth rate. The annual data in current dollars were deflated to 1992
     dollars using the construction deflators from (3) below. It should be
     noted that source (1) is actually derived from source (2), as the
     Dodge data take a sample of all types of construction permits, not
     just residential, and with some additional processing and time lags,
     transform the value of "permits" into completed construction.
(3) Deflators were computed from "Annual Value of Construction Put
     in Place in US," Annual Tables, 1964–2001, in current and constant
     dollars of 1996, from US Census website, *Current Construction
     Reports*, Series C30, Table 1. Excerpted years also appear in saus,
     Tables 928 and 929, with an explanation of the methodology. The
     series was then re-indexed to 1992 dollars.

Once sources (1) and (2) were made comparable to the REMI model data
(in terms of constant 1992 dollars), we were finally prepared to ask two key
research questions. First, to what extent does the investment series of the REMI
employment update (EU) model differ in terms of *level* and *rate of growth* in
each of the regions for those years for which we now have actual data, namely,
the Dodge data through 1999 for residential and non-residential investment
and the permits data through 2002 for residential?

Second, the EU adjustments only affect the forecasts of the REMI base
until 2010, after which the model "reverts," as it were, to the REMI base. For
the later years, should an additional "investment premium" be added or subtracted from the base? If so, what is the *level* of that premium and the *rate* of
its growth?

COMPARING DATA SERIES AND FORECASTS

The comparable absolute values for two categories of investment from the
different data sources for our seven regions are presented in Table 13.1 and
their corresponding average rates of growth in Table 13.2. The values in the
first four columns of Table 13.1 permit us to compare residential construction
for the year 1999 across four different models. For the LEC, both REMI models
(base and EU) give higher values than the Dodge data and the building permits
data, and in the ROF, REMI is higher than Permits for 1999. As a consequence,
REMI's value for the aggregated region of "All Florida" is higher than the

Table 13.1   *Residential and Non-Residential Construction, Three Sources, 1999 and 2010 (bill. 92$)*

	Residential						Non-residential				
					Forecast					Forecast	
	Building permits value 1999	Dodge data value 1999	REMI base 1999	REMI EU 1999	REMI base 2010	REMI EU 2010	Dodge data value 1999	REMI base 1999	REMI EU 1999	REMI base 2010	REMI EU 2010
	(1)	(2)	(3)	(4)	(5)	(6)	(7)	(8)	(9)	(10)	(11)
FL	12.153	n.a.	16.569	16.715	15.691	19.043	n.a.	12.945	13.484	13.862	18.264
SF	4.957	6.299	6.384	6.302	5.479	7.068	5.718	5.085	5.159	5.479	6.991
LEC	2.760	3.862	4.822	4.700	4.364	5.191	4.587	3.807	3.781	4.125	5.066
LWC	1.478	1.879	0.985	1.044	0.857	1.253	0.763	0.807	0.917	0.857	1.296
KSV	0.383	n.c.	0.213	0.210	0.198	0.246	n.c.	0.179	0.175	0.198	0.224
UEC	0.336	0.494	0.364	0.347	0.299	0.377	0.288	0.292	0.287	0.299	0.404
ROF	7.195	n.a.	10.185	10.413	8.383	11.975	n.a.	7.861	8.325	8.383	16.273

Note: n.a. = not available; n.c. = not comparable.

213

Table 13.2 *Average Rates of Growth (AROG), Different Data Sources and Models*

	Residential construction						Non-residential construction				Durable eqpt.	
	Short series				Long series		Short series		Long series		Short	Long
	Building permits 8 yr	Dodge data 10 yr	REMI EU 15 yr	REMI-p EU/base 15 yr	Dodge data 30 yr	REMI EU 40 yr	Dodge data 10 yr	REMI EU 15 yr	Dodge data 30 yr	REMI EU 40 yr	REMI EU 15 yr	REMI EU 40 yr
	1994–2002	1989–1999	1996–2010	1996–2010	1969–1999	1969–2010	1989–1999	1996–2010	1969–1999	1969–2010	1996–2010	1969–2010
	(1)	(2)	(3)	(4)	(5)	(6)	(7)	(8)	(9)	(10)	(11)	(12)
FL	8.8	n.a.	—	5.3	n.a.	—	n.a.	—	n.a.	—	—	—
SF	7.1	4.4	—	6.2	3.3	—	3.8	—	2.9	—	—	—
LEC	3.7	3.5	0.63	15.4	2.6	2.40	3.1	2.97	2.3	2.40	7.46	6.40
LWC	13.7	9.9	2.11	26.8	7.4	4.90	7.9	3.75	5.9	4.95	6.53	7.96
KSV	15.1	10.9	1.95	11.5	8.1	5.40	17.2	2.53	12.9	4.77	5.64	8.05
UEC	11.1	10.0	0.79	19.5	7.5	4.75	50.4	3.56	37.8	5.00	6.55	8.03
ROF	10.3	n.a.	1.32	17.5	n.a.	3.85	n.a.	2.97	n.a.	3.52	7.46	7.22

Note: n.a. = not available.

214

Permits estimate and the REMI-EU forecast for SF is about the same as the Dodge and higher than the Permits data for 1999.

More interesting is the case of the LWC, in which both Dodge and Permits indicate a much higher level of activity than REMI, and the KSV, in which Permits (Dodge data are not comparable) also is higher than REMI. In summary, Dodge is higher than REMI in the LWC and KSV, suggesting that at least in those three regions, some upward adjustment is warranted.

For the non-residential investment (columns 7–9 of Table 13.1), a different pattern emerges. For this category of investment, Dodge gives a higher value than the REMI base and EU for the LEC (and therefore SF), but REMI is higher in the LWC and equal in the UEC.

The REMI base and EU forecasts for 2010 are compared in columns 5–6 for residential and columns 10–11 for non-residential, showing the impact of the employment update procedures on forecasts of these variables.

Regarding rates of growth, does the REMI forecast of investment grow too slowly? The average annual rates of growth of the three categories of investment are shown in Table 13.2 for the sub-regions. The Permits data for the years 1994–2002 indicate higher AROG for the LWC and KSV than the Dodge data for roughly comparable years, 1989–1999 (columns 1–2). Both should be compared to the corresponding REMI EU model for the 15-year period 1996–2010 (column 3), which shows a much lower AROG for all regions. The long-term Dodge data for the 30-year period, 1969–99 (column 5, may be compared to REMI EU 40-year (1969–2010) series (column 6). The AROG for LEC is the same, but for the other regions Dodge has a higher AROG than REMI.

The high rates in the most recent years shown by Permits and Dodge may not be sustained in the future, but they do suggest faster growth than REMI for residential investment. To some extent, the REMI-premium, which is the investment caused by the EU adjustment (column 4), has remedied this deficiency for the 1996–2010 years. What is the correct adjustment for the future?

A similar dilemma can be seen in the case of the AROG for non-residential investment (columns 7–10 of Table 13.2). Here, the 10-year AROG for Dodge is higher than the REMI EU 15-year series (columns 7 and 8) for all the regions but the LEC. Furthermore, the Dodge 30-year AROG (column 9) is also higher than the REMI 40-year AROG (column 10) in all regions except for LEC. A comparison of the 40-year AROG and 15-year REMI reveals a lower value for the shorter AROG for every region except the LEC (columns 8 and 10). All this suggests that the recent forecasts build in a rate of growth slower than that historically achieved and that without further adjustment, even the REMI EU would understate the growth of future investment in all regions except perhaps the LEC.

In the case of producer durable equipment, the last category of investment, the long-term REMI AROGs for 1969–2010 are higher than the REMI-EU for the shorter 1996–2010 period except in the LEC and ROF (compare columns 11 and 12, Table 13.2). Again, this suggests the need for some level of adjustment if the REMI forecasts for 2010 onward are to conform to historical performance.

There is no way of knowing if the regions will, in fact, sustain the growth of investment that we have documented from the different sources. But I am convinced that simply letting the model run on into the future with no correction or adjustment would lead to serious underforecasting because the investment piece plays such an important role in the growth of the rest of the economy.

A set of illustrations may clarify our findings so far. In Figures 13.1 and 13.2, we have plotted the Dodge and REMI residential series for the LEC and LWC, respectively, for 1969–1999. The profiles for each region follow very similar patterns, except that the REMI profile in the LEC is higher at almost every point, and in the LWC, REMI is for the most part below Dodge! If Dodge is to be believed, we should subtract a "premium" from REMI in the LEC and add to it in the LWC.

This idea is illustrated in Figure 13.3, which shows the projections for residential construction generated by the REMI regional control (in triangles) from 1996 to 2030 and the upward adjustments resulting from the EU corrections (in diamonds). The "Dodge deficiency" is indicated by the dashed line in Figure 13.3, which, if subtracted, would shift the projections of LEC residential construction downward (see Figure 13.4).

The procedure is reversed in the high-growth LWC region, where the Dodge data indicate a missing positive "premium" (Figure 13.5) that should be added to the REMI-EU forecasts (Figure 13.6). Both of these adjustments assume the Dodge data are more correct than the basic REMI investment figures.

Rather than use the Dodge series to adjust the REMI, it was decided to stay within the original model framework, continuing onward from the EU-generated point for 2010. We created three scenarios that correspond to maintaining the REMI-AROG for each category of investment but at different fractions of their historical growth rates. These are given in Table 13.3. The "premiums" between each of these scenarios and the REMI-EU were then entered into the model for each region and for each of the three categories of investment.

These patterns of premiums and how they contrast with the historical series are shown in Figures 13.7–13.9 for the three investment categories in LEC, Figures 13.10–13.12 for the investment in LWC, and Figure 13.13 for durable producer equipment in the ROF.

A few observations might be made about all these illustrations. First, the forecasts made by the REMI base generally taper off or rise slightly with time. The EU model "kicks" the investment up for the first ten years of the new projection. Use of the 15-year AROG leads to a more sustained growth, while the application of the full 40-year AROG appears too extreme and overcorrects the base, suggesting unlikely and unacceptable scenarios.

In Figure 13.14, we have charted the premiums added to the basic REMI-EU model to bring total residential investment up to the "basic" levels for all the regions and an "optimistic" scenario in the case of the LEC. This illustrates the nature of the correction done for each investment category and for each region in order to replicate low, medium, and fast rates of growth. Once this "missing investment piece" is computed for each sub-region and for each "pace" and is re-inserted into REMI, then the "corrected" REMI model regenerates a "new" growth path for the entire economy.

Table 13.3   *Average Rates of Growth (AROGs) Used for Projecting Investment Categories*

	Residential construction			Non-residential construction			Producer durable eqpt.		
	Slow (1)	Med. (2)	(Histor.) Fast (3)	Slow (4)	Med. (5)	(Histor.) Fast (6)	Slow (7)	Med. (8)	(Histor.) Fast (9)
LEC	1.3	3.0	2.40	1.1	3.0	2.40	1.60	3.20	6.40
LWC	3.7	4.0	4.90	3.0	4.0	4.95	1.99	3.98	7.96
KSV	4.1	4.0	5.40	2.0	4.0	4.77	2.01	4.03	8.05
UEC	3.7	4.0	4.75	2.0	4.0	5.00	2.01	4.01	8.03
ROF	1.6	3.0	3.85	1.5	3.0	3.52	1.81	3.61	7.22

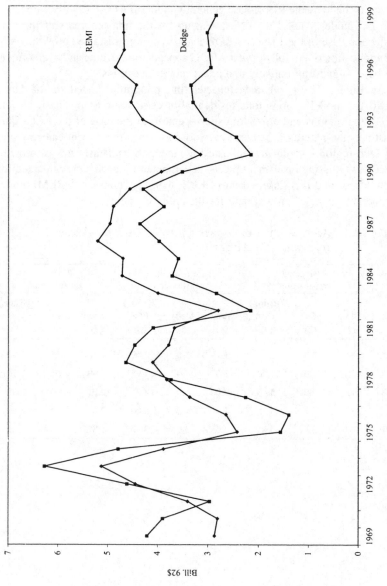

Figure 13.1   Lower East Coast Residential Construction Series, Dodge and REMI Compared

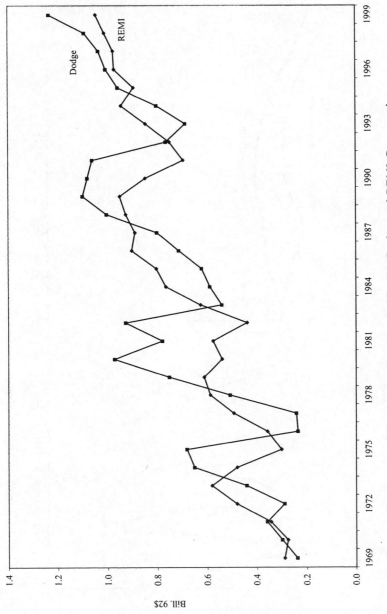

Figure 13.2   Lower West Coast Residential Construction Series, Dodge and REMI Compared

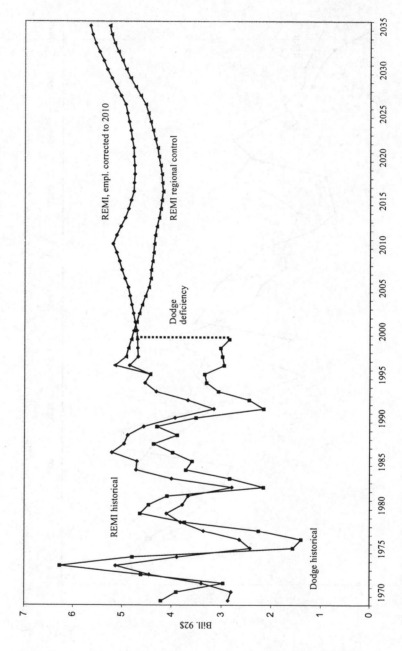

Figure 13.3   Lower East Coast Residential Construction

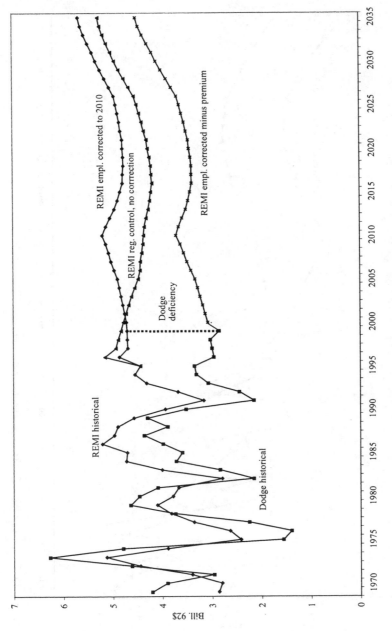

Figure 13.4 Lower East Coast Residential Construction with Premium Subtracted

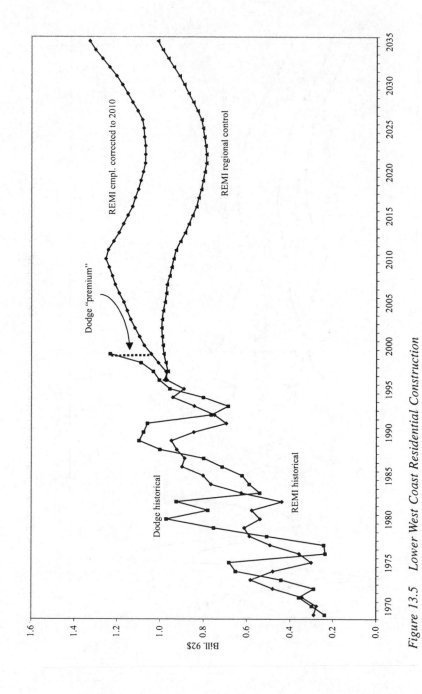

Figure 13.5 Lower West Coast Residential Construction

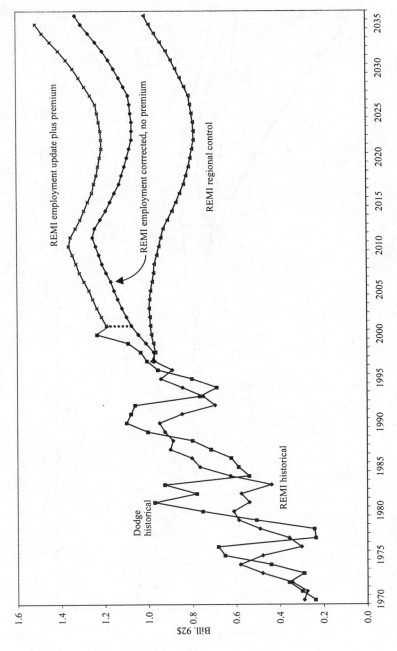

Figure 13.6   Lower West Coast Residential Construction with Premium Added

223

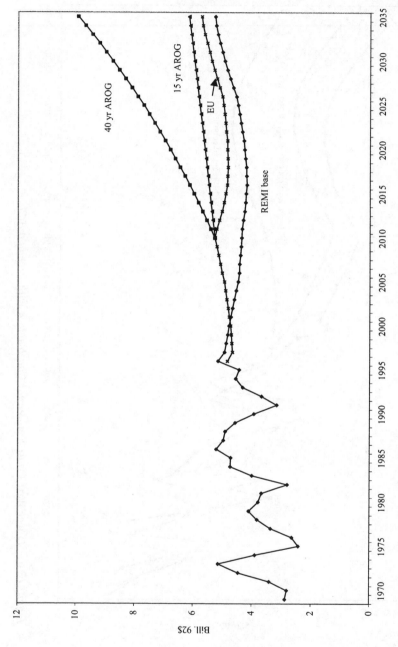

Figure 13.7 Lower East Coast Residential Construction, Different Projections

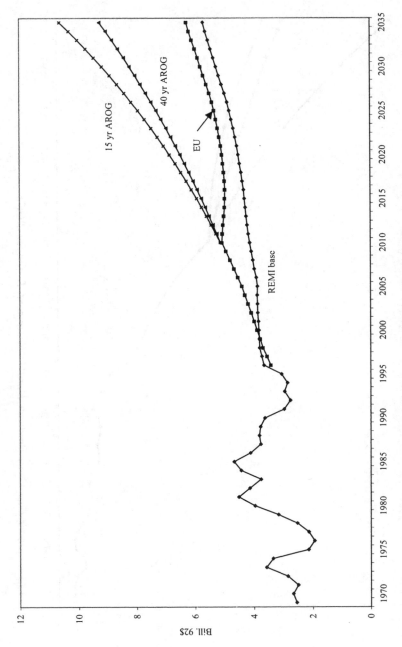

Figure 13.8 Lower East Coast Non-Residential Construction, Different Projections

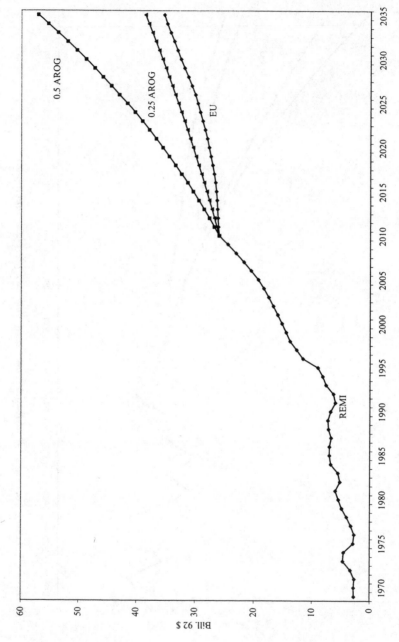

Figure 13.9   Lower East Coast Producer Durable Equipment, Different AROGs

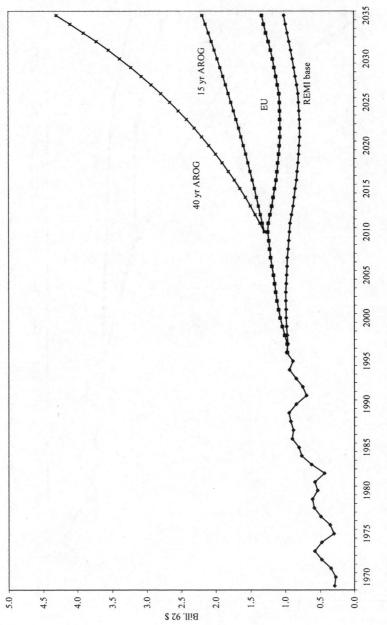

Figure 13.10   Lower West Coast Residential Construction, Different AROGs

227

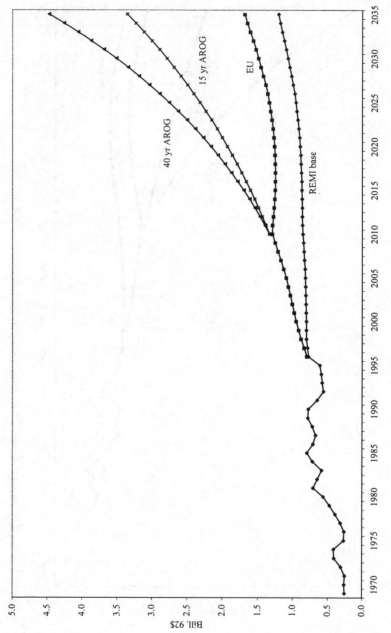

Figure 13.11 Lower West Coast Non-Residential Construction, Different AROGs

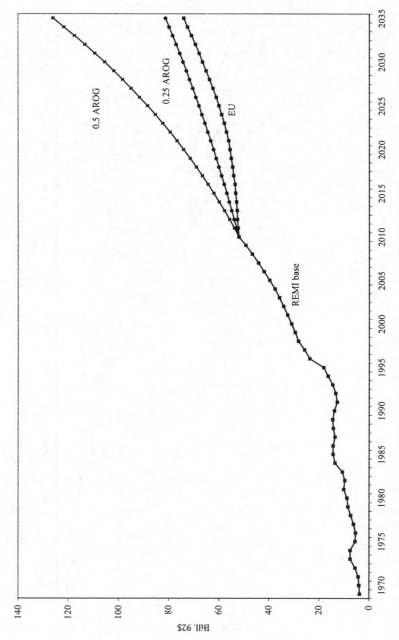

Figure 13.12 . Lower West Coast Producer Durable Equipment, Different AROGs

229

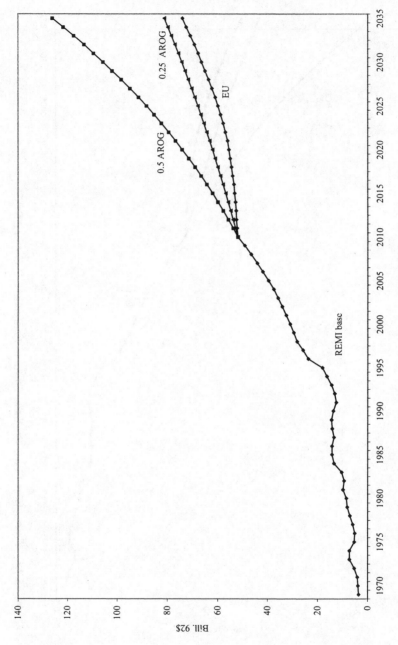

Figure 13.13   Rest of Florida Producer Durable Equipment, Different AROGs

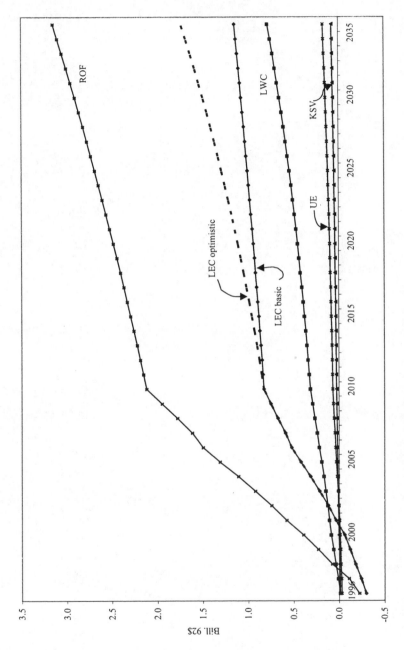

Figure 13.14   Premiums for Residential Construction, All Regions

231

14. Economics of the Third Missing Piece: Tourism

Tourism is an elusive but all pervasive activity in the economic model of Florida. There is no single "tourist" sector, as there are distinct farming and construction sectors.

Tourism is rather a collection of sectors or parts of sectors that cater primarily to the visitor, such as hotels, restaurants, car rentals, and amusement parks.

Tourist spending is nowhere identified in the REMI base, but rather spending by tourists gets mixed in with spending by local residents. Thus, in a region where tourist spending is important, it appears rather that the *local* residents are spending greater-than-normal amounts on such sectors as restaurants, car rentals, and amusement parks. As "local" disposable income increases, then so does spending on those sectors. If, however, tourist spending is actually increasing at a faster rate than local incomes, then the growth of those sectors patronized by the tourists will be underestimated in the REMI model. This omission may be serious in a region such as the LEC and, indeed, for the entire statewide model.

The correction for this "missing piece" requires data on tourist spending by sector and by region. From such data, we can then compute the growth in the levels of spending and its distribution across the sectors that can be used to adjust the REMI-EU (employment update) model.

TOURISM STATISTICS

There are two approaches to statewide tourist spending and visitation trends for Florida.[1] The annual *Florida Visitor Study*, issued now by Visit Florida, a quasi-public agency, estimates the number of visitors, their length of stay, and amount of spending. Alternatively, the state treasury reports revenue (and hence sales) in those sectors that are related to, but are not the exclusive domain of, visitors.[2] These data are published annually on a sector level but not for the counties.

The visitor counts reported in the *Florida Visitor Studies* were obtained by interviews supervised by the state's Office of Tourism Research until 1999, at which time the survey was outsourced to D.K. Shifflet & Associates. The earlier series found fewer visitors, but they stayed longer and spent much less money than the later data, which show a major increase in spending. The number of recorded spending categories is fewer, and the length of stay is shorter in the more recent studies. The newer data are considered to be more accurate and more representative of the true tourist population.[3]

The new data more closely approximate the national figures published by the Travel Industry Association of America in the Statistical Abstract of the US (saus 2001, Table 1257), which reports that $39.14 billion or 8.7 percent of the total US domestic tourist expenditures in 1999 was spent in Florida.[4] The *2000 Florida Visitor Study* (FVS) (Visit Florida Research Office, 2001) reported 51.376 million domestic visitors to the State (p. 2), staying an average of 5.3 nights (p. 16), and spending an average of $123.40 per person per day (p. 17). This computes to a total expenditure of $33.601 billion or 86 percent of the saus figure given above, but the saus estimate includes spending by Florida residents on overnight trips and on day trips more than 50 miles away. The FVS counts only out-of-state visitors. Both figures exclude Canadians and other overseas visitors.

The long-term series for tourist statistics that have been extracted from the various volumes of the *Florida Statistical Abstract* and the most recent *Florida Visitor Surveys* appear in Figures 14.1–14.5 for total number of visitors, length of stay, spending per party, number of nights, and total spending. I have drawn the graphs to highlight clearly the "breaks" and inconsistencies that appear in the various series.

In Figure 14.1, we note the increasing trend in the sheer number of visitors, from 14 million in 1963 to 70 million in 2001 and the rising importance of air travel in the most recent years.

Auto visitors historically had been noted as spending much longer staying in Florida (Figure 14.2). The recent surveys suggest a much reduced and near equivalent stay – around 5.4 nights – for both air and auto travelers.

The expenditure per person per visit (Figure 14.3) shows several discontinuities in the series since 1963. The spending *per party* for air and auto visitors (the bottom two lines of squares and triangles in Figure 14.3) appears to be extremely stable from 1979–1997, while the expenditure *per person* has risen and fallen in each "series" due to variations in the number of people in each party and the way in which spending information was gathered and reported. The recent rise in spending *per person*, shown in black diamonds in Figure 14.3, has remained stable during the 1999–2001 period.

The total number of visitor-nights reported in the last three years has increased (Figure 14.4), although the 1999 figure was lower than any *level* reported since 1980. The result of the three parameters (charted in Figures 14.1–14.3) – the number of visitors, length of stay, and spending per person-visit – determines total tourist spending (Figure 14.5), the rise of which may be due to changing methodology.

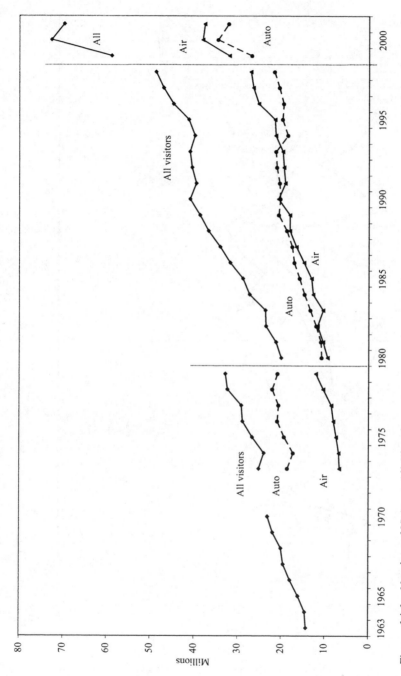

Figure 14.1 Number of Visitors, All Florida

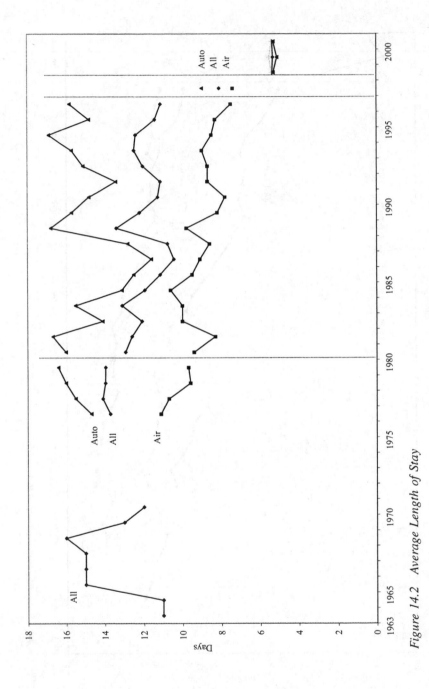

Figure 14.2 Average Length of Stay

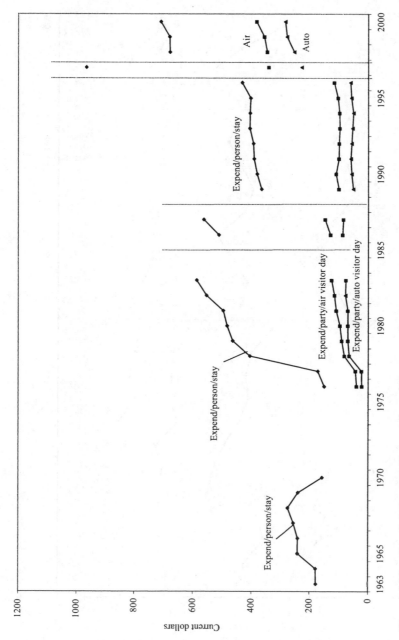

Figure 14.3   Expenditure per Party and per Person

237

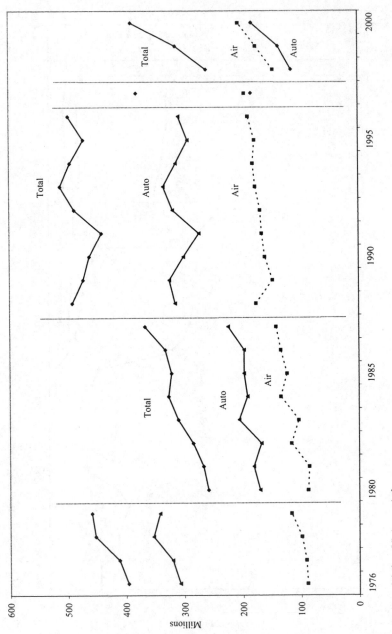

Figure 14.4   Visitor-nights

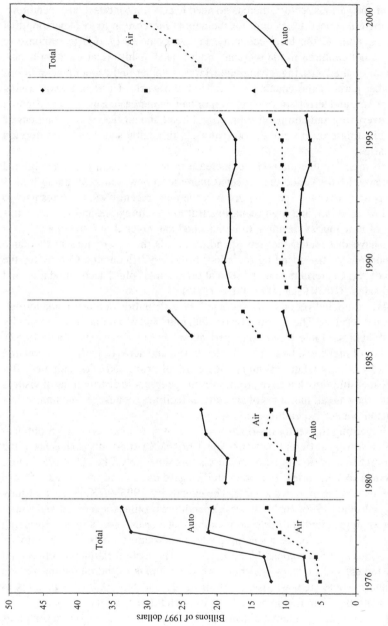

Figure 14.5 Total Tourist Spending (97$)

Since the mass of tourist spending is already captured in the REMI model within the various sectors, there is no need to account for this total expenditure. But there is a need to account for the annual *increase* in tourist spending that is exogenous to the local economy. People come to Florida in response to factors not captured in the regional model, such as historical vacation habits, promotional advertising, changing airfares, weather and economic conditions in other parts of the country and, indeed, the world. Hurricanes, war, rising gas prices, and terrorism can interrupt or halt an increase. But greater spending on advertising and competitive pricing of hotel and air tickets can compensate by attracting greater numbers of visitors from nearby states and from foreign countries.

To replicate the autonomous increase in tourist spending on the regional economy, I have varied the expected increase in new tourist spending from 1 to 3 percent over the spending given in the most recent FVS, to correspond to our low, medium, and high scenarios. But to which regions and sectors is this flow of new tourist spending to be attached and entered into the model?

I have distributed the new spending across the sub-regions in the same proportions as the spending recorded in the 1997 Economic Census for the sum of "arts, entertainment and recreation receipts" plus "accommodation and food sales" (BEBR fsa 2002, Table 19.05).[5]

We computed yet other indicators of the distribution of tourism and tourist-oriented services. The distribution of hotel units and restaurant seating capacity by county (fsa, Table 16.90), state park attendance by county (fsa, Table 19.52), number of registered boats (fsa, Table 19.45), and acres of park and recreation lands by county (state inventory file) were all processed and compared. But these measures are defective proxies for the geographic distributions of visitors in that they are all measures of capacity or facilities, not usage, and none refers to actual visitor expenditure in a specific year.

Regarding the sector distribution of tourist spending, recent FVS publications give very different patterns. The 1997 FVS pattern distributes spending over eight categories for auto and air visitors separately. The 2000 FVS pattern specifies six categories. Two other studies gave us some idea of which of these patterns was the more reasonable. The exhaustive 1995–96 Keys Visitor Study (English et al., 1996, Table 8) gives expenditure profiles for summer and winter visitors aggregated into five comparable categories. The Strategy Research Corp. (2002) breaks the spending profiles of Miami tourists in 2001 into six categories that are comparable to the FVS. There are differences between all the studies, and each study samples only a segment of the tourist market. As an intermediate step, we used *both* the 1997 and the 2000 FVS patterns to distribute the increases in annual tourist spending across the sectors.

The resulting percentage distribution of spending across our sub-regions is given in Panel A and the two distributions of tourist spending are given in Panels B and C of Table 14.1.

Table 14.1   Distribution of Tourist Spending by Region and Sector

A. Geographic distribution of tourist spending, 1997 Economic Census
("entertainment and recreation" plus "hotel and food" receipts)

	Percent
LEC	31.0
LWC	4.6
KSV	3.0
UEC	1.3
All SF	39.9
ROF	60.1
FL	100.0

B. Sectoral distribution of tourist spending, FVS 1997

	Percent	REMI variable name	REMI sector no.
1. Transport	7.76	Cons. spendg, non-res: transp	171
2. Gas	3.83	Con spend n-r: gas and oil	166
3. Food (groceries)	7.14	Con spend n-r: food and beverages	164
4. Food (restaurant)	22.58	Con spend n-r: purch. meals and bev.	T233
5. Lodging	34.40	Services (part hotels)	609
6. Entertainment	10.84	Con spend n-r: adm. to sports events	T288
7. Gifts	6.78	Con spend n-r: clothing and shoes	165
8. Other	6.67	Con spend n-r: other services	173
Total	100.00		

C. Sectoral distribution of tourist spending, FVS 2000

	Percent	REMI variable name	REMI sector no.
1. Transport	27.70	Cons. spendg, non-res: transp	171
2. Food	20.50	Con spend n-r: purch. meals and bev.	T233
3. Lodging	21.40	Services (part hotels)	609
4. Entertainment	14.10	Con spend n-r: adm. to sports events	T288
5. Gifts	13.10	Con spend n-r: clothing and shoes	165
6. Other services	3.20	Con spend n-r: other services	173
Total	100.00		

Sources and Methods: Panel A: Computed from BEBR fsa 2002, Table 19.05, by summing categories and counties. Panels B-C: Computed from *Florida Visitor Study* (FVS), 1997 and 2000, "Average Expenditures" by category of spending.

To summarize our research on the tourism "missing piece," we distributed three levels of new tourist spending (low, medium, high) across the five sub-regions according to each of two patterns, FVS 1997 and FVS 2000. Each stream was deflated to 1992 prices and entered into the model for each region. Increases for the year 2001 over the previous year were set at zero and the normal growth rate continued in 2002 and thereafter. Since it was found that the FVS 1997 pattern did not measurably affect the result, it was decided to apply only the FVS 2000 pattern to simplify the number of options computed for the tourism missing piece. The time profile of the annual increases in spending for the LEC is shown in Figure 14.6.

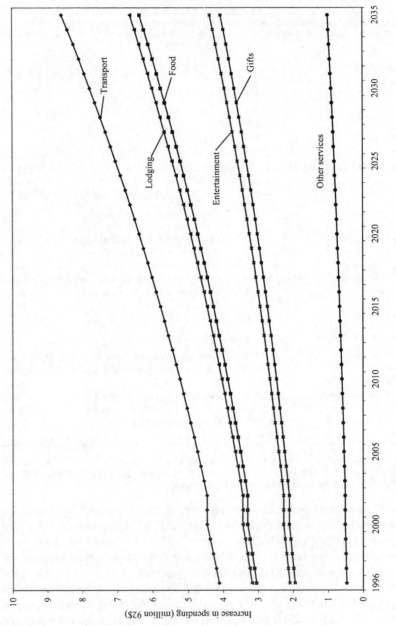

Figure 14.6 Projected Increase in Tourist Spending, Lower East Coast

242

In a subsequent interview, Dr Barry Petigoff, Vice President for Research of Visit Florida, the state's quasi-public tourist office, explained the developments that led to abandoning local surveys and the need to subscribe to national surveys and panel samples. Earlier methodology relied on interviewing auto travelers at rest stops on the interstate highways near the northern borders of the state. This sample was shown to be increasingly non-representative of the auto visitor as more resorts came to be located near the borders and fewer drivers stopped at the rest stations (the so-called "bladder factor"). Air passengers had been interviewed in the airports, but after 9/11, it became difficult to approach exiting passengers, and interviews are now confined to the waiting areas prior to boarding.

In the new composite methodology, Visit Florida still collects data on domestic air passengers from interviews in the 14 largest airports. The Travel Industry Association provides the ratio of domestic air to non-air visitors (the auto interviews have been suspended), and D.K. Shifflets provides panel data on the profile and characteristics of the domestic visitors. Data on international visitors is provided by Statistics Canada and the US Department of Commerce.

NOTES

1.   Various cities make estimates of the number of tourists and their spending. See Strategy Research Corp. for Miami (various years) and Greater Ft Lauderdale Convention and Visitors Bureau (various years). There is no uniformity in their estimating procedures.
2.   Taxes reported for the sixteen "tourist categories" include such services as book stores, music stores, and hotels. They, therefore, capture the spending (and taxes) of 16 million Florida residents as well as the tourists on these categories.
3.   Trager (1990b, 1991), in his early Florida Tourist Impact Study that used the RIMS II Model, also reported deficiencies in the early series.
4.   This made Florida the second biggest recipient of tourist spending in the nation. California was first with $57.5 billion or 12.7 percent of the total.
5.   Several other distribution schemes were tried but found defective. The FVS gives the number of visitors by "tourist district," which do not correspond to our sub-regions and do not address the issue of spending in multiple destinations. Revenue derived from "tourist development taxes," recorded for the counties in the fsa, Table 19.54, may be somewhat indicative of overall tourist spending, but not all counties have imposed such taxes, and for those that have, the rates and the years of initiation vary.

15. Economics of the Fourth Missing Piece: Everglades Restoration

INTRODUCTION

The correct modeling of expenditures on the Comprehensive Everglades Restoration Plan (CERP) in the REMI framework is a challenging exercise. The researcher must first distribute all the costs associated with the Restoration Plan to the appropriate economic sector, such as construction and real estate, and to the appropriate region that will be affected by that spending, over the entire life of the project. To balance the expenditures, the REMI model requires that the researcher devise a financing mechanism: which regions will pay how much of the cost and in what years. These "time profiles" of both spending and financing comprise our last "missing piece" to be added to the REMI model. None of this was done in the original Restudy.

BACKGROUND: IMPLAN AND THE RESTUDY IMPACT EXERCISE

In the regional impact analysis of the original Restudy (US Army Corps, 1999, Vol. E, pp. 281–310), I analyzed the composition of the construction costs for eight prototypical structures that are the basic "units," or atoms, as it were, that make up the 300 individual projects that comprise the Restudy.[1] In addition, real estate procedures, monitoring, and operation and maintenance costs (O&M) were allocated for all the projects and an estimate was made for the "losses" in output due to the reduction of sugar lands in the EAA and of the "gains" due to improved water deliveries on the remaining lands.[2]

With the use of IMPLAN software, the economic impacts were computed for the entire South Florida region as a whole. Spending was not allocated by county or distributed over time. Rather, an "average year" expenditure profile was applied to the IMPLAN software, and the impacts were compared to the total annual economic activity in the region and an adjustment was made for discounting the future stream of outputs. The purchase price of the land was excluded on the rationale that land costs represented only a "transfer of wealth," that is, the conversion of a physical asset into money, rather than the creation of new wealth. No subtraction was made for the local tax contributions from the region to pay for the project, as the financing mechanism was not yet known.

I calculated the impacts for five alternatives, each of which was composed of different configurations of the eight prototypes. The preferred alternative, D13R, consisted of 74 different pumping stations with a total capacity of 93 000 cubic feet per second (cfs), 35 pair-gated spillways, more than a mile of culverts 48 inches to 96 inches in diameter, 97 miles of channels and canal work, 502 miles of levee work, 342 ASR wells with capacity of 5 million gallons per day (mgd), 37 miles of 10-ft-deep seepage barriers and 7.8 miles of 28-ft-deep seepage barriers (see Table 11.3.1–1 of *Restudy,* Appendix E). Of the $6 billion in construction costs, 19 percent was to be spent to build the pumping plants, 21 percent for the seepage barriers, and 42 percent for the ASRs. Only 18 percent of the construction costs were to be used for the more conventional water-moving technologies used in the original C&SF Project a half-century earlier, namely, the spillways, culverts, canals, levees, and "other project elements" (see Table 11.3.1–2 of *Restudy,* Appendix E).

The $6 billion in construction costs and the $2.3 billion in land costs were calculated to amount to $301 million and $116 million per year, respectively. Other direct expenditures included O&M estimated at $165 million per year and monitoring costs at $10 million per year. "Gains" due to modified water deliveries were estimated at $1.9 million per year and "losses" due to reduction in agricultural land were estimated to be $85 million in the EAA or $154 million in the entire region. On an annual basis, all project costs would amount to $590 million per year, with the total rising to $674 million if EAA sugar "losses" were included and $743 million if all agricultural land "losses" were included.[3]

The economic dimension of the Everglades Restoration Plan is truly staggering! Here, an immense public program involving billions of dollars of new and conventional construction activity is to be played out across thirteen counties over a twenty-year period. Huge land purchases are expected to be made, and the Comprehensive Everglades Restoration Plan (CERP) is expected to change the face of South Florida by as much as the original C&SF Projects changed South Florida from the 1950s until today. Nothing as great or as grand as this has ever been attempted to fix an ecosystem on the planet!

How great, then, were the computed impacts of adding $600 to $743 million per year worth of new construction to South Florida? Not a whole lot, it turns out, since even a new $1 billion barely makes a mark on a region whose *total annual* product was already $140 billion by 1995.[4] It was not surprising, then, that the impacts of CERP, as computed by the IMPLAN software, amounted to no more than 0.13 to 0.31 of *one percent* of the total annual output, jobs, and earnings of the region. Subtraction for the local tax contribution to pay for CERP would have reduced even these meager impacts.

In retrospect, these computations may represent serious understatements. Land purchases, for example, could have a tremendous impact on a region or on other parts of Florida if the targeted land had been seriously undervalued earlier. The seller's newfound wealth might be used to purchase farmland elsewhere, in which case no net acreage would be lost to agricultural production. The mills and plants that process sugarcane or citrus would obtain their raw material from these new lands, or if the plants are already fully depreciated, they might be scrapped and new ones constructed. If the sale of land in South Florida leveraged additional funds for real estate development elsewhere in Florida (for example, the St Joe Corporation's sale of the Talisman sugar lands in the EAA), then the omission of billions of dollars in expected land purchases would lead to a serious underestimate of the true effects of CERP on promoting growth throughout Florida. Only if all the money from the land purchases were sent out of the state would such an omission be of no consequence.[5]

CERP SPENDING

The modeling of CERP spending in REMI is at once simpler and more complicated than with IMPLAN. Our REMI model allows us to allocate expenditures over 14, not 528 sectors, which means that all "construction" costs will be thrown into one aggregate sector rather than be distributed to pumps, concrete, steel, or earthmoving services, for example. The construction sector itself, through REMI's input–output relationships, will allocate the new spending among its supplying sectors automatically in the same proportion as its present composition, not according to the new project prototypes.

In addition, construction expenses for each project are assumed to occur in the county (or sub-region, in our model) where the project is located. But if the company executing the contract is based in Kansas City, for example, and its main workforce and heavy equipment are only relocated temporarily in Florida, then a substantial part of the profits, depreciation, and remitted wages may affect Kansas City, but not the Florida region. This may change over time as firms locate more of their operations in the region, for example, the assembly and repair of the pumps, pipes, and drilling equipment needed to construct the hundreds of ASR wells. Thus, the straightforward attribution of *all* annual construction costs to each sub-region will surely overstate the true impacts that the construction activity will actually cause.

The expenditures for "planning and design" were assigned to the REMI "service" sector and also allocated to the sub-region in which the projects are located. The true location, however, of the engineering firms that actually execute the designs may be elsewhere in the state or nation.

Procedural costs of land acquisition were assigned to the REMI "real estate" sector. O&M costs, which are mostly energy and repair costs, were assigned to "public utilities." The full purchase price of land was excluded from the entire analysis in the absence of survey data on the intentions of future sellers regarding the disposition of this income.

In summary, for the categories of construction, planning and design, land acquisition, and O&M, CERP and the SFWMD provided the county-by-county, year-by-year allocations of expected spending. These were aggregated into our five sub-regions (including ROF for planning and design) for the 2002 to 2035 period.

CERP FINANCING

Increased expenditures by the public sector in a region must be balanced by increased taxes in the region, except for the federal share. It was assumed that the federal government will pay half the total amount of CERP, with the remaining half split between the state as a whole and the counties of the South Florida Water Management District (SFWMD), which corresponds to our South Florida (SF) region. It was assumed that the SF contribution to CERP would be made through new taxes distributed among the four sub-regions according to the taxable value of real property assessments (BEBR fsa 2002, Table 23.91, columns 5–6).

If, however, large capital expenditures are to be financed out of new bond sales, then the appropriate modeling behavior would be to deduct a fixed annual charge for interest-plus-principal, which taxpayers would be expected to pay to bond holders. However, in the case of CERP, the state's funding arrangements may be coming from a dedicated source, such as the sale of documentary stamps required for real estate transactions as well as from funds diverted from other environmentally oriented programs. The South Florida portion may be raised by means of the property taxes that the SFWMD levies or from funds shifted to CERP through the reduction of other outlays.

Two profiles were modeled to represent the CERP tax balance. In one scenario, we assumed the non-federal portion would be met on a pay-as-you-spend basis. As projects in CERP require construction (and hence funding), so, too, the local tax bill would rise to pay these costs in those years. In a second profile, we divided the local share across the entire project lifetime and set a single, non-varying tax rate for the entire period.

The effect of the former or "annually varying tax rate" is to reduce the impact of CERP spending to that portion of CERP that is truly an "unrequited gift" from both the federal and state government. In every region except the ROF, the net effects of this will be positive in the sense that the four SF regions will receive funds for O&M, services, construction, and finance, insurance, real estate (FIRE) far in excess of the amount each region pays as its share of SFWMD taxes.

This is illustrated in Table 15.1. Total expenditures in CERP are estimated at $9.55 billion, including land costs (column 11, line 9), which is balanced by total taxes (column 1, line 9). The taxes are raised by federal and state governments and by the regions according to the distribution given in column 2, derived by the cost-sharing guidelines set forth in Table 15.2. The expenditures are summed by category for the time profiles from 2002–2035 and by region (columns 3–6) with land costs appearing in column 10.

The REMI model will measure the impact in Florida of $2.95 billion spent on the different regions over the 33 years (column 9), the expenditure net of taxes, rather than the gross spending of $7.73 billion (column 7) with no local contribution. If land costs were included (column 11), then net regional spending would be $4.78 billion (column 13) out of a total spending of $9.55 billion, again due to taxes collected throughout the regions as long as the federal government cost-shares 50 percent of the total.

Table 15.1 also indicates the percentage distribution of spending across categories (line 10). Construction will absorb 44.9 percent of spending, O&M 31.7 percent, and land 19.1 percent. Services will require 3.3 percent and FIRE 1.0 percent.

In terms of the regions, the LEC will receive 59.9 percent of all spending, including land costs (column 12), KSV 20.8 percent, UEC 10.2 percent, and the LWC 8.4 percent. Column 9, by contrast, gives the net regional dollar spending, excluding land costs, the impacts of which the REMI model will measure.

Figure 15.1 gives the profile of the spending on all CERP projects, excluding land purchases. This is the sum of all the expenditures that we have allocated by category, region, and year in the REMI model as the CERP "missing piece." The two alternative financing schemes are pictured in Figures 15.2 and 15.3. The profile in Figure 15.2 represents the "pay as you go" scheme of all CERP expenditures including land, with the allocations to each Florida sub-region. Figure 15.3 takes the total share spent in each region over the whole period and then finances it evenly, over the course of time within each region, but with no interest or finance charges added. Figures 15.4–15.6 show representative profiles for spending in the LEC on construction, land costs, and O&M, respectively, the three largest categories of spending. The profiles

Table 15.1   Distribution of Projected Taxes and Expenditures on CERP by Region and Category, 2002–2035

| | Taxes* | | Sum of projected expend. by category (mill. $) | | | | Total expend. w/o land costs (sum cols. 3–6) | | Expend. minus taxes** (col. 7 minus col. 1) | Land costs | Total expend. incl. land costs (cols. 7 + 1) | | Total less taxes (col. 11 minus col. 1) |
| | Value mill. $ | Distrib. % | O&M | Services | Construct. | FIRE | Value mill. $ | Distrib. % | (mill. $) | (mill. $) | Value (mill. $) | Distrib. % | (mill. $) |
	(1)	(2)	(3)	(4)	(5)	(6)	(7)	(8)	(9)	(10)	(11)	(12)	(13)
1. Fed	4 776	0.500											
2. LEC	2 557	0.268	2 194	162	2 357	80	4 793	62.0	2 236	933	5 727	59.9	3 169
3. LWC	461	0.048	226	20	404	0	650	8.4	189	152	802	8.4	341
4. KSV	179	0.019	453	54	1 247	13	1 766	22.9	1 588	221	1 987	20.8	1 808
5. UEC	172	0.018	151	15	285	3	453	5.9	281	520	973	10.2	801
6. SF	3 369	0.353	3 024	250	4 292	96	7 662	99.2	4 293	1 825	9 488	99.3	6 119
7. ROF	1 407	0.147	—	64	—	—	64	0.8	-1 343	—	64	0.7	-1 343
8. FL	4 776	—	3 024	315	4 292	96	7 727	100.0	2 951	1 825	9 552	—	4 776
9. Total	9 552	1.000	3 024	315	4 292	96	7 727	100.0	-1 825	1 825	9 552	100.0	—
10. Expend. (%)	—	—	31.7	3.3	44.9	1.0	80.9	—	—	19.1	100.0	—	—

Notes: *Indicates example of pay-as-you go principle. **Indicates values used in REMI model. Col. 3: O&M = Operation and maintenance. Col. 6: FIRE = Finance, insurance, and real estate.

250

Table 15.2   Regional Distribution of Taxes: Sample Cost-Sharing Guidelines

Region		Cost-sharing formula	% Total project
A. Federal govt.	pays	half of total project, and	0.500
B. Florida	pays	other half of total.	
1. State govt.	pays	half of state's share (0.25 of total), of which	
a. ROF	pays	0.589 of FL govt. (0.25) share, and	0.147
b. SF	pays	0.411 of FL govt. (0.25) share, which it divides among the four regions. Also,	
2. SFWMD	pays	the other half of state's share (0.25 of total), which it divides among the four regions. Each SF region thus pays both FL and SFWMD taxes as follows:	
a. LEC	pays	0.759 of SF (line 1b) and SFWMD (line 2)	0.268
b. LWC	pays	0.137 of SF and SFWMD	0.048
c. KSV	pays	0.053 of SF and SFWMD	0.019
d. UEC	pays	0.051 of SF and SFWMD	0.018
Total			1.000

of the other categories, such as land acquisition costs (real estate procedures) in Figure 15.7 and service costs for design and planning in Figure 15.8 are similar to the patterns in Figures 15.4 and 15.5.

The regional time patterns for all categories of expenditures minus taxes were entered into the REMI model. In addition, we modeled the impacts of the two agricultural scenarios – losses due to reductions in sugar lands and the gains due to modified water deliveries – together with their indirect impacts, which were computed by first applying the value of farm changes to the sub-regional IMPLAN model. In the final analysis, these minor scenarios were dropped for two reasons. First, there was some doubt whether our aggregate 14-sector REMI model could capture accurately these minor changes. Second, the inclusion of sugar land "losses" carried on year after year assumes that no new land is brought into production and that the purchase price of land fails to capitalize the foregone annual yields. However, sugar acreage may well expand into nearby counties, and productivity of the existing lands may also increase. Alternatively, if relations with Cuba change, foreign sugar may displace EAA production altogether and more land might be made available for water storage.

In conclusion, the final CERP profile of expenditures was limited to the basic spending categories, excluding the purchase price of land and subtracting for a constant level of SF contribution throughout the future. All of these profiles could be refined with a more disaggregated REMI model for the counties and with alternative financing schemes.

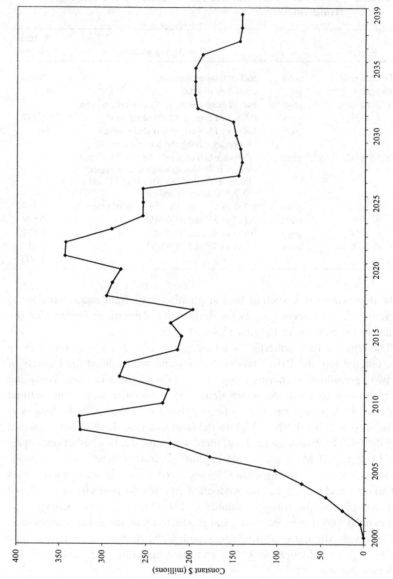

Figure 15.1 Cost of Everglades Restoration Projects (excluding land costs)

In one sense, the CERP spending can be viewed as the "icing on the cake" once the other "missing pieces" have been studied and accounted for. This in no way implies that CERP "causes" or even "enables" all the other pieces to occur. Rather, it is the confluence of all the forces of growth in the region, together with Everglades restoration, that we seek to capture in our modeling of the future of South Florida.

NOTES

1. These were pumping plants, spillways, culverts, canals and channels, levees, aquifer storage and recovery wells (ASR), seepage barriers, and "other project elements." The value of the individual components of each of these structures was specified through the MCACES software (Micro Computer Aided Cost Engineering System) for each project. The cost of the very components, for example, the concrete, pumping equipment, flood gates, electrical work, excavation, construction, and landscaping, were then distributed to one or more of the 528 economic sectors in the IMPLAN model built for the broad SF region.   In this way, a suitable "match" was created between each project and the regional economy, and the corresponding economic impacts of the various configurations of projects specified in the alternative plans could be computed.

2. These are summarized in Table 7-17, p. 7-49 in the Final Integrated Feasibility Report (Vol. I) of the *Restudy* (Yellow Book). The effects of all these program expenditures on regional output, jobs, and earnings are reported in detail in Tables 11.5.1–1 through 11.5.1–6, Appendix E of the *Restudy*.

3. See Table 11.3.4 of *Restudy*, Appendix E, alternative D13R.

4. See Table 11.4.2–2 of *Restudy*, Appendix E, which gives the 1995 input–output aggregates for the region.

5. A quick and confidential survey of past sellers of land in the SFWMD would yield some helpful answers to this question. Even a survey of prospective "seller's intentions" in CERP would ascertain the likely degree of local reinvestment and give us some real hypotheses to guide the way in which the $2 billion in land purchases should be treated in these impact models.

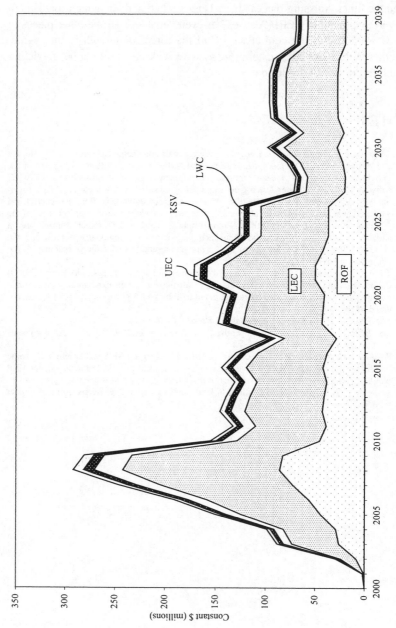

Figure 15.2   Taxes for Everglades Restoration by Region

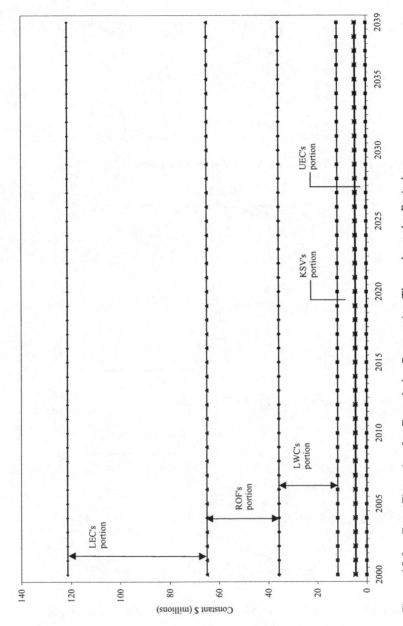

Figure 15.3   Even Financing for Everglades Restoration Throughout the Period

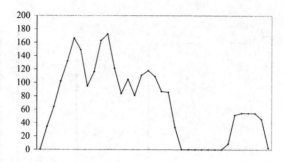

Figure 15.4   Construction Costs, Lower East Coast

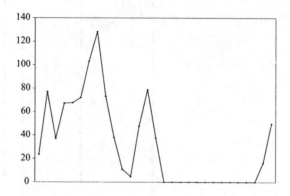

Figure 15.5   Land Costs, Lower East Coast

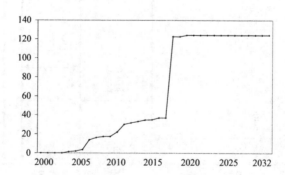

Figure 15.6   Operation and Maintenance (O&M), Lower East Coast

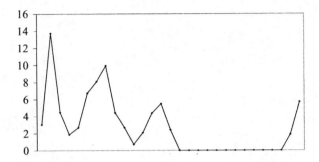

Figure 15.7   Land Acquisition (Real Estate) Costs, Lower East Coast

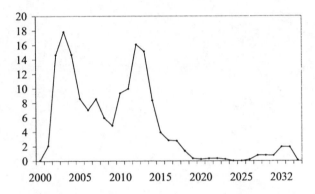

Figure 15.8   Service Costs, Lower East Coast

PART IV

Changing the Future

16. Revisions and Retrospectives

ANOTHER PHONE CALL

One hot spring day in 2003, as the Everglades restoration was just getting into gear, an unsolicited but much appreciated e-mail message came over the Professor's computer screen, The Army Corps of Engineers had just released a new water forecast entitled *CERP Update* (Gulf Engineers and Consultants (GEC), 2003), and this meant a new set of "water projections" for Miami-Dade County. The *CERP Update* was prepared by the very same engineering company using the very same computer model (IWR-MAIN) that had caught the Professor's attention six years earlier, propelling the Professor on the intellectual journey recorded in this book.[1] Now, for some reason, they had totally revised those forecasts!

The CERP update contains the most curious revelations. Its Figure 88 graphically depicts the ever-widening gap between the 1996 and 2003 population projections, similar to my Figures 8.2 and 8.3, "How Projections Fail," in this report! Then, on page 201 of the 208-page update, we find an even more disturbing contradiction.[2] The new forecasts for the entire area served are now 17 percent *higher* for 2050 than the earlier study, but they are, at the same time, 21.7 percent *lower* for 2020 than the latest Regional Water Supply Plan issued by the SFWMD. In other words, the water demands in the 1996 report, upon which the original Restudy was based, are now "updated" or increased by 17 percent on a 50-year forecast, but still 22 percent *less* than what the local water "managers" think will occur in the next twenty years! Something doesn't add up.

Why the great difference? The CERP update uses the same method as the 1996 Report. Basically, the IWR-MAIN computer model takes BEBR's population projections for 2030, extends them to 2050, and applies a set of water–people ratios to get "residential use." For industrial and commercial water use, the model takes BEBR's employment forecasts to 2015, extends them to 2050, allocates the totals among three sectors, and then applies employee-water coefficients that are neither local nor explicitly given. (They are part of the "proprietary data" that come with the model.) The new update forecasts are simply the results of higher population projections, in view of the "surprising" increases shown in the 2000 Census, and new employment projections.[3]

To the Professor's surprise, nothing had changed! South Florida's water and economic picture had indeed changed, yet the official forecasts, the forecasters, and the forecasting machinery had not. South Florida had gone through, and continues to be in, one of the strongest growth spurts in its fast-growth post-war period. All former forecasts of people, water, and economic activity have been shown to be far too low, and that might explain why the current residents – and the part-time visitors – are left wondering why the level of public services appears wanting. Setting questions of inefficiency or mismanagement aside, there is rather a singular reticence on the part of professional economists to call the shots as they are.

Table 16.1 summarizes the results of various studies computed for the identical counties as our LEC. The population estimates of the CERP update (line 2) are 4.4 percent above the original Restudy (line 1) for 2020 and 26.2 percent above the Restudy for 2050 (columns 6, 7). The update estimate for employment (line 7) is 25.7 percent above the original GEC (1996) for 2020 and 69.4 percent above the original estimate for 2050 (columns 6, 7). The result of these is a CERP update for public water supply (line 11) that is 12.7 percent above the original GEC (1996) estimate for 2020 and 38.7 percent higher than the original estimate for 2050 (compare lines 10 and 11, columns 6 and 7).

Note also that the USGS and SFWMD forecasts for 2020 (lines 12–14, columns 3 and 6) are all higher than the CERP updates for that year and much higher than the original GEC (1996) estimates.

The reason for the low water forecasts in both GEC reports can be found in the low AROGs implicit in the underlying population and employment projections (see Table 16.1, lines 1–2, 5–7, columns 8–11). Both studies demonstrate relatively high growth rates for the first decade (column 8), but these rates fall to extremely low or even negative rates for the later decades.[4]

A series of figures will demonstrate the relative configurations of the different projections. In Figure 16.1, the population forecasts made in the original Restudy (lowest long-dashed line) begin with a "handicap" in year 2000, rise steadily but slowly until 2020, and then taper off by 2030. The CERP update offers two projections (shorter-dashed lines in Figure 16.1), following BEBR's medium and high forecasts. The CERP update notes that the "medium" is the most likely forecast. My own projections from Chapter 2 for the "moderate" and "full-steam-ahead" or high scenarios are both closer to the update's medium than high projection.

The employment forecasts show a much greater spread. The original Restudy's projections (solid triangles in Figure 16.2) are based on BEBR's long-range economic model to 2010, while the employment forecasts used by

GEC (1996), which will ultimately determine water use, are adapted and extended from these. However, they are lower than the Restudy figures and actually decline after 2010. The CERP update (shorter dashed line in Figure 16.2) is higher and rises more steeply than the two earlier studies. These all contrast with my employment forecasts (solid lines) that are based on the REMI-plus-missing-pieces model.

The forecasts of public water supply for LEC are shown in Figure 16.3. The estimates used in the Restudy are from GEC (1996) and are traced out in the lowest dashed line. These are modified considerably by the CERP update (the shorter-dashed line), but they still fall below the USGS-medium and the SFWMD projections for 2020, indicated by the hollow diamonds and solid black circle. The two Weisskoff PS projections based on the medium and high population estimates give two water forecasts (W-pop-med and W-pop-hi) that fall *between* the USGS-m and SFWMD benchmarks. My W-pop-med estimate almost coincides with the CERP update for 2030, but my water forecast based on high output rather than population (W-q-hi) is measurably higher.

Table 16.2 gives the methodology and computations for comparing the IWR-MAIN estimates for the same concept (public water supply) and same geographical coverage (LEC) for the 1996 and 2003 studies. The results of these computations were used in Table 16.1 and Figures 16.1–16.3.

In Table 16.3,we compare the population and employment projections of the Restudy to my "medium" and "high" projections (W-med and W-high) for comparable years for *all* the other regions. (Only the LEC was compared in Tables 16.1 and 16.2.) The BEBR population forecasts for 2010 are similar to those of the Restudy, except for the LWC (Table 16.3, column 6). The BEBR forecasts for 2030, however, are all much higher than the Restudy, except for the UEC (column 7). My moderate and high population estimates range from 20.5 percent for the KSV to 63.1 percent for the LWC above the Restudy estimate for each corresponding region for 2030 (column 7).

The Restudy employment projections (bottom panel of Table 16.3) were made only to 2010. My projections are much higher than these (column 6), except for the KSV, which are lower, and the UEC, which are only slightly higher.

In columns 8–10 at the right-hand side of Table 16.3, the implicit annual rates of growth for each decade allow us to compare the degree to which population and employment growth tapers off over time. We note the rather steep declines in the AROG for the last Restudy decade for population (column 10) compared to all the other estimates. My own implicit population AROGs are all higher than the Restudy's, but comparable to BEBR's. For employment, my AROGs are all higher than the Restudy's for the decade 2000–2010, except for slightly lower AROGs in the case of the KSV.

Table 16.1   Comparisons of Population, Employment, and Water Projections for LEC: Various Studies

	2000* (1)	2010 (2)	2020 (3)	2030* (4)	2050 (5)	2020 % from Restudy/ GEC'96 (6)	2050 % from Restudy/ GEC'96 (7)	Implicit annual rate of growth (%)			
								2000– 2010 (8)	2010– 2020 (9)	2020– 2030 (10)	2030– 2050 (11)
Population:											
1. Restudy original (1998)	4 901	5 809	6 537	6 725	7 116	—	—	1.71	1.19	0.28	0.28
2. CERP update** GEC (2003)	5 085	5 902	6 823	7 651	8 981	4.4	26.2	1.50	1.46	1.15	0.80
3. Weisskoff – medium	5 010	6 159	7 055	7 807	n.a.	7.9	—	2.09	1.37	1.02	—
4. Weisskoff – high	5 025	6 195	7 173	8 098	n.a.	9.7	—	2.12	1.48	1.22	—
Employment:											
5. Restudy original (1998)	2 316	2 672	n.g.	n.g.	n.g.	—	—	1.44	—	—	—
6. IWR-MAIN GEC (1996)	2 280	2 532	[2 512]	2 493	2 454]	—	—	1.05	-0.08	-0.08	-0.08
7. CERP update GEC (2003)	2 358	2 750	3 158	3 541	4 158	25.7	69.4	1.55	1.39	1.15	0.81
8. Weisskoff – medium	2 792	3 397	3 574	3 836	n.a.	42.2	—	1.98	0.51	0.71	—
9. Weisskoff – high	2 808	3 423	3 663	4 036	n.a.	45.8	—	2.00	0.68	0.97	—

264

Water: Public Supply only

10. IWR-MAIN GEC (1996)	821	943	982	1 000	1 037	—	—	1.39	0.41	0.18	0.18
11. CERP Update GEC (2003)	871	963	1 107	1 233	1 438	12.7	38.7	1.01	1.40	1.09	0.77
12. USGS (1992) – medium	—	—	1 140	—	—	16.1	—	—	—	—	—
13. USGS (1992) – high	—	—	1 532	—	—	56.0	—	—	—	—	—
14. SFWMD (2000) RWSP	—	—	1 215	—	—	23.7	—	—	—	—	—
15. Weisskoff – pop-medium	882	1 066	1 176	1 253	n.a.	19.8	—	1.91	0.99	0.64	—
16. Weisskoff – pop-high	882	1 073	1 196	1 299	n.a.	21.8	—	1.98	1.09	0.83	—
17. Weisskoff – output-high	882	1 175	1 303	1 498	n.a.	32.7	—	2.91	1.04	1.40	—

Notes:

* Restudy 2000 and 2030 values are not given in the original document. They are computed here by applying the 1990–2010 AROG to the 1990 population and the 2020–2050 AROG to the 2020 population.

** Most likely forecasts based on BEBR medium projections.

Sources:

Lines 1, 5: Restudy counties selected to match our counties from US Army Corps (1998), Tables 2.3.2-1, 2.3.3-2, Appendix E.

Lines 6, 10: Employment for IWR-MAIN GEC (1996) computed from Appendix Tables on pp. A-47, 50-52, 55. Public Water Supply (line 11) is from Table 16.2, line 14.

Lines 2, 7, 11: CERP update computed from GEC (2003), Text Table 6, p. 28, for population. Employment computed from Appendix Tables by summing three sectors (commercial, industrial, govt.). Our LEC corresponds to Service Areas 1, 2, and 3 and Sub Areas 1 and 2. PS water computed by summing service area total water supply and applying ratio of PS to total water ratio for entire time series. See Table 16.2 below, line 16.

Lines 12–13: USGS from Marella (1992), Table 14.

Line 14: SFWMD LEC Regional Water Supply Plan (RWSP) (May 2000), Appendix Vol I, Table B-9, pp. 23–4.

Lines 3–4, 8–9, 15–17: This study. Population and employment from Appendix Table A.1. PS water supply for LEC, Table 3.1. Values for 1990–2000 are from USGS files.

265

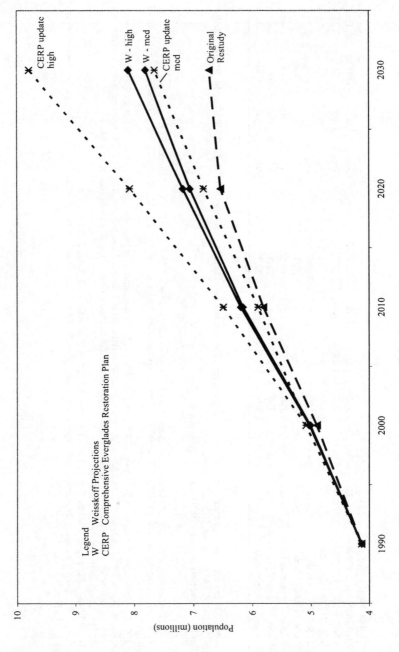

Figure 16.1   Summary of Population Forecasts, Lower East Coast

266

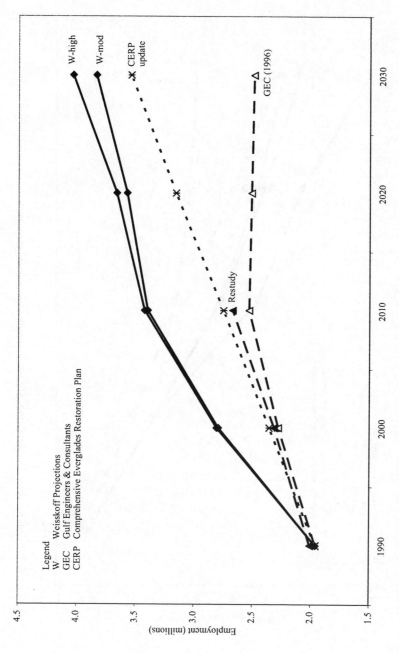

Figure 16.2 Summary of Employment Forecasts, Lower East Coast

267

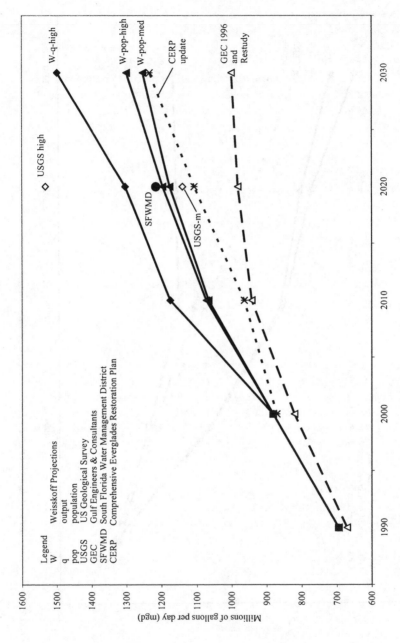

Figure 16.3 Summary of Public Water Supply Forecasts, Lower East Coast

Why do the official Army Corps water forecasts seem to be so low, especially when compared to the forecasts made by the USGS and the SFWMD, as well as my own? We have already mentioned that if the underlying population and employment projections prove too conservative, then the model is off to a bad start, so to speak. The problem is compounded, however, when these model inputs are applied to "standard" water-use coefficients that are proprietary and hence not accessible to outside examination. If these coefficients – the connection between water use and people and between water use and employment – are changing rapidly in the region or if South Florida's "usage practices" differ from the rest of the country, then the model may not perform as well here as in the more temperate zones that generated the "coefficients" in the first place.

The advantage of IWR-MAIN is that it divides residential water demand, based on population and housing types, from commercial/industrial demand, based on employment.[5] This is superior to my water model, used in Chapter 3 above, that applies either one or the other of those variables – population or employment – to each sub-region. However, there are many commercial sectors where water demand may increase to a greater extent than employment, especially if the new "employees" required to produce more output are not registered locally. In sectors such as the ports (mainly cruise ships), airports, hospitals, universities, and hotels, the value of output may prove to be a better predictor of water use, rather than officially given employment.

My point is simply that South Florida needs a "tailored" economic study of water demand, one that uses our own estimates of the economy and takes the time to develop a database which registers the current and future water needs on a sector-by-sector basis. Indeed, the tourist sector, itself a major water user in all its dimensions – car rentals, hotels, restaurants, recreation parks, golf courses – should be modeled separately for its dynamics and water usage patterns. Tourism, like agriculture, has characteristics that are quite different from the other, more locally oriented activities.

There is yet a deeper issue here. In all the series of projections – BEBR, GEC, and CERP update – we are treated to same-shaped "flat" curves. Historically, we are told, the economy has grown fast, but in some future decade, the curves will flatten out. Thirty years from now, we have been told again and again, there will be no more net growth. Indeed, as I showed in Figures 8.2 and 8.3, this has been the "patterned forecast" for the past twenty years. And in the case of South Florida, these "responsible" forecasts have proven to be quite irresponsible.

Why, if the first round of projections was off, do we continue to use the same model and the same consultants and the same methods? Who's to complain? Who's to check the old forecasts?

Table 16.2   Computations for Comparing Water Projections of Public Supply (LEC): Restudy and CERP Update (mgd)

Study and sub-region	1990 (1)	1995 (2)	2000 (3)	2010 (4)	2020 (5)	2030 (6)	% from earlier (7)	2050 (8)	% from earlier (9)	Implicit annual rate of growth (%)					
										1990–1995 (10)	1995–2000 (11)	2000–2010 (12)	2010–2020 (13)	2020–2030 (14)	2030–2050 (15)
IWR-MAIN GEC (1996) – Restudy (1999):															
1. Serv. Area 1 SE Palm Beach	192	216	252	306	325	333	—	349	—	2.38	3.13	1.96	0.60	0.24	0.23
2. Serv. Area 2 E Broward	253	295	325	370	386	393	—	408	—	3.12	1.96	1.31	0.42	0.18	0.19
3. Serv. Area 3 E Dade	355	367	393	430	440	445	—	456	—	0.67	1.38	0.90	0.23	0.11	0.12
4. Sub Area 1 NE Palm Beach	53	62	72	89	94	96	—	101	—	3.19	3.04	2.14	0.55	0.21	0.25
5. Sub Area 2 W Palm Beach	8	9	11	14	14	15	—	15	—	2.38	4.10	2.44	0.00	0.69	0.00
6. Total LEC (all water)*	861	949	1 053	1 209	1 259	1 282	—	1 329	—	1.97	2.10	1.39	0.41	0.18	0.18
IWR-MAIN GEC (2003) – CERP Update															
7. Serv. Area 1	—	—	264	301	354	401	20.4	460	31.8	—	—	1.32	1.64	1.25	0.69
8. Serv. Area 2	—	—	299	344	399	447	13.7	519	27.2	—	—	1.41	1.49	1.14	0.75

9. Serv. Area 3	—	—	375	391	436	475	6.7	568	24.6	—	—	0.42	1.10	0.86	0.90
10. Sub Area 1	—	—	86	98	115	130	35.4	150	48.5	—	—	1.31	1.61	1.23	0.72
11. Sub Area 2	—	—	31	32	36	40	166.7	44	193.3	—	—	0.32	1.18	1.06	0.48
12. Total LEC (all water)*	—	—	1 055	1 166	1 340	1 493	16.5	1 741	31.0	—	—	1.01	1.40	1.09	0.77
13. % PS of LEC for 1996 PS categories	0.780	0.780	0.780	0.780	0.780	0.780	—	0.780	—	—	—	—	—	—	—
14. PS for LEC GEC (1996) forecasts (mgd)	672	740	821	943	982	1 000	—	1 037	—	—	1.39	0.41	0.18	0.18	—
15. % PS of LEC for 2003 PS categories	0.826	0.826	0.826	0.826	0.826	0.826	—	0.826	—	—	—	—	—	—	—
16. PS for LEC GEC (2003) forecasts (mgd)	—	—	871	963	1 107	1 233	23.3	1 438	38.7	—	—	1.01	1.40	1.09	0.77

Note: * Includes public supply (PS) and certain other categories of self-supply (SS); excludes agriculture self-supply.

Sources and Methods:
Lines 1–5: from GEC (1996), Tables 36, 40, 44, 16, and 20, column 5, annual average water use mgd for residential, commercial, industrial, public administration, and unaccounted uses, based on FL employment and population projections.
Lines 7–11: from GEC (2003), Tables 14, 18, 22, 26, and 30, column 3, from baseline annual water use, no conservation.
Lines 13 & 15: computed by comparing the USGS Public Supply (PS) categories to the IWR-MAIN GEC totals for the corresponding years, and applying these fractions to the corresponding series.
Lines 14 & 16: computed by taking the PS fraction in line 13 times the IWR-MAIN GEC forecast.
Line 17: from SFWMD LEC Regional Water Supply Plan (May 2000). Append. Vol I, Table B-9, pp. 23–24.
Lines 18–20: from Table 3.1, above, this study. Values for 1990–2000 are from USGS historical files.

Table 16.3 Population and Employment Projections, Various Regions and Studies

	2000* (1)	2010 (2)	2020 (3)	2030* (4)	2050 (5)	2010 % from Restudy (6)	2030 % from Restudy (7)	Implicit AROG (%)		
								2000–2010 (8)	2010–2020 (9)	2020–2030 (10)
LWC pop										
Restudy	664	846	1 008	1 052	1 146	—	—	2.45	1.77	0.43
B m '02	739	954	1 172	1 381	—	12.8	31.2	2.58	2.08	1.65
W–med	773	1 135	1 395	1 586	—	34.2	50.8	3.92	2.08	1.29
W–high	789	1 173	1 467	1 715	—	38.6	63.1	4.04	2.26	1.58
KSV pop										
Restudy	274	365	445	462	499	—	—	2.93	2.00	0.38
B m '02	296	375	459	538	—	2.8	16.4	2.41	2.02	1.61
W–med	299	409	489	557	—	12.1	20.5	3.18	1.81	1.30
W–high	301	413	501	582	—	13.2	26.0	3.21	1.95	1.51
UEC pop										
Restudy	313	391	464	485	529	—	—	2.24	1.73	0.44
B m '02	319	386	452	515	—	-1.4	6.1	1.90	1.61	1.30
W–med	335	451	537	602	—	15.3	24.0	3.01	1.78	1.13
W–high	336	455	549	630	—	16.3	30.0	3.08	1.89	1.40
SF pop										
Restudy	6 155	7 411	8 454	8 724	9 290	—	—	1.87	1.33	0.31
B m '02	6 444	7 654	8 909	10 089	—	3.3	15.6	1.74	1.53	1.25
W–med	6 417	8 156	9 482	10 559	—	10.1	21.0	2.43	1.52	1.08
W–high	6 450	8 235	9 688	11 021	—	11.1	26.3	2.47	1.64	1.30

FL pop										
Restudy	15 389	18 252	20 778	21 453	22 889	—	—	1.72	1.30	0.32
B m '02	15 982	18 867	21 793	24 529	—	3.4	14.3	1.67	1.45	1.19
W–med	16 338	21 002	24 598	27 530	—	15.1	28.3	2.54	1.59	1.13
W–high	16 405	21 164	25 088	28 732	—	16.0	33.9	2.58	1.72	1.37
LWC empl										
Restudy	345	390	n.g.	n.g.	—	—	—	1.22	—	—
W–med	422	554	609	678	—	42.4	—	2.78	0.94	1.08
W–high	439	578	648	748	—	48.5	—	2.80	1.14	1.45
KSV empl										
Restudy	121	160	n.g.	n.g.	—	—	—	2.83	—	—
W–med	115	145	161	180	—	–9.3	—	2.35	1.04	1.14
W–high	116	148	167	190	—	–7.8	—	2.41	1.25	1.32
UEC empl										
Restudy	127	154	n.g.	n.g.	—	—	—	1.95	—	—
W–med	145	187	201	221	—	9.2	—	2.61	0.71	0.93
W–high	146	190	208	237	—	9.9	—	2.71	0.91	1.30
SF empl										
Restudy	2 910	3 375	n.g.	n.g.	—	—	—	1.49	—	—
W–med	3 473	4 284	4 545	4 914	—	26.9	—	2.12	0.59	0.78
W–high	3 508	4 339	4 686	5 212	—	28.6	—	2.15	0.77	1.07
FL empl										
Restudy	7 239	8 631	n.g.	n.g.	—	—	—	1.77	—	—
W–med	8 855	11 002	11 767	12 820	—	27.5	—	2.19	0.67	0.86
W–high	8 925	11 100	12 113	13 599	—	28.6	—	2.20	0.88	1.16

Note: *Restudy values for 2000, 2030 estimated on basis of AROGs of values given for surrounding years.
n.g. = not given. B m '02 = BEBR fsa 2002 medium forecast.

If the area suffers a water shortage, we can always blame Nature or the Feds, and get Everglades restoration to bail the cities out. If that fails, then desalinate or purify ocean brine when the aquifer gives out.

There is much to be said for this position. The conservative forecasts lead the public to expect that the future of our water supply is secure. Only the water utilities are uneasy – they know more about what's happening on the ground. They know intuitively, if not factually, that the forecasts are unrealistic and they could be left holding the bag when actual demand grows faster than expected. The new forecast places a great burden on "passive conservation," on new water-saving fixtures that use much less water once they are installed. But there is no real measurement of this or its opposite – the *increased use* of water due to larger buildings, more bathrooms, more tourists, and the *increased use* due to low prices, conspicuous consumption, and rising incomes. The result is a fanciful forecast, designed to lead the naive down the path of complacency when the entire historical record screams to the public agencies to take notice.

There is something to be said for not being overly pessimistic or alarmist. If the consultant or modeler finds that the forecast is too radical or too extreme, his projection may be "rejected" by his clients, leaving him unemployed and unemployable. Besides, conservative projections have a way of working out. Or do they?

If the forecasts are too dramatic, we are warned, the present generation may become discouraged. "We will need THAT MUCH infrastructure! THAT many schools! THAT much sewage treatment!" This will result in denial and dismay, and the consequences may be to reject the first doctor's advice and continue on our merry way.[6]

The ultimate crisis, the breakdown, has a different scenario in each region. In Tampa, the land around the well fields dramatically caved in.[7] In Milwaukee, an entire city got sick from the *Cryptosporidium* microbe that is not killed by chlorination and for which utilities are not yet required to test.[8] Other cities suffer from gridlock, rising crime, homelessness, power failures, bad air …

I believe we *should* know our history, our economic record, and where our customs are taking us. We should be prepared for the *worst-case* scenario that, hopefully, will *not* occur, for am I not a willing collaborator in the crackup if you drive full-speed ahead and I fail to tell you what lies ahead, especially if I am sitting next to you?

NOTES

1. Compare Gulf Engineers and Consultants (GEC) (1996) and (2003).
2. See GEC (2003), Tables 47 and 48.
3. Someone seems to have noticed that the original GEC 1996 study had expected employment to *decline* after 2020! See my analysis below.
4. The employment numbers from GEC (1996) for 2020–2050 must be errors and are therefore bracketed in Table 16.1, line 6, columns 3–5.
5. For a discussion of the IWR-MAIN Water Demand Analysis Software, see Baumann et al. (1998), pp. 94-135. For an application of the IWR-MAIN model to the ACT-ACF River Basins of Alabama, Florida, and Georgia, see Planning and Management Consultants, Ltd (1996).
6. Indeed, the Nevada Division of Water Planning was disbanded when its Public Water Use Projections for Washoe County (Reno area) contradicted the forecasts made by the local utility by 300 percent. See Nevada Research Associates (1999).
7. On Tampa, see Chapter 5, " Tampa Bay's Avarice," in Glennon (2002) and also Rand (2003) for an insider's account of the Tampa Bay developments. Her book, *Water Wars*, is not to be confused with other recent books with a similar title, for example, Shiva (2002) which deals with the consequences of privatization in India. See also the video *Thirst* by Snitow-Kaufman Productions (2004) for the cases of privatization in Stockton, CA, and in Japan, Bolivia, and India.
8. The Milwaukee "attack" occurred in April, 1993, and sickened some 400 000 residents. See Garrett (1995), p. 430. But by the beginning of 2005, a new rule to treat water to "reduce disease incidence associated with *Cryptosporidium* and other pathogenic microorganisms in drinking water," had still not been put into effect by the Environmental Protection Agency . For the proposed rule, see http://www.epa.gov/safewater/lt2/pdfs/fact_lt2.pdf.

17. Conclusions

This book has been about understanding the future economy – how many people are likely to live here, how much employment and how much business will occur in the next decades. I have argued that this knowledge is crucial to the success of Everglades restoration because a fast-growing economy will put greater pressure on the ecosystem, using more water and land and demanding higher levels of flood protection and drainage. At the same time, fresh surface water must be pumped out to tide through the canals to allay further saltwater intrusion.

Upstream from the Everglades, the great agricultural emporium thrives, and new farm bills will undoubtedly protect the future for commercial farming in the region. For those farms located near cities, the opportunity to convert cropland into residential subdivisions and business development – malls, office buildings, warehouse parks – will prove irresistible, so that any decline in agriculture means a rise in urbanization or, rather, sub-urbanization and sprawl. This will require a greater supply of treated water, replacing the irrigation wells of the farm and producing a different type of runoff and pollutants that flow downstream.

SUMMARY OF OUR MODEL

The major thrust of this study has been forecasting: to estimate the economy, we applied the REMI model to our sub-regions and then used our results to estimate the amount of water and land that would be needed by the future economy and its people.

To do this, we introduced several innovations in the methodology of forecasting. We reviewed the data available regarding agriculture (Chapter 12), investment (Chapter 13), tourism (Chapter 14), and CERP spending (Chapter 15) in order to establish trends and make forecasts for each "missing piece" for each of our sub-regions. We utilized the IMPLAN model to estimate each region's backward and forward agricultural linkages, correcting the REMI model for this relatively minor sector, whose growth is of critical importance in determining the future demand for water. We then created a high, medium, and low "overall program" for each region for all the missing pieces bundled together. The high represents a "full steam ahead!" scenario, allowing the historically achieved rates of growth to continue for the next thirty years. The medium and low scenarios assume lower growth rates for each of the pieces. The low scenario would be equivalent to a prolonged recession in all the regions.

For each scenario we measured population, employment, and output over time and then used these variables to estimate the future demand for water (Chapter 3) and land (Chapter 4). The estimates for water demand are based also on projections of the historical coefficients of water consumption for each region. These water forecasts were compared to projections made by other agencies.

The forecast demand for land (Chapter 4) was made on the basis of two land-use studies for South Florida from which urban land for each county was extracted. This gave us some historical evidence for estimating the future population–land relationship, which, together with the forecast population, allowed us to estimate probable urban land needs for each region.

All these projections are indicators of the future only to the extent that present trends continue and that no major transformations occur. If the current zoning laws remain in place and the dominant consumption patterns are not altered, these forecasts provide, I believe, a likely road map of where we are headed.

In Table 17.1 we summarize the major findings of the full-steam-ahead scenario, which may be the environmentalist's nightmare and every developer's dream. In the overall South Florida region, today's population of roughly six million can be expected to grow by 71 percent to eleven million by 2030, and today's employment of 3.5 million could grow by 48 percent to five million by 2030 (lines 1–2, columns 1, 4, 5).

Public water supply for SF can be expected to increase by 59 percent, from the current 1000 mgd or one *billion* gallons per day for all of South Florida to 1.7 billion gallons a day in 2030 (line 4). The demand for *all* fresh water (public utility-supplied plus other self-supplied fresh water drawn from ground and surface sources, line 5) will increase by 74 percent from around 4000 mgd to almost 7000 mgd in SF by 2030!

The amount of urban land needed by the growing population (line 6) can be expected to increase by 79 percent from 1.3 million acres to 2.3 million acres, a growth of 1.01 million acres or 1578 square miles of new urban land spread over the four sub-regions in the next thirty years.

The bulk of these increases will be concentrated in the LEC with the exception of total fresh water demand and new urban land (Table 17.1, LEC, lines 4–5, column 6). Forty-nine percent of all new fresh water and 47 percent of all new urban land will be needed by the LWC. The KSV will require

12 percent of all new urban land, which is double the percentage increase in its population over the next thirty years.

Where will this land come from – agriculture? Nature? the ocean?

CHANGING THE FUTURE

Our economic growth model addresses only the demand side of this question, and in a very rigid manner at that. We have made no allowance for the impact of skyrocketing urban land prices, the continued low interest rate, rising construction costs, and increasing travel time. To avoid these projections, a rapid revolution would have to occur in the redesign of the South Florida infrastructure, one that emphasizes urban infill, alternative transport modes, and compact, pedestrian-friendly development. If this happens, and design standards are radically altered, then the consumption of urban land could change dramatically. But in the absence of such innovations, our projections of the historical record would suggest continuing pressure on the lands surrounding the cities and increased land absorption. Building codes and zoning practices in South Florida have yet to recognize the consequences of urban expansion on the fragile ecosystem.

Can the region handle it? The implications of growth on space find their expression not in the stark ratios and coefficients emphasized here, but rather in the breakdown of urban services, longer commuting times, and degeneration of all dimensions of our quality of life.

THE NEED TO GROW

Others who are also alarmed by these prospects have reacted by opposing growth, emphasizing the need for quality of life instead and urging us to be circumspect about what it is we strive for.[1] In South Florida, hypergrowth has become a way of life for many of the governing agencies. Growth is viewed as a solution for many of the ills, rather than seeing the cause of the social ills in the very imperative to grow. Any dip in tourism, housing starts, or new investment is viewed with alarm. Any questioning of their value is regarded as heresy and backward thinking.

The cities and counties compete with one another, falling over themselves to provide yet more infrastructure to accommodate the stated desires of the private sector.

"Build us another runway, another seaport, another highway, another power plant."

Table 17.1   Summary of "Full-Steam Ahead!" Forecasts, All Regions

	Actual 2000 (1)	Weisskoff projections			% change 2000–2030 (5)	% of SF absolute change 2000–2030 (6)
		2010 (2)	2020 (3)	2030 (4)		
SF						
1. Population (thou.)	6 450	8 235	9 688	11 021	70.9	100.0*
2. Employment (thou.)	3 508	4 337	4 685	5 208	48.4	100.0*
3. Output (bill. 92$)	233	326	386	475	103.7	100.0*
4. Water: Pub. sup.(mgd) pop-hi	1 070	1 355	1 540	1 695	58.5	100.0
5. Water: All fresh (mgd) pop-hi	3 996	5 280	6 191	6 966	74.3	100.0
6. Urban land (thou. acres) pop-hi	1 279	1 809	2 068	2 289	78.9	100.0
LEC						
1. Population (thou.)	5 025	6 195	7 173	8 098	61.2	67.2
2. Employment (thou.)	2 808	3 423	3 663	4 036	43.7	72.3
3. Output (bill. 92$)	195	271	321	394	101.7	82.1
4. Water: Pub. sup. (mgd) pop-hi	882	1 073	1 196	1 299	47.3	66.7
5. Water: All fresh (mgd) pop-hi	2 150	2 619	2 986	3 321	54.5	37.7
6. Urban land (thou. acres) pop-hi	721	902	998	1 085	50.6	36.1
LWC						
1. Population (thou.)	788.8	1 172.7	1 467.0	1 715.5	117.5	20.3
2. Employment (thou.)	438.6	578.3	647.8	748.2	70.6	18.2
3. Output (bill. 92$)	24.5	35.4	42.5	53.6	118.9	12.0
4. Water: Pub. sup. (mgd) pop-hi	110.0	161.7	185.4	198.5	80.5	14.2
5. Water: All fresh (mgd) pop-hi	977.4	1 736.3	2 156.3	2 502.7	156.1	49.1
6. Urban land (thou. acres) pop-hi	299.8	554.9	677.6	778.3	159.6	47.4

KSV						
1. Population (thou.)	300.7	413.3	501.4	582.0	93.5	6.2
2. Employment (thou.)	116.3	147.6	167.1	190.4	63.7	4.4
3. Output (bill. 92$)	5.5	7.8	9.5	11.8	113.6	2.6
4. Water: Pub. sup. (mgd) pop-hi	41.4	65.0	83.6	102.8	148.5	9.8
5. Water: All fresh (mgd) pop-hi	254.1	338.0	414.8	487.3	91.8	7.5
6. Urban land (thou. acres) pop-hi	136.3	203.9	232.7	257.7	89.1	12.0
UEC						
1. Population (thou.)	335.8	454.8	548.7	630.3	87.7	6.4
2. Employment (thou.)	145.5	190.1	208.1	236.8	62.7	5.4
3. Output (bill. 92$)	8.1	11.5	13.6	16.9	109.3	3.6
4. Water: Pub. sup. (mgd) pop-hi	36.4	56.2	75.1	94.7	160.2	9.3
5. Water: All fresh (mgd) pop-hi	478.6	586.5	633.9	655.3	36.9	5.7
6. Urban land (thou. acres) pop-hi	122.5	148.6	159.3	167.5	36.7	4.5
FL						
1. Population (thou.)	16 405	21 164	25 088	28 732	75.1	—
2. Employment (thou.)	8 925	11 100	12 113	13 599	52.4	—
3. Output (bill. 92$)	563	792	949	1 181	109.6	—
4. Water: Pub. sup. (mgd) pop-hi	2 437	3 212	3 822	4 394	80.3	—
5. Water: All fresh (mgd) pop-hi	16 512	22 854	27 107	31 061	88.1	—
6. Urban land (thou. acres) pop-hi	n.a.	n.a.	n.a.	n.a.	n.a.	—

Notes: * May not sum to 100 due to rounding; n.a. = not available.

Sources: Lines 1–3 from Appendix Tables A.1–3; line 4 from Table 3.1; line 5 from Table 3.5; line 6 from Appendix Table C.1, below.

The cities, shorthanded for cash, think that more commercial development will bring them more taxes to pay for the schools, fire services, and water that the growing population expects. The treadmill, they find, never stops.

The new development scarcely seems to pay for the services it needs. The cities find themselves no better off, still looking for further sources of revenue, promoting even more development, spending public money to attract yet more business.

Private enterprise also gets public agencies to compete with one another:

"Build me a bigger seaport, or I'll move my cruise ships to another place that *will* build me one."

"Build me a bigger airport, with more parking space, and an intermodal center."

"Build me..."

When will it stop?

The economic model, as we have tried to show, suggests *that it doesn't need to stop*. There is no inherent *economic* reason. There may be logistical difficulties, personnel, financing, transport, even security problems, but the economy can keep chugging along, creating jobs, income, products, and services, together with the inherent drawbacks. The apparatus of the local and state governments, the lobbying groups of the private sector, even the universities, are all into growth.

Is that really what's best in the long run?

ALTERNATIVE PATHS: ZERO GROWTH

Is there another path besides an attempt at zero growth?

Even "zero growth," as currently practiced in the Florida Keys, for example, fails to solve the problem. By prohibiting any "net" increase in built-up land, the market has driven up the price of existing sites, which are then "renovated" and upscaled by their new owners. Adjacent sites get "consolidated" and a single new structure is built. This results in skyrocketing values, the replacement of modest structures with luxury homes, while large, box-like commercial developments displace blocks of traditional, "old-fashioned" stand-alone businesses. The gentrification of the "zero growth" region leads to an even greater need for affordable housing for those who work in the growing businesses, hotels, and restaurants. There is a need also for more modest housing for the not-so-wealthy retiree. The market pressure to provide sleeping quarters for the labor force is satisfied by the illegal subdivision of apartments and spare rooms, and by the use of non-permitted structures – warehouses, garages, walled-in porches – as rented space. Working people need to live in the Keys, too.

TWO CURRENT PATHS: OUTWARD AND INWARD

In the rest of South Florida, the market, constrained by current zoning codes and real estate practices, is taking two complementary turns. First, suburban sprawl continues unabated. New subdivisions, bearing such imaginative names as Hawks Landing, Sunset Lakes, Harbor Isles, and Marbella Cove are built on limestone fill around the deep inland lakes that were dug to extract the fill! These are estates primarily of single-family houses and some attached town-houses that will draw people away from the traditional centers and closer to the natural areas at the outer edge of the development boundaries. In the case of Miami-Dade County, the last frontier is the "deep south," near Homestead and Florida City, at the very end of Florida's Turnpike.

A second movement, equally impressive in its building and design, is occurring away from the Everglades at the other extreme, on the coastline and on the mainland overlooking Biscayne Bay, the Intracoastal Waterway, along the Miami River, the New River in Ft Lauderdale, and on the barrier islands from Key Biscayne northward – Miami Beach, Surfside, Sunny Isles, Aventura, Hollywood, Ft Lauderdale, and onward. These are multi-storied condominiums, luxury apartments with water view or water access, hotels, rental apartments, and some retail space.

The coastal towers provide living and parking space, residences for a part-year clientele who will patronize local businesses and for those who prefer a shorter commute or even a walk to work. Within a few years, the occupants of these new buildings will contribute considerable tax revenue for the cities that have so enthusiastically provided their permits.

THE MIAMI CASE

There is a not-so-hidden drawback to all this buoyant construction. The new buildings have successfully blockaded the land-based public from access to the water. Aside from the short boardwalks of Miami Beach and Hollywood and the famous Ocean Avenue of South Beach, the Atlantic Ocean and Biscayne Bay have been virtually "privatized" and the premium for water-view property has been captured in the luxury prices. The public, too, can catch a glimpse of the water – between the hotel and condo towers. High fences and limited parking areas prevent non-residents from "penetrating" the ocean beaches north of the City of Miami. Access to Biscayne Bay south of downtown Miami is also blocked from public access, save for a single park kept inconspicuously hidden among the mansions and the well-used causeway parking strips. In downtown Miami alone, which includes the Brickell Avenue and lower Miami River areas, nearly 3000 new residential units, 1.7 million square feet of new office space, and 725 new hotel rooms were constructed between 2000 and 2004.[2]

And this was just a start. Three hundred thousand square feet of retail space and 5000 new condo and rental units were under construction by the end of 2004. Another 800 000 square feet of retail space, 12 000 more condo units, and 700 new hotel rooms are planned or already permitted.[3]

Part of the boom is due to the crash in the stock market and low interest rates. In the late 1920s, hurricanes and severe flooding led to the collapse of the Florida real estate market and drove speculative money north to Wall Street, contributing in some measure to the Great Crash of 1929. In our era, it is the reverse. The burst Wall Street bubble has sent money south to Florida, fueling the housing boom. How will this boom end? No one hastens to answer.

But speculation is only part of the story. The attractiveness of the Florida weather, the aging of the baby-boomers, the decay of the northern urban environments, and the ease of air travel to Florida airports from all over the world, make South Florida a destination for wealthy and not-so-wealthy Canadians, Americans, Europeans, Asians, and South Americans in search of a new or at least another home. All this is occurring under the current regime of incentives. New programs, such as the Miami River Commission's Urban Infill Plan[4] can be expected to *accelerate* the availability of so-called "affordable" housing and intensify settlement in the traditional cities along the coast.

THE NEED FOR OPEN SPACE: URBAN PARKLAND

The future, then, which we are currently programming and building, promises both an unending sprawl inland away from the coasts until the natural limit is reached and *also* a densely packed urban corridor along the coast as the older cities build and rebuild upward. In this scenario, public or open space will become extremely scarce, parks having been for some time the neglected stepchild of the cities. Budgets and bond issues for acquiring large regional parks have been left almost entirely to the counties.

Among the seven US cities with populations of 3–400 000, Miami has the fewest acres of parkland per thousand people (Table 17.2, Panel A, column 2). In fact, five of the seven Florida cities shown (Panel B of Table 17.2) would rank below Atlanta in acres per thousand people. Only Orlando and St Petersburg would rank near the top of the list of other US cities in terms of parkland per person.

In Miami-Dade County, it is the Miami River corridor that is the last frontier of water-accessible, underutilized urban land, and this too may

Table 17.2 *Parkland per Person: Comparable Sized US Cities and Other Florida Cities*

	Acres/thou. persons col. (2)/(3) (1)	Park (acres) (2)	Population (thou.) (3)
A. Middle-size US cities			
1. Cincinnati	21.4	7 391	346
2. Minneapolis	15.9	5 694	359
3. St Louis	9.6	3 385	352
4. Pittsburgh	7.8	2 735	350
5. Atlanta	7.8	3 147	402
6. Tampa	5.9	1 821	308
7. Miami	4.1	1 493	364
B. Florida cities			
1. Orlando	17.6	3 313	188
2. St Petersburg	11.1	2 786	250
3. Tallahassee	7.4	1 144	154
4. Tampa	5.9	1 821	308
5. Ft Lauderdale	5.4	837	155
6. Hollywood	5.2	732	140
7. Miami	4.1	1 493	364

Note: Florida cities include city and county parklands; Harnik's sample includes regional, state, and federally owned lands also

Sources: Panel A cities from Harnik (2000), Table 5; Panel B Florida cities from Florida, Office of Recreation and Parks Inventory, unpublished data (Aug. 2002) and population from BEBR fsa 2001.

eventually be "privatized" into a "condo canyon" similar to that along Brickell Avenue. At best, the public will get an "average" 15-foot wide walkway in the shadow of the 40-story towers along the downtown portion of the river's edge.

Upstream, only riverside condos can pay the prices that many of the derelict and absentee owners have been asking. There is at the present time no provision that requires these new mid-size condos to be "set back" from the river. An off-the-river publicly financed greenway may provide some shade from which pedestrians may catch an occasional glimpse of the river. Unless the riverbanks themselves are purchased by the city or county, the "march of the condos" – which has already begun – will continue and the vision of a true urban riverwalk or greenway will be lost completely.[5] The city may even sell off its older, underused parklands in search of yet more tax revenue.

None of this, of course, need occur.

ALTERNATIVE PATTERNS OF GROWTH

If the economy continues to grow – or even if it does not – relief must be sought from other fronts.

The redeveloping cities and the new suburbs must be built differently so that the "vertical" growth can create truly livable urban space. New mass transport networks can reduce the cars on the road and the amount of land dedicated exclusively to vehicles, as rising densities makes integrated mass transit more workable. Zoning codes that now restrict and segregate new communities according to "use" as residential, commercial, or industrial of varying intensities can give way to an integrated mix of these activities along a creative line of new urbanist principles to achieve higher densities, reduce congestion, and provide more public open space.

If the Everglades is to be saved, then the cities have to be redesigned so that the movement from both coasts inland towards the remaining natural area is interrupted. Some European alternatives are contrasted with conventional South Florida practices listed in Table 17.3.

CHANGING WATER NEEDS

The increasing demands for water by the growing economy must also be slowed. This can be done through equitable and correct pricing, in which both households and businesses pay the full cost of this depletable resource. Correct pricing of water will reward the frugal consumer, penalize the waster, and activate the private sector to promote water-saving practices.

Conservation of our water resources must be sought on a "permanent crisis" basis, rather than waiting for an occasional drought to "force" reluctant consumers to revise their lawn-sprinkling or car-washing habits. Indeed, the very ideal of the perfect green lawn in a region where a dry season is part of the climate must be re-examined. Native ground cover, less water-dependent than the pervasive, water-thirsty St Augustine variety, might provide an acceptable water-saving alternative.

Individual condo units rarely have water meters. Rather, water use of an entire building or set of buildings is usually measured by a single meter. This structural feature alone can result in massive wasting of water, as leaky plumbing in one unit or in the swimming pool or sprinkling systems can go undetected. The cost is factored into everyone's bill. The savings resulting from a simple unit-by-unit metering system might postpone the need for future desalinization and water treatment plants, especially in those coastal communities where wells are already being depleted or suffering from saltwater intrusion.

Savings in water *use* also saves water disposal, the need to treat, recycle, or inject wastewater into deep wells. At some time in the not-so-distant future, the counties of South Florida that have been relying on deep-well-injection on an "emergency basis" for several decades[6] will turn to massively expensive state-of-the-art wastewater treatment facilities, and the treated water will be recycled. But much of the expected expenditure could be reduced through more modest consumption now and well-metered, correctly priced water to begin with.

Despite the current metering and billing practices, much of the water for backyard pools, gardens, and lawns is provided by individual, unmetered wells. Again, a comprehensive program of water conservation would encourage new practices that could reduce lawn consumption through drip irrigation rather than the automatically clocked, traditional sprinklers. The promotion of native plants and trees that thrive on the natural water cycle could reduce the need for well water, especially during the natural dry season. The present practice of "maxi-scaping" – planting luxuriant, water-thirsty foliage on median strips, along highways, and around schools and public buildings as private gardens – could give way to xeriscaping, rock gardens, and native plants.[7]

The promoters of the current "Florida lifestyle" will have to set the pace for such changes, with water-consciousness and Everglades-saving in their mind's eye, as well as an appreciation for natural beauty and a reduced need for heavy spraying.

A lesson might be learned from the recent developments in the Tampa Bay area. There, the largest seawater desalination plant in North America, 25 million gallons *per day* (mgd), is being completed and a second plant of a similar size is being sited for construction.[8] The first plant cost $110 million to build; the second is estimated to cost $189 to $310 million. What happened to the underground water? Could a more aggressive conservation program instituted ten years ago have extended the life of the underground supplies enough to offset the need for this "technological fix"?

"It's a question of demand and supply," I am told. "No one could have foreseen the rapid growth in the 1990s. No one could have known about the rapid depletion of the underground water."

No one? Were there no warning voices?

The same cannot be said about South Florida today. There are many warning voices. The coral reefs die. The roads are impassable. Bottled water sales are booming. The pumps draining the lands on which the new mansions are built – all former Everglades – run overtime, all the time! The people keep coming.

It all has to do with how we choose to live. If we believe the ecosystem is immutable, there is no reason to change. If we believe our surroundings are fragile, then our every action, our whole lifestyle and our public decision-making must be up for re-examination: how we spend our money; how we can spend our time; how we build our homes and cities.

Table 17.3 Comparison of South Florida Practices with Some European Alternatives

Current South Florida Practice	Alternative
1. Rapid flushing of rain runoff into canals and pumped out to estuaries. Old cisterns in remote Keys replaced by long-distance piping.	1. Creative use of rainwater by homes and businesses.
2. Mega-traffic jams on all virtually all highways during rush hours.	2. Reduce CO_2 emissions. Intra-city delivery services to reduce reliance on private shopping trips. Mass transit, bicycles, and more use of curbside rental vehicles.
3. Reliance on nuclear and thermal power, with large purchases of conventional power from states selling excess.	3. Wind park for electricity.
4. Roofs are already structurally reinforced roofs due to strict code for hurricane protection, but no practice of planting on roofs. Cities designed to reduce the time that water stands in urban areas. Periodic flooding of rural and urban areas due to limited canal and pumping capacity to carry rainwater to coastal estuaries.	4. Rooftop greenery and trickle recharge of underground water.
5. Widespread use of exotics for ornamentals. Release of exotics into natural areas, endangering vast regions, especially by melaleuca and Brazilian pepper.	5. Local vegetation for landscaping.
6. Energy-intensive life-style in housing, transport, sports, shopping, schools, and hospitals. New hotels, offices, schools built with unopenable or no windows at all, requiring year-round power for light and air. Little awareness of the implications of climate change and sea-level rise.	6. Energy awareness. "At the beginning, remember the end."

7. Rejection of "New Urbanism" criteria by local zoning boards. Giant new residential towers built at ocean's edge and sprawling single-family housing extended into flood-prone interior areas, which must be protected by drainage canals and continuous pumping. Low prices for water, land, electricity, and gasoline encourage resource-intensive design; low taxes and municipal fracturing reduce public sector capabilities to deliver needed services. Weak multi-county planning structures.	7. Sustainability awareness in project design.
8. Reliance on traditionally heated, chlorinated urban pools and new water parks. Heavy investment in preserving natural lands and in maintaining an extensive network of public parks, lakes, and ocean beaches on city, county, state, and federal levels.	8. Conversion of conventional swimming pool into natural bathing lagoon.
9. Use of public funds to build new sports stadiums and cultural centers. New upscale malls and warehouse parks built to the west on natural lands, while "Eastward Ho!" concept is promoted for urban infill.	9. Conversion of obsolete industrial structures.
10. Many grass roots movements active to preserve natural areas and improve urban settings (for example, Everglades Alliance; Biscayne Bay Partnership Initiative; Miami River Partnership). Demonstration self-help projects for urban minorities (Habitat for Humanity) and year-round farmworkers (Centro Campesino). Royalities from casino gambling on lands owned by Native American tribes (Miccosukee and Seminole) have extended the South Florida lifestyle to the most marginalized groups. Local vegetable and fruit growers donate excess produce gleaned by volunteers directly to the urban poor (Farm Share) and to networks of privately-funded soup kitchens (Camillus House, Miami River Mission).	10. Urban renewal and citizen participation, esp. of marginal groups. "Climate Alliances" bring together experts on emissions, forestry, and social and economic effects of climate change.

Source: "Alternatives" from author's notes at the United Nations-sponsored "Urban 21: Global Conference on the Urban Future," Berlin, 2000.

OTHER SCENARIOS

The last remaining, potentially "developable" lands in South Florida are the vast tracts of sugar and vegetable lands south of Lake Okeechobee, the Everglades Agricultural Area (EAA). Once the cities fill up and their surrounding pasturelands and greenhouses are all turned into shopping centers and townhouses, then the "heavy" agricultural regions – sugarcane and vegetables in western Palm Beach County, even the citrus lands in the Upper East Coast counties – too will be up for grabs.

When the Cuban sugar lands, neglected and underutilized since the 1960s, come back into the US orbit and its sugar is again allowed to enter the US market as a "foreign aid" mechanism to help that economy grow, we might expect momentous changes in South Florida. If the Florida cane producers become co-partners in the Cuban expansion, Everglades sugar cultivation may be curtailed, the aging sugar mills sold off, and their lands turned into golf-course developments, "lakeside" retirement communities and the like, providing housing for the future population that our model shows will be coming to South Florida. This "new frontier" will also need more freshwater, and the runoff from the golf courses and urban "civilization" downstream into the Everglades can create a problem several magnitudes greater than that caused by current sugar and vegetable growing. Rapid transit, improved east–west superhighways, and an expanded north-south Turnpike also would allow residents to commute up and down the coast to keep South Florida growing.

If, on the other hand, sugar yields decline due to the subsiding topsoil, Cuban sugar replaces "Everglades sugar" in the US market, and the US government purchases the development rights to the EAA,[9] then the area may be allowed to revert to marshland and be used for extensive water storage. This may be especially important if the key role of ASR (aquifer storage and recovery) wells in the overall Everglades restoration plan proves unrealizable for some technological, geological, or economic reason.

Any disruption in the Middle Eastern oil supplies could drive energy prices upward and make the current engineering solution to Everglades restoration much more expensive to operate and maintain. Such an eventuality will throw an added advantage to less energy-intensive water storage contingencies such as added surface reservoirs. All these considerations raise the public's stake in the preservation of the present agricultural lands assumed in the Everglades Plan.

We can imagine, of course, a range of other "grand compromises" that involve the future of the sugar lands. A part could be reserved for organic rice, which needs less drainage than sugarcane and no chemical pesticides. A part could be made into deep reservoirs for water storage needed for Everglades restoration, and a part could be turned into new hotels, vacation homes, condos, golf courses, and equestrian communities. South Florida would get the land it needs to continue growing. The Caribbean would provide the sugar. The northern pasture lands in the Kissimmee Valley could be irrigated for growing vegetables and citrus, and the public could continue the charade of paying to keep the remaining Everglades "pristine."

It is indeed ironic that the solution to the Everglades or its ruin depends entirely on the future of our cities and farms and on all the policies and programs that keep them growing. As we come to understand more thoroughly the costs and consequences of our current lifestyles, we need to examine the alternatives that are now before us, while there is still time to choose.

Only in this way will our own future be compatible with a restored Everglades.

NOTES

1. See the works of Herman Daly, for example, and the zero-growth school. He often cites J.S. Mill's positive view of the stationary-state in contrast to a dismal end to economic society.
2. Construction data for projects from Miami Downtown Development Agency (DDA) (2004b).
3. Data from Miami Downtown Development Agency (DDA) (2004a), Spread sheets "Under Construction" and "Planned."
4. See Kimberly-Horn and Associates (2002).
5. Compare Metropolitan Dade County (1962), City of Miami (1992), and Greenways, Inc. (2001) to Harnick (2000) for a review of urban parks. See Crompton (2000), and Ross-Miller (2001) on the value of open space.
6. See Sydney Bacchus (2002).
7. As promoted in the SFWMD literature but not by our local nurseries.
8. See www.tampabaywater.org.
9. See *Miami Herald*, Jan. 12, 2003, p. 6B. "Plan Would Block Loss of Farmland: Senator Proposes Buying Development Rights in Glades."

APPENDICES

Appendix A

Table A.1 Summary of Scenarios: All Rates, South Florida and All Florida, Four Years

Scenario element	V*	South Florida				All Florida			
		2000	2010	2020	2030	2000	2010	2020	2030
1. REMI base totals	P	6 228.0	7 105.9	7 721.8	8 391.2	15 901.6	18 425.6	20 251.4	22 123.2
	E	3 210.1	3 506.6	3 628.6	3 839.9	8 224.8	9 098.0	9 483.8	10 102.8
	M	61.9	20.3	−10.2	2.1	185.0	78.7	−6.6	24.1
	Q	212.1	254.4	287.1	331.1	515.4	624.1	707.5	819.6
2. EMPLOYMENT update totals	P	6 326.5	7 818.5	8 871.9	9 690.6	16 126.7	20 191.3	23 113.4	25 387.6
	E	3 351.9	4 069.7	4 215.8	4 473.6	8 568.5	10 473.4	10 941.2	11 699.3
	M	93.2	95.2	0.6	−1.2	262.9	261.4	23.5	21.2
	Q	224.1	308.0	347.9	403.2	542.8	751.8	853.5	994.4
3. Final low	P	6 366.8	8 028.6	9 224.3	10 159.7	16 245.3	20 754.0	24 024.4	26 557.1
	E	3 419.3	4 210.0	4 393.9	4 701.6	8 755.0	10 843.3	11 403.8	12 271.8
	M	111.6	111.3	7.9	5.0	310.8	302.0	40.5	33.8
	Q	228.0	317.4	360.1	419.7	553.4	775.8	884.4	1 035.1
4. Final medium	P	6 416.7	8 155.6	9 481.9	10 558.8	16 337.7	21 001.7	24 597.5	27 530.1
	E	3 473.3	4 289.3	4 547.7	4 918.5	8 854.7	11 001.9	11 767.0	12 820.0
	M	121.9	118.6	18.9	14.3	329.9	317.1	71.9	63.3
	Q	231.3	322.6	373.2	441.3	559.3	785.7	915.3	1 088.8
5. Final high	P	6 450.2	8 235.2	9 688.3	11 021.3	16 405.4	21 163.9	25 087.9	28 731.9
	E	3 508.4	4 337.0	4 684.9	5 208.0	8 925.3	11 100.2	12 113.4	13 598.8
	M	128.7	123.4	34.3	41.2	343.6	327.0	114.6	140.8
	Q	233.4	325.6	386.3	475.5	563.3	791.8	948.8	1 180.5

Table A.1 Summary of Scenarios: All Rates, South Florida and All Florida, Four Years (Continued)

Scenario element	V*	South Florida				All Florida			
		2000	2010	2020	2030	2000	2010	2020	2030
Add:									
6a. FARM low	P	23.58	107.1	170.9	234.7	64.29	278.6	430.2	565.8
	E	42.87	62.21	85.68	114.3	111.1	163.7	219	279.5
	M	12.57	5.645	3.828	4.3	30.8	14.22	8.361	8.394
	Q	2.43	3.367	4.758	6.556	5.881	8.597	12.26	16.74
6b. FARM medium	P	24.61	132.6	224.7	312.5	68.94	345	575.4	794.3
	E	46.51	84.98	122	161.6	121.2	220.4	315.4	417.2
	M	13.25	8.112	5.879	5.527	32.62	20.66	14.81	14.23
	Q	2.68	4.906	7.426	10.45	6.542	12.2	18.7	26.65
6c. FARM high	P	24.76	143.3	260.7	390.5	69.28	368.1	652.7	960.2
	E	47.19	94.41	145.7	207.5	122.6	240.8	366.2	515.4
	M	13.4	9.675	8.647	9.541	32.95	24.04	20.73	22.79
	Q	2.723	5.532	9.065	13.8	6.635	13.57	22.26	33.91
7a. INVESTMENT low	P	-1.844	64.02	124.6	167.1	6.245	185.2	339.7	438.2
	E	6.018	52.17	64.59	81.93	26.57	144.8	175.3	215.3
	M	2.321	7.97	3.293	1.976	7.662	20.84	7.802	4.046
	Q	0.4868	4.354	5.399	7.129	2.068	11.65	14.18	18.17
7b. INVESTMENT medium	P	-1.844	64.02	185.6	321.5	6.245	185.2	512.5	883.5
	E	6.018	52.17	115.7	177.3	26.57	144.8	321.4	490.1
	M	2.321	7.97	10.95	9.671	7.662	20.84	30.23	26.79
	Q	0.4868	4.354	11.43	19.55	2.068	11.65	30.77	52.45
7c. INVESTMENT high	P	-1.844	64.02	259.2	593	6.245	185.2	730.4	1691
	E	6.018	52.17	184.2	370.7	26.57	144.8	524.7	1067
	M	2.321	7.97	22.63	32.38	7.662	20.84	65.03	95.06

296

V								
8a. TOURISM low								
Q	0.4868	4.354	19.87	46.83	2.068	11.65	54.72	129.8
P	18.52	37.42	51.92	60.15	48.11	98.21	136.5	158.8
E	18.53	21.09	24.75	27.6	48.82	55.46	65.5	73.42
M	3.584	1.703	0.4655	0.1302	9.469	4.53	1.317	0.4983
Q	1.042	1.268	1.592	1.908	2.66	3.218	4.06	4.888
8b. TOURISM medium								
P	67.47	138.9	194.7	227.1	135.8	279.5	391.6	458
E	68.91	77.62	91.2	101.9	138.4	157.3	186.2	209.1
M	13.21	6.489	1.783	0.4812	26.73	13.14	3.887	1.434
Q	4.076	4.887	6.05	7.201	7.895	9.542	11.97	14.38
8c. TOURISM high								
P	100.8	207.8	291.5	340.1	203.2	418.6	586.8	686.4
E	103.3	115.9	136.2	152.1	207.6	235.2	278.5	312.8
M	19.82	9.738	2.68	0.7224	40.11	19.71	5.841	2.15
Q	6.111	7.299	9.035	10.76	11.84	14.27	17.91	21.51
9. CERP minus taxes								
P	0.006836	1.602	5.024	7.152	0.01172	0.6504	4.656	6.754
E	0.0271	4.866	3.012	4.118	0.04297	5.939	2.795	4.296
M	0.006332	0.8202	-0.3517	-0.2584	0.01025	1.046	-0.529	-0.3155
Q	0.001465	0.414	0.4243	0.8723	0.00238	0.487	0.4277	0.9274

Notes: *V = variables: P = population (thou.); E = employment (thou.); M = economic migrants (thou.); Q = output (bill. 92$).

Table A.2 Summary of Scenarios: All Rates, LEC, LWC, Four Years

Scenario element	V*	LEC				LWC			
		2000	2010	2020	2030	2000	2010	2020	2030
1. REMI base totals	P	4 890.6	5 453.9	5 898.3	6 420.3	723.2	906.7	1 001.9	1 080.9
	E	2 619.0	2 835.6	2 932.0	3 099.2	353.5	403.8	419.5	446.2
	M	33.1	9.0	-5.5	4.8	17.2	7.3	-2.6	-1.0
	Q	180.4	215.5	243.7	281.2	19.2	23.6	26.3	30.2
2. EMPLOYMENT update totals	P	4 968.4	5 991.1	6 741.7	7 354.6	736.4	1 016.1	1 193.2	1 309.4
	E	2 731.2	3 281.0	3 386.3	3 581.4	375.1	483.4	509.3	548.9
	M	56.8	64.6	1.1	1.2	22.3	19.3	0.1	-0.6
	Q	190.4	260.7	294.6	341.3	20.7	29.6	33.3	38.7
3. Final low	P	4 992.4	6 105.2	6 911.0	7 551.3	742.5	1 069.4	1 301.5	1 478.4
	E	2 773.0	3 361.3	3 473.8	3 680.7	389.1	521.6	566.3	635.0
	M	67.8	72.6	2.2	1.2	26.2	24.5	3.8	3.6
	Q	193.1	266.9	302.0	350.7	21.5	31.9	36.7	44.4
4. Final medium	P	5 009.5	6 158.9	7 054.7	7 807.1	772.8	1 135.2	1 395.2	1 586.1
	E	2 791.8	3 397.4	3 573.8	3 835.7	421.6	554.5	608.8	677.6
	M	71.3	76.1	11.7	10.0	32.5	27.0	5.2	3.6
	Q	194.3	269.3	311.0	366.6	23.5	33.9	39.6	47.4
5. Final high	P	5 024.8	6 195.0	7 172.5	8 098.2	788.8	1 172.7	1 467.0	1 715.5
	E	2 807.9	3 423.2	3 663.1	4 036.2	438.6	578.3	647.8	748.2
	M	74.3	78.7	21.8	28.4	35.8	29.5	8.0	8.9
	Q	195.3	271.1	320.9	393.9	24.5	35.4	42.5	53.6

Add:

6a. FARM low	P	13.53	49.03	61.06	64.1	1.381	26.69	56.52	93.01
	E	25.47	27.82	29.88	30.64	7.575	17.89	31.28	49.12
	M	7.251	1.53	-0.1462	-0.3426	2.418	2.298	2.465	2.887
	Q	1.677	2.022	2.494	2.975	0.3871	0.7519	1.354	2.255
6b. FARM medium	P	14.58	71.67	116.4	157.8	1.228	27.93	51.69	73.81
	E	27.89	48.15	67.97	89.23	8.102	17.93	26.52	35.07
	M	7.704	4.052	2.744	2.654	2.542	2.082	1.576	1.296
	Q	1.856	3.343	5.083	7.252	0.4197	0.8123	1.18	1.536
6c. FARM high	P	14.67	77.58	135.4	197.5	1.263	30.7	61.55	95.79
	E	28.29	53.53	81.02	113.9	8.269	20.35	32.83	47.69
	M	7.798	4.89	4.144	4.636	2.577	2.503	2.365	2.462
	Q	1.885	3.763	6.166	9.445	0.4281	0.9383	1.52	2.245
7a. INVESTMENT low	P	-3.973	36.43	67.63	83.2	2.649	21.58	43.24	63.09
	E	1.503	32.99	36.93	43.23	4.364	15.05	21.56	29.81
	M	1.094	4.827	1.349	0.2912	1.052	2.272	1.426	1.24
	Q	0.1539	2.906	3.29	4.053	0.3224	1.138	1.648	2.374
7b. INVESTMENT medium	P	-3.973	36.43	114.9	200.9	2.649	21.58	51.21	86.03
	E	1.503	32.99	78.45	119.5	4.364	15.05	27.86	42.99
	M	1.094	4.827	7.222	6.023	1.052	2.272	2.542	2.578
	Q	0.1539	2.906	8.407	14.52	0.3224	1.138	2.235	3.685
7c. INVESTMENT high	P	-3.973	36.43	171.1	400.6	2.649	21.58	62.12	130.5
	E	1.503	32.99	133	268.8	4.364	15.05	37.31	72.47
	M	1.094	4.827	15.92	22.27	1.052	2.272	4.369	6.598
	Q	0.1539	2.906	15.52	37.16	0.3224	1.138	3.122	6.724
8a. TOURISM low	P	14.36	28.27	38.69	44.51	2.101	4.623	6.716	7.976
	E	14.73	16.63	19.4	21.57	2.052	2.446	2.959	3.353
	M	2.739	1.246	0.3259	0.09199	0.4247	0.2343	0.07318	0.0214
	Q	0.853	1.032	1.293	1.55	0.1055	0.1342	0.1707	0.2052

Table A.2   Summary of Scenarios: All Rates, LEC, LWC, Four Years (Continued)

Scenario element	V*	LEC				LWC			
		2000	2010	2020	2030	2000	2010	2020	2030
8b. TOURISM medium	P	30.47	59.73	81.65	93.77	32.6	69.55	99.18	116.9
	E	31.22	35.28	41.05	45.54	34.02	38.11	45.1	50.64
	M	5.763	2.638	0.6785	0.183	6.55	3.376	0.9593	0.2593
	Q	1.891	2.304	2.884	3.458	2.007	2.365	2.891	3.414
8c. TOURISM high	P	45.68	89.55	122.4	140.6	48.56	103.9	148.3	174.9
	E	46.83	52.88	61.53	68.26	50.92	56.68	67.08	75.36
	M	8.648	3.958	1.019	0.2752	9.835	5.066	1.444	0.3887
	Q	2.837	3.452	4.321	5.181	3.007	3.52	4.301	5.08
9. CERP minus taxes	P	0.004883	0.3682	1.896	4.899	0.004883	0.3682	1.896	4.899
	E	0.01953	2.794	1.227	3.791	0.01953	2.794	1.227	3.791
	M	0.004543	0.3939	-0.3482	0.02304	0.004543	0.3939	-0.3482	0.02304
	Q	0.001114	0.2554	0.2506	0.8055	0.001114	0.2554	0.2506	0.8055

Notes: *V = variables: P = population (thou.); E = employment (thou.); M = economic migrants (thou.); Q = output (bill. 92$).

Table A.3 Summary of Scenarios: All Rates, KSV, UEC, Four Years

Scenario element	V*	KSV				UEC			
		2000	2010	2020	2030	2000	2010	2020	2030
1. REMI base totals	P	287.6	360.0	405.0	444.9	326.5	385.2	416.6	445.1
	E	105.1	121.7	128.9	139.0	132.5	145.5	148.2	155.5
	M	6.5	2.7	-0.3	0.3	5.0	1.3	-1.9	-1.9
	Q	5.0	6.4	7.3	8.5	7.5	8.9	9.8	11.2
2. EMPLOYMENT update totals	P	290.5	382.3	442.2	488.5	331.2	429.0	494.7	538.0
	E	107.2	130.9	139.8	151.7	138.4	174.3	180.4	191.6
	M	7.4	5.1	0.2	0.3	6.6	6.2	-0.8	-2.1
	Q	5.2	7.0	8.1	9.5	7.7	10.6	11.8	13.6
3. Final low	P	297.7	407.3	489.6	560.1	334.2	447.2	523.5	574.6
	E	113.4	144.6	162.0	182.6	143.9	184.8	192.9	207.0
	M	9.3	7.0	2.0	2.0	8.3	7.5	-0.3	-1.8
	Q	5.4	7.6	9.0	10.8	8.0	11.3	12.6	14.6
4. Final medium	P	299.3	409.1	489.4	556.9	335.1	450.8	537.5	601.6
	E	115.0	145.1	160.9	180.2	144.9	187.5	201.3	220.8
	M	9.7	6.8	1.7	1.8	8.5	7.9	0.7	-0.8
	Q	5.5	7.6	9.1	11.0	8.0	11.3	13.1	15.5
5. Final high	P	300.7	413.3	501.4	582.0	335.8	454.8	548.7	630.3
	E	116.3	147.6	167.1	190.4	145.5	190.1	208.1	236.8
	M	10.0	7.1	2.7	3.0	8.6	8.3	1.6	1.0
	Q	5.5	7.8	9.5	11.8	8.1	11.5	13.6	16.9

Table A.3 Summary of Scenarios: All Rates, KSV, UEC, Four Years (Continued)

Scenario element	V*	KSV				UEC			
		2000	2010	2020	2030	2000	2010	2020	2030
Add:									
6a. FARM low	P	5.865	19.11	35.85	57.03	2.808	12.28	17.5	20.56
	E	4.833	10.31	17.13	26.25	4.99	6.197	7.379	8.291
	M	1.472	1.278	1.384	1.741	1.425	0.5391	0.1248	0.01447
	Q	0.1448	0.3143	0.5582	0.913	0.2211	0.2785	0.3521	0.4139
6b. FARM medium	P	5.871	17.78	30.08	43.31	2.934	15.26	26.51	37.54
	E	5.152	10.04	14.55	19.7	5.368	8.864	13.01	17.57
	M	1.531	1.029	0.8633	0.9427	1.469	0.9494	0.6954	0.6346
	Q	0.1613	0.3561	0.5563	0.8029	0.2432	0.3945	0.6063	0.859
6c. FARM high	P	5.877	18.25	31.76	47.12	2.954	16.79	32.05	50.01
	E	5.173	10.36	15.4	21.44	5.459	10.18	16.45	24.44
	M	1.537	1.1	1.001	1.153	1.488	1.182	1.137	1.29
	Q	0.1623	0.3711	0.5979	0.8916	0.2476	0.4596	0.7814	1.221
7a. INVESTMENT low	P	-0.05215	2.517	5.228	7.668	-0.4684	3.496	8.552	13.14
	E	0.1329	1.256	1.912	2.865	0.01878	2.881	4.187	6.022
	M	0.1005	0.318	0.1776	0.1681	0.07479	0.5528	0.3411	0.2773
	Q	0.008418	0.08509	0.1334	0.2123	0.002047	0.2255	0.3281	0.4894
7b. INVESTMENT medium	P	-0.05215	2.517	7.687	13.85	-0.4684	3.496	11.84	20.77
	E	0.1329	1.256	3.099	5.02	0.01878	2.881	6.276	9.742
	M	0.1005	0.318	0.4972	0.4547	0.07479	0.5528	0.6853	0.6152
	Q	0.008418	0.08509	0.2397	0.4282	0.002047	0.2255	0.5433	0.914

	*V								
7c. INVESTMENT high	P	-0.05215	2.517	11.34	27.83	-0.4684	3.496	14.68	34.01
	E	0.1329	1.256	5.27	11.58	0.01878	2.881	8.666	17.8
	M	0.1005	0.318	1.092	1.663	0.07479	0.5528	1.249	1.851
	Q	0.008418	0.08509	0.4346	1.088	0.002047	0.2255	0.798	1.864
8a. TOURISM low	P	1.385	3.068	4.405	5.187	0.6795	1.455	2.102	2.483
	E	1.205	1.353	1.601	1.793	0.5482	0.6561	0.7892	0.8849
	M	0.2878	0.152	0.04709	0.01541	0.1324	0.07017	0.01932	0.001376
	Q	0.05599	0.06699	0.08361	0.09945	0.02773	0.03519	0.04484	0.05361
8b. TOURISM medium	P	2.968	6.57	9.463	11.17	1.432	3.05	4.407	5.204
	E	2.532	2.861	3.401	3.818	1.142	1.366	1.645	1.845
	M	0.6151	0.3281	0.1043	0.03579	0.2771	0.1472	0.0405	0.003117
	Q	0.1189	0.1432	0.1799	0.2148	0.05933	0.07503	0.09566	0.1146
8c. TOURISM high	P	4.446	9.852	14.2	16.76	2.147	4.575	6.61	7.807
	E	3.798	4.287	5.098	5.724	1.713	2.048	2.466	2.767
	M	0.9232	0.493	0.157	0.05373	0.4159	0.2209	0.06089	0.00468
	Q	0.1784	0.2147	0.2696	0.322	0.08904	0.1125	0.1434	0.1718
9. CERP minus taxes	P	0.001709	0.3792	1.866	1.737	0.00009155	1.032	0.574	0.4106
	E	0.007545	0.7446	1.521	0.03014	0.00004578	0.6859	0.1859	0.1692
	M	0.001744	0.1377	0.2213	-0.2175	0.00005913	0.09698	-0.04126	-0.02024
	Q	0.0003514	0.04679	0.1129	-0.002537	0.000004292	0.06844	0.02984	0.03142

Notes: *V = variables: P = population (thou.); E = employment (thou.); M = economic migrants (thou.); Q = output (bill. 92$).

303

Appendix B

Table B.1   Public Supply Withdrawals: USGS, SFWMD Comparisons of Actual and Forecasts (2000, 2020)

	2000				2020			
	USGS	USGS earlier forecast			SFWMD	USGS forecast		
	Actual	Low	Medium	High	Forecast	Low	Medium	High
	(1)	(2)	(3)	(4)	(5)	(6)	(7)	(8)
Florida	2 199.4	2 040.3*	2 306.4	2 570.7	n.g.	1 879.6	2 887.8	3 895.9
Broward	258.1	231.7	257.4 ^	283.1	312.6	221.3 ^	316.2	411.0
Miami-D	394.3	356.2 ^	395.8	435.3	616.6	330.0	471.4 ^	612.9
Monroe	0.0	10.7	11.9	13.1		9.8	14.0	18.2
Palm Bch.	229.8	215.1 ^	253.1	291.0	285.7	185.9 ^	338.0	490.0
LEC	882.2	813.7*	918.2	1 022.5	1 214.9	747.0	1 139.6*	1 532.1
Collier	52.4	31.5	37.0	42.6 ^	82.0	27.6	50.3	72.9 ^
Glades	0.6	0.3	0.4	0.4 ^	0.5	0.2	0.5 ^	0.7
Hendry	4.7	3.4	4.0	4.6 ^	6.0	2.7	4.9 ^	7.2
Lee	52.4	49.1 ^	57.8	66.5	66.3	42.9 ^	78.0	113.1
LWC	110.1	84.3	99.2*	114.1	154.8	73.4	133.7 *	193.9
Highland	9.1 ^	10.2	11.4	12.5	0.0 ^	10.3	14.8	19.2
Okee.	2.2 ^	2.5	3.2	3.8	3.0	1.6 ^	4.1	6.5
Osceola	30.0	12.0	14.1	16.3 ^	37.1	10.7	19.5	28.3 ^
KSV	41.4	24.7	28.7	32.6 *	40.1	22.6	38.4*	54.0

Table B.1   Public Supply Withdrawals: USGS, SFWMD Comparisons of Actual and Forecasts (2000, 2020) (Continued)

	2000				2020			
	USGS Actual	USGS earlier forecast			SFWMD Forecast	USGS forecast		
		Low	Med	High		Low	Med	High
	(1)	(2)	(3)	(4)	(5)	(6)	(7)	(8)
Martin	18.5	13.8	16.3	18.7	22.4	11.8	21.5^	31.1
St Lucie	18.0	17.5	20.6	23.7	32.0	15.2	27.7^	40.2
UEC	36.4	31.3*	36.9	42.4	54.4	27.0	49.2*	71.3
All SF	1 070.1	954.0	1 083.0	1 211.6	1 464.5	870.0	1 360.9*	1 851.3
ROF	1 129.3	1 086.3*	1 223.4	1 359.1	n.g.	1 009.6	1 526.9	2 044.6

Notes: ^ indicates location of values of "USGS actual" (column 1) or "SFWMD forecast" (column 5) in relation to USGS forecasts (columns 2–4, 6–8) for each county estimate; * indicates location of values of "USGS actual" (column 1) or "SFWMD forecast" (column 5) in relation to USGS forecasts (columns 2–4, 6–8) for Florida and regional estimates. "n.g." = not given.

Sources: Column 1 from "Total public supply water withdrawals by County, 2000" USGS; totals from "Total water withdrawals by County, 2000" 11/21/2002 USGS files. Public supply forecasts for 2000–2030 from Marella (1992), T. 14, "Projected range of public-supply water use in Florida by county." SFWMD projections for 2020 for LEC from *LEC Regional Water Supply Plan* (May 2000), Append Vol. I, T. B-9, p. 23–4. (We excluded part of Hendry County which is within LEC and converted "million gallons per year (mgy to mgd). SFWMD projections for 2020 for LWC from *LWC Water Supply Plan*, Support Document (April 2000b), T. 15, p. 66, "Public Water Supplied," 2020, given in mgd. SFWMD projections for 2020 for KSV, UEC and all SF from *Districtwide Water Supply Assessment* (July 1998). KSV has been slightly updated in *Kissimmee. Basin Water Supply Plan* (April 2000a), Table 18, p. 65, but these updates are not published on a county level.

Table B.2   *Comparing PS and RF Estimates, SFWMD and USGS, 1995*

	1995 mgd Public supply (PS)		1995 mgd Rest of fresh (RF)		% Ground in RF
	SFWMD (1)	USGS (2)	SFWMD (3)	USGS (4)	(5)
Miami-Dade	387.4		607.0		
Broward	222.3		369.6		
Monroe	0.0		2.7		
Palm Beach	175.0		834.6		
LEC total	784.7 <	795.8	1 813.8 >	1 022.4	0.270
E Hendry	0.0		234.5		
N Glades	0.0		26.2		
LWC unit	91.6		765.8		
LWC total	91.6 >	84.4	1 026.6 >	914.4	0.436
Highland	0.0		93.6		
W Okeechobee	2.0		31.6		
E Okeechobee	0.0		8.6		
Osceola	18.1		44.8		
KSV total	20.0 <	29.4	178.6 <	240.4	0.887
Martin	13.1		177.4		
St Lucie	14.0		328.9		
UEC total	27.1 <	29.3	506.2 >	450.6	0.225
All SF	923.5 <	938.9	3 525.2 >	2 627.8	0.371

Sources: SFWMD from *Regional Water Supply Plans and Districtwide Assessment.* USGS from Marella (1999). Column 5 above is computed from USGS data.

Appendix C

Table C.1 Urban Land Forecasts at Different Projected Rates of Population Increase

	Population (thou.)		Urban land (ac.)		Land/person	
	Medium (1)	High (2)	Medium pop. (3)	High pop. (4)	Medium pop. (5)	High pop. (6)
Lower East Coast (LEC)						
1995 model base	4 517	4 517	720 709	720 709	0.1596	0.1596
2010 forecast	6 157	6 195	897 729	901 830	0.1458	0.1456
2020 forecast	7 055	7 173	986 305	998 145	0.1398	0.1392
2030 forecast	7 807	8 098	1 057 427	1 085 221	0.1354	0.1340
1995 abs. change	3 290	3 581	336 718	364 512		
2030 % change	72.8	79.3	46.7	50.6		
Short-run elasticity (1988–95)			0.6765			
Long-run elasticity (1995–2030)			0.6414	0.6380		
Lower West Coast (LWC)						
1995 model base	595	595	299 830	299 830	0.5035	0.5035
2010 forecast	1 135	1 172	538 525	554 894	0.4745	0.4735
2020 forecast	1 395	1 467	646 911	677 608	0.4637	0.4619
2030 forecast	1 586	1 715	724 732	778 253	0.4570	0.4538
1995 abs. change	991	1 120	424 902	478 423		
2030 % change	166.4	188.0	141.7	159.6		
Short-run elasticity (1988–95)			0.8786			
Long-run elasticity (1995–2030)			0.8519	0.8487		

Kissimmee Valley (KSV)						
1995 model base	236	236	136 264	136 264	0.5765	0.5765
2010 forecast	409	413	202 335	203 865	0.4947	0.4936
2020 forecast	489	501	228 609	232 704	0.4675	0.4645
2030 forecast	557	582	249 715	257 682	0.4483	0.4428
1995 abs. change	321	346	113 451	121 418		
2030 % change	135.6	146.2	83.3	89.1		
Short-run elasticity (1988–95)		0.6639				
Long-run elasticity (1995–2030)		0.6138	0.6094			
Upper East Coast (UEC)						
1995 model base	282	282	122 546	122 546	0.4339	0.4339
2010 forecast	451	455	148 012	148 586	0.3282	0.3267
2020 forecast	537	549	157 837	159 265	0.2939	0.2903
2030 forecast	602	630	164 487	167 510	0.2732	0.2658
1995 abs. change	320	348	41 941	44 964		
2030 % change	113.2	123.2	34.2	36.7		
Short-run elasticity (1988–95)		0.3481				
Long-run elasticity (1995–2030)		0.3024	0.2978			
South Florida (SF)						
1995 model base	5 631	5 631	1 279 349	1 279 349	0.2272	0.2272
2010 forecast	8 152	8 235	1 786 600	1 809 176	0.2192	0.2197
2020 forecast	9 476	9 690	2 019 663	2 067 722	0.2131	0.2134
2030 forecast	10 552	11 025	2 196 361	2 288 666	0.2081	0.2076
1995 abs. change	4 921	5 394	917 012	1 009 317		
2030 % change	87.4	95.8	71.7	78.9		
Short-run elasticity (1988–95)		0.6822				
Long-run elasticity (1995–2030)		0.8203	0.8236			

Table C.2   Comparisons of Land/Person Elasticities and Marginal Coefficients

| | Population (thou.) | | | Land (thou. acres) | | | Marg. coeff. d(land)/ d(people) (6)/(3) | Average land per person at midpt. | Implicit 1973–84 elasticity land w/r/t people at midpt. | Weisskoff comparable |
	1973 (1)	1984 (2)	Chge. pop. (3)	1973 (4)	1984 (5)	Chge. land (6)	(7)	(8)	(9)	(10)
Reynolds et al. (1990)										
1. MSA counties	5 785.2	8 206.9	2 421.8	1 445.1	2 499.9	1 054.9	0.4356	0.2819	**1.5449**	**0.6765** LEC
2. Non-MSA	610.0	911.0	301.0	240.5	641.7	401.2	1.3331	0.5800	**2.2983**	**1.4201** Okeechobee.
3. All Florida	6 395.1	9 117.9	2 722.7	1 685.6	3 141.6	1 456.1	0.5348	0.3112	**1.7186**	
South & Central:										
4. MSA							**0.3470**			**0.1067** LEC
5. Non-MSA							**0.6820**			**0.9031** Okeechobee.
North:										
6. MSA							0.8030			
7. Non-MSA							2.0260			
8. All Florida							0.5348			
Burchell et al. (1999)	1995	2020	Chge. pop	1995	2020	Chge. land				
9. LEC	4 398.0	6 590.0	2 192.0			231.9	**0.1058**			**0.1067**
10. UEC	285.0	465.0	180.0			79.2	0.4402			0.1592
Burchell et al. (2003)			(Sprawl scenario)							
11. Central GEER			2 509.8			438.9	**0.1749**			0.1067 LEC / **0.1592** UEC
12. Peripheral GEER			2 219.6			409.6	0.1845			0.2958 KSV / 0.9286 LWC
13. Total GEER			4 729.4			848.5	**0.1794**			**0.1264** All SF
14. Non-GEER			2 396.6			615.2	0.2567			n.c.
15. FL total			7 126.0			1 463.7	**0.2054**			**0.2220** All FL

0.3404 Martin
0.0636 St. Lucie

Burchell et al. (2002)			(2000–2025)			(2000–2025)	
16. Miami–Ft Laud. EA			1 744.7	246.2	**0.1411**	**0.1067**	LEC
17. Collier County	251.4	502.0	250.6	60.3	**0.2404**	**0.9286**	(LWC)
18. Broward County	1 623.0	2 416.9	793.9	52.5	**0.0661**	**0.0766**	Brow
19. PB County	863.5	1 746.0	882.5	49.0	0.0555	0.1085	PB

Sources and Methods:

Reynolds et al. (1990): Lines 1–3: Columns 1–7 are from Reynolds (1990), Table 2; lines 4–9, column 7 are given in his Table 3. Lines 4–5: South & Center include Planning Districts 6–11, which corresponds to 24 counties in Burchell's GEER. Reynolds, however, excludes Dade (now, Miami–Dade) and Monroe Counties. Lines 6–7: North includes Planning Districts 1–5, the northern half or non-GEER part of FL.

Burchell et al. (1999): Lines 9–10: Population summed from 6 components in each of 3 counties for LEC (omits Monroe) and 2 counties for UEC. Acreage from summing county totals, bottom lines, Table IV-J-1, p. 166. Burchell's projected population (people, households, employment), including seasonal population (Table II-S) by county, then placed these in 6 geographical areas (Eastward Ho, middle area, hurricane hazard, ag, conservation, or public area). He estimated the number of residential structures by type and county for existing (sprawl) and "compact" scenarios. He computed residential space based on needed housing units and non-residential space by converting employees space into building space. Available land was estimated in categories: vacant, agricultural, fragile, and other (p. 160). He computed roads, railroads, utility infrastructure (water, sewer), development cost saved by compact scenario over sprawl.

Burchell et al. (2003): Lines 11–15: Similar methodology to (1999) study. Population and employment are estimated and translated into new residential and non-residential "units" (Table 7), that are located in areas (inner, existing development, county peripheral, p. 19) and by type (single family detached: attached single-family, multi-family). New employment by 1-digit SIC category is translated into non-residential growth as office, industrial/warehouse, and retail space. Infrastructure and development costs are then computed. Line 11: Central GEER (Greater Everglades Ecosystem Region) includes 12 counties in Central, Treasure Coast, and South RPCs. These are compared here to the 8 lower counties (LEC, UEC) in this study. Line 12: Peripheral GEER includes 12 counties in East Central and SW RPCs, and are compared to 5 counties in LWC. Line 13: Burchell's Total GEER includes 24 counties, which include my 13 counties and 11 counties which I do not include. Weisskoff's comparables are computed from "missing pieces," moderate population, and land estimates for 2000–2030. Burchell's new population is from his Table 6 and his land acreage is from his Table 10. Weisskoff coefficients are from Table 4.1, this study.

Burchell et al. (2002): Line 16: Population computed for 10 counties from number of households, T. 5.17, and household size, Table 3.7 (S. Atlantic region). Acreage from Table 6.29. Lines 17–19: I used BEBR, fsa 2002, T. 1.20, 1.41 for county populations here, since Burchell gives only changes of "units" and acreage, his Table 6.33. Note that Miami–Ft Lauderdale EA covers 10 counties, larger than our LEC.

311

Appendix D

Table D.1   Threatened and Endangered Animals in South Florida

Listings found in South Florida (of the 57 species on federal listing for Florida)	Status	Sub-region of South Florida			
		LEC	LWC	KSV	UEC
1. Alligator, American (*Alligator mississippiensis*)	T(S/A)	x	x	x	x
2. Butterfly, Schaus swallowtail (*Heraclides aristodemus ponceanus*)	E	x			
3. Caracara, Audubon's crested (*Polyborus plancus audubonii*)	T	x	x	x	x
4. Crane, whooping USA (*Grus americana*)	XN			x	
5. Crocodile, American (*Crocodylus acutus*)	E	x	x		
6. Deer, key (*Odocoileus virginianus clavium*)	E	x			
7. Eagle, bald (*Haliaeetus leucocephalus*)	T	x	x	x	x
8. Jay, Florida scrub (*Aphelocoma coerulescens*)	T	x	x	x	x
9. Kite, Everglade snail (*Rostrhamus sociabilis plumbeus*)	E	x	x	x	x
10. Manatee, West Indian (*Trichechus manatus*)	E	x	x	x	x
11. Mouse, Key Largo cotton (*Peromyscus gossypinus allapaticola*)	E	x			
12. Mouse, St. Andrew beach (*Peromyscus polionotus peninsularis*)	E				x
13. Panther, Florida (*Puma (=Felis) concolor coryi*)	E	x	x	x	x
14. Plover, piping (*Charadrius melodus*)	T	x	x	x	x
15. Rabbit, Lower Keys marsh (*Sylvilagus palustris hefneri*)	E	x			
16. Rice rat (lower FL Keys) (*Oryzomys palustris natator*)	E	x			

Species		29	21	13	21
17. Sea turtle, green (*Chelonia mydas*)	T	x	x		x
18. Sea turtle, hawksbill (*Eretmochelys imbricata*)	E	x	x		x
19. Sea turtle, Kemp's ridley (*Lepidochelys kempii*)	E	x	x		x
20. Sea turtle, leatherback (*Dermochelys coriacea*)	E	x	x		x
21. Sea turtle, loggerhead (*Caretta caretta*)	T	x	x		x
22. Skink, bluetail mole (*Eumeces egregius lividus*)	T			x	
23. Skink, sand (*Neoseps reynoldsi*)	T			x	
24. Snail, Stock Island tree (*Orthalicus reses*, not incl. *nesodryas*)	T	x			x
25. Snake, Atlantic salt marsh (*Nerodia clarkii taeniata*)	T				
26. Snake, eastern indigo (*Drymarchon corais couperi*)	T	x	x	x	x
27. Sparrow, Cape Sable seaside (*Ammodramus maritimus mirabilis*)	E	x	x		
28. Sparrow, Florida grasshopper (*Ammodramus savannarum floridanus*)	E	x	x	x	
29. Stork, wood (*Mycteria americana*)	E	x	x	x	x
30. Tern, roseate (*Sterna dougallii dougallii*)	T	x		x	x
31. Whale, finback (*Balaenoptera physalus*)	E	x			x
32. Whale, humpback (*Megaptera novaeangliae*)	E	x	x		x
33. Whale, right (*Balaena glacialis* incl. *australis*)	E	x			x
34. Woodpecker, red-cockaded (*Picoides borealis*)	E	x	x	x	x
35. Woodrat, Key Largo (*Neotoma floridana smalli*)	E	x			x
Total number found in each sub-region		29	21	13	21

Method: Species on the county files, summed for our regions, from EnviroTools, Inc (1998) CD-ROM, were compared to the Florida listings of TESS, posted by the US Fish & Wildlife Service, wwww.fws.gov accessed 23 January 2003.

Table D.2 Threatened and Endangered Plants in South Florida

Listings found in South Florida (of the 57 species on federal listing for Florida)	Status	Sub-region of South Florida			
		LEC	LWC	KSV	UEC
1. Lead-plant, Crenulate (Amorpha crenulata)	E	x			
2. Pawpaw, four-petal (Asimina tetramera)	E				x
3. Bonamia, Florida (Bonamia grandiflora)	T			x	
4. Prickly-apple, fragrant (Cereus eriophorus var. fragrans)	E	x			x
5. Spurge, deltoid (Chamaesyce deltoidea ssp. deltoidea)	E	x			
6. Spurge, Garber's (Chamaesyce garberi)	T	x			
7. Fringe-tree, pygmy (Chionanthus pygmaeus)	E			x	
8. Cladonia, Florida perforate (Cladonia perforata)	E			x	x
9. Pigeon wings (Clitoria fragrans)	T			x	
10. Rosemary, short-leaved (Conradina brevifolia)	E			x	
11. Harebells, Avon Park (Crotalaria avonensis)	E			x	
12. Gourd, Okeechobee (Cucurbita okeechobeensis ssp. okeechobeensis)	E		x		
13. Pawpaw, beautiful (Deeringothamnus pulchellus)	E		x		
14. Mint, Garrett's (Dicerandra christmanii)	E			x	
15. Mint, scrub (Dicerandra frutescens)	E			x	
16. Mint, Lakela's (Dicerandra immaculata)	E				x

#	Species	Status				
17.	Buckwheat, scrub (*Eriogonum longifolium* var. *gnaphalifolium*)	T			x	
18.	Snakeroot (*Eryngium cuneifolium*)	E			x	
19.	Milkpea, Small's (*Galactia smallii*)	E	x			
20.	Seagrass, Johnson's (*Halophila johnsonii*)	T	x			
21.	Hypericum, highlands scrub (*Hypericum cumulicola*)	E			x	
22.	Jacquemontia, beach (*Jacquemontia reclinata*)	E	x			
23.	Blazingstar, scrub (*Liatris ohlingerae*)	E			x	
24.	Beargrass, Britton's (*Nolina brittoniana*)	E			x	
25.	Whitlow-wort, papery (*Paronychia chartacea*)	T			x	
26.	Polygala, Lewton's (*Polygala lewtonii*)	E			x	
27.	Polygala, tiny (*Polygala smallii*)	E	x			x
28.	Wireweed (*Polygonella basiramia*)	E			x	
29.	Sandlace (*Polygonella myriophylla*)	E			x	
30.	Plum, scrub (*Prunus geniculata*)	E			x	
31.	Chaffseed, American (*Chwalbea americana*)	E			x	
32.	Warea, wide-leaf (*Warea amplexifolia*)	E			x	
33.	Mustard, Carter's (*Warea carteri*)	E		x	x	
34.	Ziziphus, Florida (*Ziziphus celata*)	E			x	
	Total number found in each sub-region:		9	3	22	7

Method: See notes to Table D.1.

315

Appendix E

Table E.1   Sub-Regions of South Florida: Historical Growth, 1970–2000 and Projections, 2010–2030

	Historical				Projections			Annual growth rate for period					
								Historical			Projections		
	1970	1980	1990	2000	2010	2020	2030	1970–1980	1980–1990	1990–2000	2000–2010	2010–2020	2020–2030
	(1)	(2)	(3)	(4)	(5)	(6)	(7)	(8)	(9)	(10)	(11)	(12)	(13)
1. Population by sub-region (thou.)													
LEC	2 289	3 284	4 134	5 090	6 159	7 055	7 807	3.68	2.33	2.10	1.92	1.37	1.02
LWC	159	316	521	739	1 135	1 395	1 586	7.11	5.13	3.56	4.38	2.08	1.29
KSV	66	117	206	296	409	489	557	5.89	5.82	3.69	3.29	1.80	1.31
UEC	79	151	251	319	451	537	602	6.69	5.21	2.43	3.52	1.76	1.15
ROF	4 198	5 879	7 826	9 538	12 846	15 116	16 971	3.43	2.90	2.00	3.02	1.64	1.16
SF	2 593	3 868	5 112	6 444	8 156	9 482	10 559	4.08	2.83	2.34	2.38	1.52	1.08
FL	6 791	9 747	12 938	15 982	21 002	24 598	27 530	3.68	2.87	2.14	2.77	1.59	1.13
2. Output by subregion (bill. $92)													
LEC	65.0	103.6	141.7	190.4	260.7	294.6	341.3	8.01	5.96	3.93	3.63	1.19	1.52
LWC	3.7	7.9	14.1	20.7	29.6	33.3	38.7	7.76	7.07	3.87	3.10	1.42	1.63
KSV	0.9	1.8	3.6	5.2	7.0	8.1	9.5	8.68	4.95	2.71	3.26	1.06	1.40
UEC	1.6	3.6	5.9	7.7	10.6	11.8	13.6	5.06	4.98	3.38	3.37	1.31	1.58
ROF	85.7	140.5	228.5	318.7	443.8	505.6	591.2	5.10	3.52	3.09	3.23	1.22	1.49
SF	71.1	116.9	165.3	224.1	308.0	347.9	403.2						
FL	156.8	257.4	393.8	542.8	751.8	853.5	994.4	5.08	4.34	3.26	3.31	1.28	1.54

3. Output per capita by subregion ($92)

	1970	1980	1990	2000	2010	2020	2030	Each year as ratio to LEC base					
								1970	1980	1990	2010	2020	2030
LEC	28 158	31 205	34 127	38 329	43 520	43 702	46 413	1.00	1.00	1.00	1.00	1.00	1.00
LWC	22 567	24 655	26 788	28 146	29 124	27 927	29 584	0.80	0.79	0.78	0.67	0.64	0.64
KSV	12 638	15 034	17 019	17 878	18 432	18 346	19 530	0.45	0.48	0.50	0.42	0.42	0.42
UEC	19 914	23 730	23 251	23 320	24 816	23 916	25 260	0.71	0.76	0.68	0.57	0.55	0.54
ROF	20 276	23 704	29 014	32 521	35 870	35 500	37 661	0.72	0.76	0.85	0.82	0.81	0.81
SF	27 162	29 882	32 144	35 419	39 396	39 213	41 609	0.96	0.96	0.94	0.91	0.90	0.90
FL	22 908	26 160	30 250	33 658	37 235	36 925	39 168	0.81	0.84	0.89	0.86	0.84	0.84

4. Employment by subregion (thou.)

	1970	1980	1990	2000	2010	2020	2030	Annual growth rate for period					
								1970	1980	1990	2010	2020	2030
LEC	1 079	1 703	2 222	2 731	3 281	3 386	3 581	4.67	2.69	2.08	1.85	0.32	0.56
LWC	72	154	274	375	483	509	549	7.89	5.90	3.19	2.57	0.52	0.75
KSV	23	45	82	107	131	140	152	6.78	6.24	2.75	2.02	0.66	0.82
UEC	33	69	111	138	174	180	192	7.57	4.90	2.19	2.34	0.34	0.61
ROF	1 759	2 735	4 129	5 217	6 404	6 725	7 226	4.52	4.20	2.37	2.07	0.49	0.72
SF	1 208	1 971	2 689	3 352	4 070	4 216	4 474	5.02	3.15	2.23	1.96	0.35	0.60
FL	2 967	4 707	6 818	8 569	10 473	10 941	11 699	4.72	3.78	2.31	2.03	0.44	0.67

5. Econ migrants by subregion (thou.)

	1970	1980	1990	2000	2010	2020	2030	As % of employment in sub-region and year					
								1970	1980	1990	2010	2020	2030
LEC	0	21.0	53.8	56.8	64.6	1.1	1.2	—	1.23	2.42	1.97	0.03	0.03
LWC	0	6.6	20.4	22.3	19.3	0.1	-0.6	—	4.30	7.45	3.99	0.03	-0.11
KSV	0	2.1	8.3	7.4	5.1	0.2	0.3	—	4.60	10.13	3.88	0.14	0.22
UEC	0	4.8	8.4	6.6	6.2	-0.8	-2.1	—	6.95	7.56	3.58	-0.42	-1.09
ROF	0	38.0	140.4	169.7	166.2	22.9	22.3	—	1.39	3.40	2.59	0.34	0.31
SF	0	34.4	91.0	93.2	95.2	0.6	-1.2	—	1.75	3.38	2.34	0.02	-0.03

Sources and Methods: For 1970–2000, line 1, population, is from Census; lines 2, 4, 5 are from REMI regional control. For 2010–2030, lines 1, 2, 4, 5 are from REMI runs of Weisskoff, medium projections. Line 3 is line 2 divided by line 1.

Appendix F

Table F.1   REMI and IMPLAN Sectors and their SIC Codes: A "Cross-Walk"

REMI sector name	SIC codes	IMPLAN sector no.
1. Durables	24, 25, 32–39	133–160, 230–432
2. Non-durables	20–23, 26–31	58–132, 161–229
3. Mining	10, 12–14	28–47
4. Construction	15–17	48–57
5. Transport, Public Utilities (incl. air, shipping, truck)	40–42, 44–49	433–446
6. Finance/Insurance/Real Estate (FIRE!)	61–65, 67	456–462
7. Retail Trade (incl. eating and drinking)	52–59	448–455
8. Wholesale Trade	50–51	447
9. Services (incl. hotels, personal, auto, business, recreational, medical, other professional, educational services, and other non-profit organizations)	70–89	463–509, 522
10. Agricultural, Forestry, Fishing Services	07–09	24–27
11. State and Local Government		510–512, 523
12. Federal Government (civilian)		513–515, 520–521
13. Federal Government (military)		519
14. Farm		1–23

Sources: Aligned from REMI (1999) and Minnesota IMPLAN Group (1999), Appendix A.

Bibliography

Alvarez, Jose (1978), *Potential for Commercial Rice Production in the Everglades*, Economics Information Report 98, Gainesville: Agricultural Experimental Station, Institute of Food and Agricultural Sciences, University of Florida.

Alvarez, Jose and George H. Snyder (1984), 'Effect of prior rice culture on sugarcane yields in Florida,' *Field Crops Research*, **9**, 315–21.

Alvarez, Jose, George H. Snyder, and D.B. Jones (1989), 'The integrated program approach in the development of the Florida rice industry,' *Journal of Agronomic Education*, **18** (1), 6–11.

Anderson, David L. and Peter C. Rosendahl (1997), 'The development and application of environmental policy: South Florida, the Everglades, and the Florida sugar industry,' in B.A. Keating and J.R. Wilson (eds), *Intensive Sugarcane Production: Meeting the Challenges Beyond 2000*, Wallingford, UK: CAB International, pp. 381–402.

Anderson, David L. and Peter C. Rosendahl (1998), 'Development and management of land/water resources: the Everglades, agriculture, and South Florida' *Journal of the American Water Resources Association*, **34** (2), 235–49.

Bacchus, Sydney T. (2002), 'The "ostrich" component of the multiple stressor model: undermining South Florida,' in James W. Porter and Karen G. Porter (eds), *The Everglades, Florida Bay, and Coral Reefs of the Florida Keys: An Ecosystem Sourcebook*, Boca Raton, FL: CRC Press, pp. 677–748.

Baumann, Duane D., John J. Boland, and W. Michael Hamemann (1998), *Urban Water Demand Management and Planning*, New York: McGraw Hill.

Beach, Dana (2002), *Coastal Sprawl: The Effects of Urban Design on Aquatic Eco-systems in the United States*, Arlington, VA: Pew Oceans Commission.

Biscayne Bay Partnership Initiative (2000), *Social and Economic Team Report*, Miami, FL: BBPI.

Blake, Nelson Manfred (1980), *Land into Water – Water into Land: A History of Water Management in Florida*, Tallahassee: University Presses of Florida.

Bosselman, Fred P., Craig A. Peterson, and Claire McCarthy (1999), *Managing Tourism Growth: Issues and Applications*, Washington, DC and Covelo, CA: Island Press.

Bottcher, A.B. and F.T. Izuno (1994), *Everglades Agricultural Area (EAA): Water, Soil Crop, and Environmental Management*, Gainesville, FL: University Press of Florida.

Brown, Lester R. (2001), *Eco-Economy: Building an Economy for the Earth*, New York: W.W. Norton.

Brown and Caldwell Consultants (1999), *Water Price Elasticity Study*, Brooksville, FL: Southwest Florida Water Management District.

Buffalo Tiger and Harry A. Kersey, Jr. (2002), *Buffalo Tiger, A Life in the Everglades*, Lincoln, NE: University of Nebraska Press.

Burchell, Robert W., Nancy Neuman, Alex Zakrewsky, and Stephanie E. DiPetrillo (1999), *Eastward Ho! Development Futures: Paths to More Efficient Growth in Southeast Florida*, Tallahassee, FL: Department of Community Affairs.

Burchell, Robert W., G. Lowenstein, W.R. Dolphin, C.C. Galley, A. Downs, S. Seskin, K.G. Still, and T. Moore (2002), *Costs of Sprawl – 2000,* Transit Cooperative Research Program TCRP Report 74, Washington, DC: National Academy Press.

Burchell, Robert W., William R. Dolphin, and Sahan Mukherji (2003), *Projected Development in the GEER (Greater Everglades Ecosystem Restoration) Region and Potential Resource Savings by Employing a Compact Development Growth Regimen*, New Brunswick, NJ: Rutgers University, Center for Urban Policy Research.

Bureau of Economic Analysis (BEA) (1997), 'State Projections of Employment, Earnings, and Product,' http://www.bea.doc.gov/gsp/gspdata/.

Bureau of Economic and Business Research (BEBR) (1998b), 'Number of Households and Average Household Size in Florida, April 1, 1997,' *Florida Population Studies* Vol. 30, No. 3, Bulletin 120, Gainesville, FL.

Bureau of Economic and Business Research (BEBR) (1998c), 'Projections of Florida Population by County in the Years 1997–2020,' *Florida Population Studies* Vol. 31, No. 1, Bulletin 119, Gainesville, FL.

Bureau of Economic and Business Research (BEBR) (2002a), *Florida Long-Term Economic Forecast 2002*, Vol. 1: State and MSAs; Vol. 2: State and Counties, Gainesville, FL: BEBR.

Bureau of Economic and Business Research (BEBR) (2002b), *2002 Florida Statistical Abstract*, Gainesville, FL: BEBR.

Bureau of Economic and Business Research (BEBR) (2003), *Building Permit Activity in Florida,* Monthly Cumulative Totals (diskette).

Burns and McDonnell, Inc. (1994), *Everglades Protection Project, Palm Beach County, Fla.* 'Conceptual Design,' (February 15), Kansas City, Mo.

Carson, Rachel (1998), *Lost Woods: The Discovered Writing of Rachel Carson*, Linda Lear (ed.), Boston: Beacon Press.

Catanese Center for Urban and Environmental Solutions (2004), *Regional Shift: South Florida in Transition,* Ft Lauderdale, FL: Florida Atlantic University.

City of Miami (1992), *Miami River Master Plan* (January), Miami, FL: Department of Planning, Building & Zoning.

Cleo, Frank and Hank Mesouf (1964), *Florida: Polluted Paradise*, Philadelphia: Chilton Books.

Congress for the New Urbanism (2000), *Charter of the New Urbanism*, New York: McGraw-Hill.

Congress for the New Urbanism (2001), *Greyfields into Goldfields: Dead Malls Become Living Neighborhoods*, San Francisco, CA: CNU.

Congress for the New Urbanism (2002), *A Guidebook to New Urbanism in Florida*, Prepared for the Tenth Congress for the New Urbanism in Miami Beach, Ft Lauderdale and Miami, FL: Anthony James Catanese Center for Urban & Environmental Solutions and University of Miami School of Architecture.

Conservation Fund (1994), *Sustainable Everglades Initiative. Strategic Issues Assessment: Environmental, Economic, and Social*, Report prepared for the John D. and Catherine T. MacArthur Foundation.

Costanza, Robert, R. D'Arge, R. De Groot, S. Farber, M. Grasso, B. Hannon, K. Limburg, S. Naeem, R.V. O'Neill, J. Paruelo, R.G. Raskin, P. Sutton, and M. van den Belt (1997), 'The value of the world's ecosystem services and natural capital,' *Nature*, **387**, 253-60.

Crompton, John L. (2000), *The Impact of Parks and Open Space on Property Values and the Property Tax Base*, www.wrpts.tamu.edu/rpts/faculty/crompton.htm, Texas A&M University.

Daly, Herman E. (1999), 'Uneconomic growth and the built environment: in theory and in fact,' in Charles J. Kibert (ed.), *Reshaping the Built Environment: Ecology, Ethics, and Economics*, Washington, DC and Covelo, CA: Island Press, pp. 73–86.

Daly, Herman E. and Kenneth N. Townsend (eds) (1993), *Valuing the Earth: Economics, Ecology*, Ethics, Cambridge, MA: MIT Press.

Daly, Herman E. and John B. Cobb, Jr. (1994), *For the Common Good: Redirecting the Economy Toward Community, the Environment, and a Sustainable Future*, 2nd edn, Boston: Beacon Press.

Davis, Steven M. and John C. Ogden (eds) (1994), *Everglades: The Ecosystem and Its Restoration*, Boca Raton, FL: St Lucie Press.

DeAngelis, Donald L., L.J. Gross, M.A. Huston, W.F. Wolff, D.M. Fleming, E.J. Comiskey, and S.M. Sylvester (1998), 'Landscape modeling for Everglades ecosystem restoration,' *Ecosystems*, **1**, 64–75.

Degner, Robert L., Susan D. Moss, and W. David Mulkey (1997), *Economic Impact of Agriculture and Agribusiness in Dade County, Florida*, FAMRC Industry Report 97-1, Gainesville, FL: Food and Resource Economics Department, Institute of Food and Agricultural Sciences, University of Florida.

Deren C.W., G.H. Snyder, J.D. Miller, and P.S. Porter (1991), 'Screening for heritability of flood-tolerance in the Florida (CP) sugarcane breeding population,' *Euphytica*, **56**, 155–160.

Deren, C.W., B. Glaz, and G.H. Snyder (1995), 'Wetland agriculture in the Everglades: a concept for sustaining agriculture and the ecosystem,' in Kenneth L. Campbell (ed.), *Versatility of Wetlands in the Agricultural Landscape*, American Society of Agricultural Engineers Conference Volume.

Derr, Mark (1989), *Some Kind of Paradise: A Chronicle of Man and the Land in Florida*, New York: William Morrow.

Dixon, John A. and Paul B. Sherman (1990), *Economics of Protected Areas: A New Look at Benefits and Costs*, Washington DC and Covelo, CA: Island Press.

Douglas, Marjory Stoneman (1947), *The Everglades: River of Grass*, revised edition (1988), Sarasota, FL: Pineapple Press.

Douglas, Marjory Stoneman (1958), *Hurricane*, New York: Rinehart & Co.

Douglas, Marjory Stoneman (1987), *Voice of the River: An Autobiography*, Sarastoa, FL: Pineapple Press.

Douglas, Marjory Stoneman (1990), *Nine Florida Stories*, Kevin M. McCarthy (ed.), Jacksonville, FL: University of North Florida Press.

Doyle, Mary and Donald E. Jodrey (2002), 'Everglades restoration: forging new law in allocating water for the environment,' *The Environmental Lawyer*, **8** (2), 255–302.

Duchin Faye and Glenn-Marie Lange (1994), *The Future of the Environment: Ecological Economics and Technological Change*, New York: Oxford University Press.

Duplaix, Nicole (1990), 'South Florida water: paying the price,' *National Geographic*, **178** (1), 89–114.

Englehardt, James D. (1996), *Benefit-Risk Analysis of Everglades Stormwater Treatment Area Phase I Discharge Alternatives*, Washington, DC: US EPA.

English, Donald B.K., Warren Kriesel, Vernon R. Leeworthy and Peter C. Wiley (1996), 'Economic contribution of recreating visitors to the Florida Keys/Key West,' *Linking the Economy and Environment of Florida Keys/Florida Bay* (November), Silver Spring, MD: National Oceanic and Atmospheric Administration (NOAA).

EnviroTools Inc. (1998), *Threatened and Endangered Species Software (TESS)*, CD-ROM, Gainesville, FL.

Fernald, Edward A. and Donald J. Patton (eds) (1984), *Water Resources Atlas of Florida*, Tallahassee, FL: Institute of Science and Public Affairs, Florida State University.

Fernald, Edward A. and Elizabeth D. Purdum (eds) (1996), *Atlas of Florida*, Gainesville, FL: University Press of Florida.

Fernald, Edward A. and Elizabeth D. Purdum (eds) (1998), *Water Resources Atlas of Florida*, Tallahassee, FL: Institute of Science and Public Affairs, Florida State University.

Florida Agricultural Statistics Service (FASS) (2001), *Florida Agricultural Statistics: Vegetable Summary*, Tallahassee, FL: Florida Department of Agriculture and Consumer Services.

Florida Agricultural Statistics Service (FASS) (2002), *Citrus Summary 2000–2001*, Tallahassee, FL: Florida Department of Agriculture and Consumer Services.

Florida Council of 100 (2003), *Improving Florida's Water Supply Management Structure: Ensuring and Sustaining Environmentally Sound Water Supplies and Resources to Meet Current and Future Needs*, Tampa, FL. (September).

Florida Department of Labor and Employment Security, Office of Labor Market Statistics (2000), *Florida Industry and Occupational Employment Projections to 2007*, Tallahassee, FL.

Florida Department of Transportation, State Topographic Bureau, Thematic Mapping Section (1985), *Florida Land Use, Cover and Forms Classification System* (September), West Palm Beach, FL: South Florida Water Management District.

Florida Fish and Wildlife Conservation Commission (2000), *Monetary Value of Nature: An Economic Impact Assessment of Three Lakes Wildlife Management Area Osceola County, Florida* (August) Tallahassee, FL.

Florida Fish and Wildlife Conservation Commission and National Oceanic Atmospheric Administration (2001), *Socioeconomic Study of Reefs in Southeast Florida*, Hollywood, FL: Hazen and Sawyer.

Foresta, Ronald A. (1984), *America's National Parks and Their Keepers*, Washington, DC: Resources for the Future.

Fulton, George A. and Donald R. Grimes (2001), *The Economic Outlook for Wayne County in 2001–2003* (October), Ann Arbor, MI: Institute of Labor and Industrial Relations, University of Michigan.

Galbraith, John Kenneth (1954), *The Great Crash 1929*, 2nd edn (1961), Boston: Houghton Mifflin.

Gannon, Michael (1993), *Florida: A Short History*, Gainesville, FL: University Press of Florida.

Garreau, Joel (1981), *The Nine Nations of North America*, Boston: Houghton Mifflin Co.

Garrett, Laurie (1994), *The Coming Plague: Newly Emerging Diseases in a World Out of Balance*, New York: Penguin Books.

Gee and Jenson, Inc. (1996), *Lower East Coast Regional Conveyance Alternatives*. Prepared for the South Florida Water Management District.

George, Jean Craighead (1983), *The Talking Earth*, New York: HarperCollins.

George, Jean Craighead (1992), *The Missing 'Gator of Gumbo Limbo: An Ecological Mystery*, New York: HarperCollins.

Glaz, Barry (1995), 'Research seeking agricultural and ecological benefits in the Everglades,' *Journal of Soil and Water Conservation*, **50** (6), 609–12.

Glennon, Robert (2002), *Water Follies: Groundwater Pumping and the Fate of America's Fresh Waters,* Washington, DC and Covelo, CA: Island Press.

Governor's Commission for a Sustainable South Florida (1995), *Initial Report* (October 1), Coral Gables, FL.

Governor's Commission for a Sustainable South Florida (1996), *A Conceptual Plan for the C&SF Project Restudy* (August 28), Coral Gables, FL.

Governor's Commission for a Sustainable South Florida (1998), *A Report on Full Cost Accounting* (December 19), Coral Gables, FL.

Greater Fort Lauderdale Convention and Visitors Bureau (various years), *Year-End Tourism Marketing Research,* Ft Lauderdale, FL.

Greenways, Inc. (2001), *Miami River Greenway Action Plan,* Miami, FL: Trust for Public Land.

Gulf Engineers and Consultants (1996), *Municipal and Industrial (M&I) Water Use Forecast, Lake Okeechobee Regulation Schedule Study (LORSS),* Jacksonville, FL: US Army Corps of Engineers.

Gulf Engineers and Consultants (2003), *Municipal and Industrial (M&I) Water Use Forecast, Comprehensive Everglades Restoration Plan (CERP) Forecast Update,* Jacksonville, FL: US Army Corps of Engineers (March).

Gunderson, Lance H. (2001), 'Managing surprising ecosystems in southern Florida,' *Ecological Economics,* **37** (3), 371–8.

Grunwald, Michael (2002), 'Series on the Everglades,' *Washington Post,* June 23–26, 2002.

Hagelberg, G.B. (1974), *The Caribbean Sugar Industries: Constraints and Opportunities,* Occasional Paper 3, New Haven, CT: Antilles Research Program, Yale University.

Harnik, Peter (2000), *Inside City Parks,* Washington, DC: Urban Land Institute.

Haydu, John J. and Alan W. Hodges (2002), *Economic Impacts of the Florida Golf Course Industry,* Economic Information Report EIRO2-4, Gainesville, FL: IFAS.

Hazen and Sawyer (1992), *Economic Benefit Evaluation of Everglades Restoration and Preservation,* West Palm Beach, FL: South Florida Water Management District.

Hazen and Sawyer (1993), *Twenty Year Evaluation: Economic Impacts from Implementing the Marjory Stoneman Douglas Everglades Restoration Act and the US vs. SFWMD Settlement Agreement,* West Palm Beach, FL: South Florida Water Management District.

Hazen and Sawyer (1996), *Full Cost Evaluation Methodology for Public Water Supply in Northern Tampa Bay,* Brooksville, FL: Southwest Florida Water Management District.

Hazen and Sawyer (1997), *Economic Incentive Approaches to Water Resource Management,* Brooksville, FL: Southwest Florida Water Management District.

Hazen and Sawyer (1998), *National Audubon Society Report on the Status and Preservation of the Agricultural Industry in South Florida,* Hollywood, FL.

Hazen and Sawyer (2001), *Socioeconomic Study of Reefs in Southeast Florida, Final Report for Broward County, Palm Beach County, Miami-Dade County, Monroe County, Florida Fish and Wildlife Conservation Commission, and the National Oceanic and Atmospheric Administration,* posted on www.noaa.gov/research.html.

Hendrickson, Chris, A. Horvath, S. Joshi, and L. Lave (1998), 'Economic input-output models for environmental life cycle assessment,' *Environmental Science and Technology,* **32** (7), pp. 184A–191A.

Hodges, Alan W. and John J. Haydu (1999), *Economic Impact of Florida's Environmental Horticulture Industry, 1997*, Economic Information Report EIR 99-1, Gainesville, FL: IFAS, University of Florida.

Hodges, Alan W., W. David Mulkey, and Effie Philppakos (2000), *Economic Impacts of Florida's Agricultural and Natural Resource Industries*, EIR 00-4, Gainesville, FL: IFAS, University of Florida.

Hodges, Alan W., Effie Philippakos, David Mulkey, Tom Spreen, and Ron Muraro (2001), *Economic Impact of Florida's Citrus Industry, 1999–2000*, EIR 01-2, Gainesville, FL: IFAS, University of Florida.

Horvath, Arpad and C. Hendrickson (1998), 'A comparison of the environmental implications of asphalt and steel-reinforced concrete pavements,' Transport Research Board, Washington, DC (January).

Hymans, Saul H., Joan P. Crary, and Janel C. Wolfe (2001), *The US Economic Outlook for 2002–2003*, Ann Arbor, MI: Research Seminar in Quantitative Economics, University of Michigan.

Institute for Environmental Modeling and US Geological Survey (1998), *Across Trophic Level System Simulation (ATLSS) Model Outputs for the Central and Southern Florida Comprehensive Study Review*, Knoxville, TN: University of Tennessee.

Institute for Water Resources (1994), *Analyzing Employment Effects of Stream Restoration Investments*, The Federal Infrastructure Strategy Program, US EPA and the US Army Corps of Engineers, IWR Report 94-FIS-18 (November).

Izuno, F.T. and L.T. Capone (1995), 'Strategies for protecting Florida's Everglades: the best management practices approach,' *Water Science and Technology*, **31** (8), pp. 123–81.

Izuno, F.T., R.W. Rice, and L.T. Capone (1999), 'Best management practices to enable the coexistence of agriculture and the Everglades environment,' *HortScience*, **34** (1), 27–33.

Jacobs, Jennifer M. and Sudheer Reedy Satti (2001), *Evaluation of Reference Evapotranspiration Methodologies and AFSIRS Crop Water Use Simulation Model*, Palatka, FL: St Johns River Water Management District (April).

Johnson, Lamar (1974), *Beyond the Fourth Generation*, Gainesville, FL: University Press of Florida.

Juarez-Espinosa, Octavio, J. Garrett, and C. Hendrickson (1997), 'A software tool for economic input–output life-cycle assessment,' Green Design Initiative, Dept. of Civil and Environmental Engineering, Carnegie-Mellon University.

Keasler, John (1958), *Surrounded on Three Sides*, reprinted (1999), Gainesville, FL: University Press of Florida.

Kelbaugh, Douglas (1997), *Common Place: Toward Neighborhood and Regional Design*, Seattle, WA: University of Washington Press.

Kiker, Clyde F. J. Walter Milo, and Alan W. Hodges (2001), 'Adaptive learning for science-based policy: the Everglades restoration,' *Ecological Economics*, **37** (3), 403–16.

Kimberley-Horn and Associates (2002), *Miami River Corridor Urban Infill Plan* (June), Miami, FL.

Lakshmanan, T.R and Roger Bolton (1986), 'Regional energy and environmental analysis,' in Peter Nijkamp (ed.), *Handbook of Regional and Urban Economics*, Amsterdam: Elsevier, pp. 581–628.

Landell Mills Commodities Studies (1994), *The Importance of the Sugar and Corn Sweentener Industry to the US Economy*, New York, for the American Sugar Alliance.

Lave, Lester B., E. Cobas-Flores, C. Hendrickson, and F. McMichael (1995), 'Life-cycle assessment: using input–output analysis to estimate economy-wide discharges,' *Environmental Science and Technology*, **29** (9), 420–26.

Leach Stanley (1978), *Map of Freshwater Use in Florida, 1975*, Tallahassee, FL: US Geological Survey.

Leeworthy, Vernon R. and J.M. Bowker (1997), 'Nonmarket economic user values of the Florida Keys/Key West,' *Linking the Economy and Environment of Florida Keys/Florida Bay* (Oct.), Silver Spring, MD: National Oceanic and Atmospheric Administration (NOAA).

Leeworthy, Vernon R. and Patrick Vanasse (1999), 'Economic contribution of recreating visitors to the Florida Keys/Key West: updates for years 1996–97 and 1997–98,' *Linking the Economy and Environment of Florida Keys/Florida Bay* (June), Silver Spring, MD: National Oceanic and Atmospheric Administration (NOAA).

Leeworthy, Vernon R. and Peter C. Wiley (1997), 'A socioeconomic analysis of the recreation activities of Monroe County residents in the Florida Keys/Key West,' *Linking the Economy and Environment of Florida Keys/Florida Bay* (August), Silver Spring, MD: National Oceanic and Atmospheric Administration (NOAA).

Leontief, Wassily (1970), 'Environmental repercussions and the economic structure: an input-output approach,' *Review of Economics and Statistics*, **52** (3), 262–71, reprinted in W. Leontief (1986), *Input–Output Economics*, New York: Oxford University Press (2nd edn), pp. 241–72.

Leontief, Wassily and D. Ford (1972), 'Air pollution and the economic structure: empirical result of input–output computations,' in A. Brody and A.P. Carter (eds), *Input-Output Techniques*, Amsterdam: North-Holland, pp. 9–30, reprinted in W. Leontief (1986), *Input–Output Economics*, New York: Oxford University Press (2nd edn), pp. 273–93.

Leontief, Wassily, Ann P. Carter, and Peter A. Petri (1977), *The Future of the World Economy*, New York: Oxford University Press.

Letson, David and J. Walter Milon (2002), *Florida Coastal Environmental Resources: A Guide to Economic Valuation and Impact Analysis*, Gainesville, FL: Florida Sea Grant College Program, University of Florida.

Light, Stephen S. and J. Walter Dineen (1994), 'Water Control in the Everglades: a historical perspective,' in Steven M. Davis and John C. Ogden (eds), *The Everglades: The Ecosystem and Its Restoration*, Boca Raton, FL: St Lucie Press, pp. 47–84.

Light, Stephen S., Lance H. Gunderson, and C.S. Holling (1995), 'The Everglades: evolution of management in a turbulent ecosystem,' in Lance H. Gunderson, C.S. Holling, and Stephen S. Light (eds), *Barriers and Bridges to the Renewal of Ecosystems and Institutions*, New York: Columbia University Press, pp. 102–68.

Lissakers, Karin (1991), *Banks, Borrowers, and the Establishment: A Revisionist Account of the International Debt Crisis*, New York: Basic Books.

Lodge, Thomas E. (1998), *The Everglades Handbook: Understanding the Ecosystem*, Boca Raton, FL: St Lucie Press.

Lynch, Thomas A., Neil Sipe, Steven E. Polzin, and Xuehao Chu (1997), *An Analysis of the Economic Impacts of Florida High Speed Rail*, Tallahassee, FL: Institute of Science and Public Affairs, Florida State University.

Mairson, Alan (1994), 'The Everglades: dying for help,' *National Geographic*, **185** (4), 2–35.

Marella, Richard L. (1982), *Map of Estimated Water Use in Florida, 1980*, Tallahassee, FL: US Geological Survey.

Marella, Richard L. (1989), *Map of Freshwater Withdrawals and Water-Use Trends in Florida, 1985*, Tallahassee, FL: US Geological Survey.

Marella, Richard L. (1992), *Factors that Affect Public-Supply Water Use in Florida, with a Section on Projected Water Use to the Year 2020*, Water-Resources Investigations Report 91-4123, Tallahassee, FL: US Geological Survey.

Marella, Richard L. (1995), *Water-Use Data by Category, County, and Water Management District in Florida, 1950–90*, Open-File Report 94-521, Tallahassee, FL: U.S. Geological Survey.

Marella, Richard L. (1997a), *Map of Irrigated Crop Acreage and Water Withdrawals in Florida, 1990*, Tallahassee, FL: US Geological Survey.

Marella, Richard L. (1997b), *Map of Freshwater Withdrawals and Water-Use Trends in Florida, 1990*, Tallahassee, FL: US Geological Survey.

Marella, Richard L. (1999), *Water Withdrawals, Use, Discharge, and Trends in Florida, 1995*, Water-Resources Investigations Report 99-4002, Tallahassee, FL: US Geological Survey.

Marella, Richard L. (2000), *Map of Freshwater Withdrawals and Water-Use Trends in Florida, 1995*, Tallahassee, FL: US Geological Survey.

Marella, Richard L., Michael F. Mokray, and Michael Hallock-Solomon (1998), *Water Use Trends and Demand Projections in the Northwest Floirda Water Management District*, Open-File Report 98-269, Tallahassee, FL: US Geological Survey.

Matthiessen, Peter (1991), *Killing Mister Watson*, New York: Vintage Books.

McCally, David (1999), *The Everglades: An Environmental History*, Gainesville, FL: University Press of Florida.

McCluney, William R. (ed.) (1969), *The Environmental Destruction of South Florida*, Coral Gables, FL: University of Miami Press.

McLarty, Carol L. and Janet Galvez (1994), 'A profile of Florida's temporary residents', *Economic Leaflets*, **53** (12), 1–6, Gainesville, FL: BEBR.

Metropolitan Dade County (1962), *A Planning Study of the Miami River* (April), Miami, FL: Planning Department.

Miami-Dade County Lake Belt Plan Implementation Committee (1999), *1999 Progress Report*, West Palm Beach, FL: SFWMD.

Miami Downtown Development Authority (DDA) (2004a), *DDA District Projects Breakdown Report*, Miami, FL (dated 10/7/04).

Miami Downtown Development Authority (DDA) (2004b), *District Developments Presentation* (CD-ROM), Miami, FL (dated October).

Miernyk, William H., K.L. Shellhammer, D. M. Brown, R.L. Coccari, C.J. Gallagher, and W.H. Wineman (1970), *Simulating Regional Economic Development: An Interindustry Analysis of the West Virginia Economy*, Lexington, MA: Heath Lexington Books.

Mill, John Stuart (1871), *Principles of Political Economy* (reprinted 1909), London: Longmans, Green & Co.

Milon, J. Walter, Alan W. Hodges, Arbindra Rimal, Clyde F. Kiker, and Frank Casey (1999), *Public Preferences and Economic Values for Restoration of the Everglades/South Florida Ecosystem*, (August) Economics Report 99-1, Gainesville, FL: Food & Resource Economics Department, University of Florida.

Mines, Samuel (1971), *The Last Days of Mankind: Ecological Survival or Extinction*, New York: Simon and Schuster. See chapter 3, 'The Everglades,' pp. 66–88.

Minnesota IMPLAN Group Inc. (1999), *IMPLAN Professional Version 2.0 Social Accounting & Impact Analysis Software*, Stillwater, MN.

Mintz, Sidney W. (1985), *Sweetness and Power: The Place of Sugar in Modern History*, New York: Penguin Books.

Moseley, Anne E. (1990), *Economic Impact of Agriculture and Agribusiness in Dade County, Florida*, Gainesville, FL: Food and Resource Economics Dept., for the Special Agricultural Advisory Committee and the Dade County Farm Bureau.

Muir, Helen (1953), *Miami, USA*, expanded edn (2000), Gainesville, FL: University Press of Florida.

Myers, Ronald L. and John J. Ewel (eds) (1990), *Ecosystems of Florida*, Orlando, FL: University of Central Florida Press.

National Research Council (2001), *Aquifer Storage and Recovery in the Comprehensive Everglades Restoration Plan: A Critique of the Pilot Projects and Related Plans for ASR in the Lake Okeechobee and Western Hillsboro Areas*, Washington, DC: National Academy Press.

National Research Council (2002), *A Review of the Florida Keys Carrying Capacity Study*, Washington, DC: National Academy Press.

National Research Council (2003), *Science and the Greater Everglades Ecosystem Restoration: An Assessment of the Critical Ecosystem Studies Initiative*, Washington, DC: National Academy Press.

National Research Council (2004), *Valuing Ecosystem Services: Toward Better Environmental Decision-Making*, Washington, DC: National Academies Press.

Natural Resources Conservation Service (2000), *Summary Report, 1997 National Resources Inventory*, USDA, accessed at http://www.nrcs.usda.gov/technical/NRI/1997/summary_report/.

Nevada Research Associates (1999), *Washoe County Commercial Water Use Analysis by SIC Code*, Reno, NV: Business and Economic Research Group.

Nijkamp, Peter, Piet Rietveld, and Folke Snickars (1986), 'Regional and multiregional economic models: a survey,' in Peter Nijkamp (ed.), *Handbook of Regional and Urban Economics*, Amsterdam: Elsevier, pp. 257–94.

Nijman, Jan (1996), 'Breaking the rules: Miami in the urban hierarchy,' *Urban Geography*, **17** (1), 5–22.

Nijman, Jan (1997), 'Globalization to a Latin beat: the Miami growth machine,' *The Annals of the American Academy of Political and Social Science*, 551 (May), 164–77.

Odum, Howard T., Elisabeth C. Odum, and Mark T. Brown (1998), *Environment and Society in Florida*, Boca Raton, FL: Lewis Publishers.

Office of Tourism Research (various years), *Florida Visitor Study*, Tallahassee, FL: Florida Dept. of Commerce.

Pierce Neal and Curtis Johnson (2000), *The CitiStates Project*, Ft Lauderdale and Miami, FL: Sun-Sentinel and Collins Center for Public Policy.

Planning and Management Consultants, Ltd (1996), *Alabama-Coosa-Tallapoosa and Apalachicola-Chattahoochee-Flint River Basins Comprehensive Study, Municipal and Industrial Water Use Forecasts, Final Summary Report*, Carbondale, IL.

Polenske, Karen R. (1970), *A Multiregional Input–Output Model for the United States*, Cambridge, MA: Harvard Economic Research Project.

Polenske, Karen R., C.W. Anderson, R. Berner, W.R. Buechner, B. Carlsson, O. Dixon, P. Dixon, W.N. Grubb, F.J. Kok, M.M. Shirley, J.F. Smith, and I.B. Whiston (1972), *State Estimates of the Gross National Product 1947, 1958, 1963*, Lexington, MA: Lexington Books.

Polenske, Karen R., C.W. Anderson, O. Dixon, R.M. Kubarych, M.M. Shirley, and
    J.V. Wells (1974), State Estimates of Technology, 1963, Lexington, MA: Lexington
    Books.
Polenske, Karen R., K. Robinson, Y.Y. Hong, X. Lin, J. Moore, and B. Stedman (1992),
    *Evaluation of the South Coast Air Quality Management District's Methods for
    Assessing Socioeconomic Impacts of District Rules and Regulations*, Report 67,
    Cambridge, MA: Department of Urban Studies and Planning, MIT.
Polopolus, Leo C. and Jose Alvarez (1991), *Marketing Sugar and Other Sweeteners*,
    Amsterdam: Elsevier.
Porter, James W. and Karen G. Porter (eds) (2002), *The Everglades, Florida Bay and
    Coral Reefs of the Florida Keys: An Ecosystem Sourcebook*, Boca Raton, FL: CRC
    Press.
Porter, P.S., George H. Snyder, and C.W. Deren (1991), 'Flood-tolerant crops for low
    input sustainable agriculture in the Everglades Agricultural Area,' *Journal of Sus-
    tainable Agriculture*, **2** (1), 77–101.
Portes, Alejandro and Alex Stepick (1993), *City on the Edge: The Transformation of
    Miami*, Berkeley: University of California Press.
Power, Thomas Michael (1996), *Lost Landscapes and Failed Economies: The Search
    for a Value of Place*, Washington, DC and Covelo, CA: Island Press.
Rand, Honey (2003), *Water Wars: A Story of People, Politics, and Power*, Philadelphia,
    PA: Xlibris.
Randazzo, Anthony F. and Douglas S. Jones (eds) (1997), *The Geology of Florida*,
    Gainesville, FL: University Press of Florida.
Regional Economic Models, Inc. (1995), *The REMI Policy Analysis Handbook*,
    Amherst, MA.
Regional Economic Models, Inc. (1997), *Model Documentation for the REMI EDFS-
    14 Forecasting and Simulation Model*, (March–April), 2 vols, Amherst, MA.
Regional Economic Models, Inc. (1999), *REMI Policy Insight User Guide Version*,
    Amherst, MA.
Regional Economic Models, Inc. (2000), *REMI Reprints*, 3 vols (articles, reviews,
    documentation), Amherst, MA.
Reynolds, John E. (1992), 'Urban land conversion in Florida: will agriculture survive,'
    Soil Crop Science Society of Florida Proceedings, **52**, 6–9.
Reynolds, John E. (1999), *Urban Land Conversion and Competition for Rural Land
    Use* (December), Staff Paper SP 99-15, Gainesville, FL: Institute for Food and
    Agricultural Sciences, University of Florida.
Reynolds, John E. and Buddy L. Dillman (1990), *Urban Land Conversion in Florida's
    Metropolitan Areas*, (December), Staff Paper 401, Gainesville, FL: Institute for
    Food and Agricultural Sciences, University of Florida.
Reynolds, John E., J. Richard Conner, Keeneth C. Gibbs, and Clyde F. Kiker (1973),
    Water Allocation Models Based on an Analysis for the Kissimmee River Basin,
    (December), Publication 26, Gainesville, FL: Water Resources Research Center,
    University of Florida.
Ridenour, James M. (1994), *The National Parks Compromised: Pork Barrel Politics
    and America's Treasures*, Merrillville, IN: ICS Books, Inc.
Rieff, David (1987), *Going to Miami: Exiles, Tourists, and Refugees in the New
    America*, New York: Penguin Books.
Ripple, Jeff (1996), *Southwest Florida's Wetland Wilderness: Big Cypress Swamp and
    the Ten Thousand Islands*, Gainesville, FL: University Press of Florida.

Robertson, William B., Jr (1989), *Everglades: The Park Story*, Miami, FL: Florida National Parks and Monuments Association, Inc.

Rose, Adam, Brandt Stevens, and Gress Davis (1988), *Natural Resource Policy and Income Distribution*, Baltimore, MD: Johns Hopkins University Press.

Rosebank Research and Statistical Analysis (1997), *Total Pollution Pounds per Employee Coefficients*, Marshfield, NC (May).

Ross-Miller, Andrew (2001), 'Valuing open space: land economics & neighborhood parks,' Cambridge, MA: unpublished MA thesis, MIT.

Salamone, Debbie (2002), *Florida's Water Crisis* (reprint), Orlando, FL: *Orlando Sentinel*, 1–28.

Sayles, John (2002), *Sunshine State*, DVD, Culver City, CA: Sony Pictures Classics.

Schmandt, Jurgen, Ernest T. Smerdon, and Judith Clarkson (1988), *State Water Policies: A Study of Six States*, New York: Praeger.

Schueneman, Thomas (2001), *Rice in the Crop Rotation*, Document SS-AGR-23, Gainesville, FL: IFAS, Florida Cooperative Extension Service.

Scoggins, J.F. and Ann C. Pierce (eds) (1995), *The Economy of Florida*, Gainesville, FL: Bureau of Economic & Business Research, University of Florida.

Shih, S.F., B. Glaz, and R.E. Barnes, Jr (1997), *Subsidence Lines Revisited in the Everglades Agricultural Area, 1997*, Technical Bulletin 902, Gainesville, FL: Agricultural Experiment Station, University of Florida.

Shiva, Vandana (2002), *Water Wars: Privatization, Pollution, and Profit*, Cambridge, MA: South End Press.

Simpson, R. David and Norman L. Christensen, Jr (eds) (1997), *Ecosystem Function and Human Activities: Reconciling Economics and Ecology*, New York: Chapman & Hall.

Sklar, F.H., H.C. Fitz, Y. Wu, R. Van Zee, and C. McVoy (2001), 'The design of ecological landscape models for Everglades restoration,' *Ecological Economics*, **37** (3), 379–401.

Smajstrla, A.G. (1990), *Technical Manual: Agricultural Field Scale Irrigation Requirements Simulation (AFSIRS) Model Version 5.5* (January), Gainesville, FL: Agricultural Engineering Department, University of Florida.

Smajstrla, A.G. and F.S. Zazueta (1995), *Estimating Crop Irrigation Requirements for Irrigation System Design and Consumptive Use Permitting* (March), Report AE-257, Gainesville, FL: Florida Cooperative Extension Service, Institute of Food and Agricultural Sciences, University of Florida.

Smith, Patrick D. (1973), *Forever Island*, reprinted in Patrick D. Smith (1987), *Forever Island and Allapattah: A Patrick Smith Reader*, Sarasota, FL: Pineapple Press.

Smith, Patrick D. (1978), *Angel City*, reprinted in Patrick D. Smith (1989), *The River is Home and Angel City: A Patrick Smith Reader*, Sarasota, FL: Pineapple Press.

Smith, Stanley K. (1984), *Population Projections: What do We Really Know?*, Gainesville, FL: BEBR.

Smith, Patrick D. (1987), *Allapattah*, reprinted in Patrick D. Smith (1987), *Forever Island and Allapattah: A Patrick Smith Reader*, Sarasota, FL: Pineapple Press.

Smith, Stanley K. (1986), 'A review and evalution of the housing unit method of population estimation,' *Journal of the American Statistical Association*, **81** (394), 287–96.

Smith, Stanley K. (1987), 'Tests of forecasts accuracy and bias for county population projections,' *Journal of the American Statistical Association*, **82** (400), 991–1012.

Smith, Stanley K. (1989), 'Toward a methodology for estimating temporary residents,' *Journal of the American Statistical Association*, **84** (406), 430–36.

Smith, Stanley K. (1991), 'An evaluation of population forecast errors in Florida and its counties,' *Special Population Reports*, 2, Population Program, Gainesville, FL: BEBR.

Smith, Stanley K. and Scott Cody (2002), 'Number of households and average household size in Florida: April 1, 2001,' *Florida Population Studies*, **35** (1) Bulletin 131 (January), 1–4.

Smith, Stanley K. and June M. Nogle (2002), 'Projections of Florida Population by County, 2001–2030,' *Florida Population Studies*, **35** (2) Bulletin 132 (February), 1–8.

Smith, Stanley K. and June M. Nogle (2003), 'Projections of Florida Population by County, 2001–2030,' *Florida Population Studies*, **36** (1) Bulletin 134 (January), 1–8.

Smith, Stanley K. and Stefan Rayer (2004), 'Projections of Florida population by county, 2003–2030,' Florida Population Studies, **37** (2) Bulletin 138 (February), 1–8.

Smith, Stanley K. and Mohammed Shahidullah (1991), 'Revised annual population estimates by county in Florida, 1980–1990, with components of growth,' *Special Population Reports* 1 (May), Population Program, Gainesville, FL: BEBR.

Smith, Stanley K. and Terry Sincich (1988), 'Stability over time in the distribution of population forecast errors,' *Demography*, **25** (3), 461–74.

Smith, Stanley K. and Terry Sincich (1992), 'Forecasting state and household populations; Evaluating the forecast accuracy and bias of alternative population projections for states' *International Journal of Forecasting*, **8**, 495–508.

Snitow-Kaufman Productions (2004), DVD, *Thirst*, Oley, PA: Bullfrog Films.

Snyder, George H. and J.M. Davidson (1994), 'Everglades agriculture: past, present, and future,' in Steven M. Davis and John C. Ogden (eds), *Everglades: The Ecosystem and Its Restoration*, Boca Raton., FL: St. Lucie Press, pp. 85–115.

Snyder, George, H.W. Burdine, J.R. Crockett, G.J. Gascho, D.S. Harrison, G. Kidder, J.W. Mishoe, D.L. Myhre, F.M. Pate, and S.F. Shih (1978), *Water Table Management for Organic Soil Conservation and Crop Production in the Florida Everglades*, Bulletin 801, Gainesville, FL: Agricultural Experimental Stations, Institute of Food and Agricultural Sciences.

Solecki, William D. (2001), 'The role of global-to-local linkages in land use/land cover change in South Florida,' *Ecological Economics*, **37** (3), 339–56.

Solley, Wayne B., Robert R. Pierce, and Howard A. Perlman (1998), *Estimated Use of Water in the United States in 1995*, US Geological Survey Circular 1200, Denver, CO: US Geological Survey.

South Florida Ecosystem Restoration Task Force Working Group (various years), *Cross-Cut Budget FY South Florida Ecosystem Restoration Program*, formerly published as *Integrated Financial Plan: South Florida Ecosystem Project Activities*, Office of the Executive Director, Miami, FL.

South Florida Ecosystem Restoration Task Force Working Group (2002), *Co-ordination Success: Strategy for Restoration of the South Florida Ecosystem and Tracing Success: Biennial Report of FY 2001–2002* (August), Miami, FL: Office of the Executive Director.

South Florida Water Management District (SFWMD) (February 1992), *Lower East Coast Regional Water Supply Plan*, 'Appendices and supporting technical information,' (March 1993), 'Working document'; (March 1997) 'Draft,' West Palm Beach, FL: SFWMD.

South Florida Water Management District (SFWMD) (July 1992), *Water Supply Needs and Sources, 1990–2010*, West Palm Beach, FL: Planning Department Staff.

South Florida Water Management District (SFWMD) (February 1994), *Lower West Coast Water Supply Plan*, vol 2 'Background document,' West Palm Beach, FL: Planning Department Staff, SFWMD.

South Florida Water Management District (SFWMD) (1996), *Land Use/Land Cover – 1988*, West Palm Beach, FL.

South Florida Water Management District (SFWMD) (October 1996), *Kissimmee Basin Water Supply Plan*, 2 vol 'Background Document, Appendices,' West Palm Beach, FL: Upper East Coast/Kissimmee Planning Division.

South Florida Water Management District (SFWMD) (1997a), *Everglades Best Management Practices Program*, West Palm Beach FL (September).

South Florida Water Management District (SFWMD) (1997b), *Geographic Information Systems Data*, CD-ROM #1, 'Land use, national wetlands inventory,' West Palm Beach, FL.

South Florida Water Management District (SFWMD) (1998), *1995 Land Use/Land Cover GIS Coverages*, West Palm Beach, FL.

South Florida Water Management District (SFWMD) (February 1998), *Upper East Coast Water Supply Plan*, 3 vols 'Planning Document, Support Document, Appendices,' West Palm Beach, FL: Upper District Planning Division, SFWMD.

South Florida Water Management District (SFWMD) (July 1998), *Districtwide Water Supply Assessment*, West Palm Beach, FL: Districtwide Water Supply Assessment Team, SFWMD.

South Florida Water Management District (SFWMD) (April 2000a), *Kissimmee Basin Water Supply Plan*, 3 vols 'Planning Document, Support Document, Appendices,' West Palm Beach, FL: Water Supply Planning and Development Department, SFWMD.

South Florida Water Management District (SFWMD) (April 2000b), *Lower West Coast Water Supply Plan*, vol 2 'Support Document,' West Palm Beach, FL: Water Supply Planning and Development Department, SFWMD.

South Florida Water Management District (SFWMD) (May 2000), *Lower East Coast Regional Water Supply Plan*. 'Planning Document and Appendices,' West Palm Beach, FL: Water Supply Planning and Development Department, SFWMD.

South Florida Water Management District (SFWMD) (August 2000), *District Water Management Plan*, West Palm Beach, FL: SFWMD.

South Florida Water Management District (SFWMD) (2001), *South Florida Water Management Model* (SFWMM), model documentation from http://www.sfwmd. gov/org/pld/hsm/models/sfwmm/fact_sht.htm, accessed 6/3/01, also Review of the Documentation for SFWMM (peer reviews of version 2.10) (Mar. 1998), accessed at http://www.sfwmd.gov/org/pld/hsm/pubs/pubs_subj.htm#Sensitivity.

South Florida Water Management District (SFWMD) (2003a), *2003 Everglades Consolidated Report*, Executive Summary and CD ROM, West Palm Beach, FL.

South Florida Water Management District (SFWMD) (2003b), *Water Resource Protection Strategies for the Implementation of CERP Under Federal and State Law*, West Palm Beach, FL: SFWMD (April).

Southern DataStream, Inc. (2000), *Agricultural Water Use Estimates for Levy County Final Report* (August 31), posted on www.srmd.com, Live Oak, FL: Suwannee River Management District.

Stakhiv, Eugene Z. (2003), 'Disintegrated water resources management in the US: Union of Sisyphus and Pandora,' *Journal of Water Resources Planning and Management*, **129** (3) 151–54.

Stamper, Judith Bauer (1993), *Save the Everglades*, Austin, TX: Raintree Steck-Vaughn Publishers.

Stevens, Tom, Alan Hodges, and David Mulkey (2003), *Economic Impact of Tyson foods' Plant Closure in Northeast Florida, 2002*, Gainesville, FL: IFAS, University of Florida.

Strategy Research Corporation (various years), *Visitor Profile and Tourism Impact: Greater Miami and the Beaches, Annual Reports*, Miami, FL.

Sun-Sentinel (2002), 'Getting nowhere fast: South Florida's transportation crisis' (June 2–7), Special Supplement, Ft Lauderdale, FL, pp. 1–10.

Taylor, Lance (ed.) (1990), *Socially Relevant Policy Analysis: Structuralist Computable General Equilibrium Models for the Developing World*, Cambridge, MA: MIT Press.

Tebeau, Charlton W. (1966), *Florida's Last Frontier: the History of Collier Country*, rev. edn, Coral Gables, Fl: University of Miami Press, Copeland Studies in Florida History.

Thomas, Michael and Nicolas Stratis (2001), *Assessing the Economic Impact & Value of Florida's Public Piers and Boat Ramps* (March), Tallahassee: Florida Fish and Wildlife Conservation Commission.

Trager, Kenneth (1990a), *The 1989 Impact of Florida's Sugarcane Industry on the State's Economy*, Joint Legislative Management Committee, Division of Economic and Demographic Research, Florida Legislature.

Trager, Kenneth (1990b), *The Impact of Fiscal Year 1988–89 Out-of-State Tourism on the Florida Economy*, Tallahassee, FL: Joint Legislative Management Committee, Division of Economic and Demographic Research, Florida Legislature.

Trager, Kenneth (1991), 'Estimating the impact of out-of-state tourism on Florida's economy,' *Journal of Star Research*, **2** (April), 81–98, Tallahassee, FL.

Trager, Kenneth (1999), *A Measure of the Competitiveness of Florida Business Acitivity: A REMI Model Perspective*, Tallahassee, FL: Joint Legislative Management Committee, Division of Economic and Demographic Research, Florida Legislature.

Treyz, George I. (1993), *Regional Economic Modeling: A Systematic Approach to Economic Forecasting and Policy Analysis*, Boston, MA: Kluwer Academic Publishers.

US Army Corps of Engineers (1948), *Comprehensive Report on Central and Southern Florida for Flood Control and Other Purposes*, reprinted from 80th Congress, 2nd session, House Doc. 643. Washington, DC: US Government Printing Office.

US Army Corps of Engineers (1991), *National Economic Development Procedures Manual – Overview Manual for Conducting Nation Economic Development*, IWR Report 91-R-11, Fort Belvoir, VA: Water Resources Support Center, Institute for Water Resources.

US Army Corps of Engineers (1994), *Central and South Florida Project, Comprehensive Review Study. Reconnaissance Report*, Jacksonville, FL.

US Army Corps of Engineers (1996), *National Review of Corps Environmental Restoration Projects*, IWR Report 96-R-27, Alexandria, VA: Water Resources Support Center, Institute for Water Resources.

US Army Corps of Engineers (1999), *Central and Southern Florida Project, Comprehensive Review Study*, Jacksonville, FL.

US Army Corps of Engineers (2001), *Monitoring and Assessment Plan, Comprehensive Everglades Restoration Plan*, (March), Jacksonville, FL.

US Census Bureau (2001). *Statistical Abstract of the United States: 2001*, Washington, DC: US Government Printing Office.

US Department of Agriculture (various years), *Census of Agriculture – Florida – County Data*, Washington, DC.

US Department of Agriculture, National Agricultural Statistical Service (NASS) (2001), *Florida Agricultural Facts*, Washington, DC, accessed at http://www.nass.usda.gov/fl/.

US Department of Commerce, Bureau of Economic Analysis (2002), *REIS Regional Economic Information System*, CD-ROM, Washington, DC.

US Fish and Wildlife Service and US Department of Commerce, Bureau of the Census, (1993), *1991 National Survey of Fishing, Hunting, and Wildlife-Associated Recreation, Florida* (August), Washington, DC: US Government Printing Office.

US Fish and Wildlife Service and US Department of Commerce, Bureau of the Census (1998), *1996 National Survey of Fishing, Hunting, and Wildlife-Associated Recreation, Florida* (March), Washington, DC: US Government Printing Office.

Vileisis, Ann (1997), *Discovering the Unknown Landscape: A History of America's Wetlands*, Washington, DC and Covelo, CA: Island Press.

Visit Florida Research Office (various years), *Florida Visitor Study*, Tallahassee, FL (through 1999, published by Office of Tourism Research, Bureau of Economic Analysis, Florida Department of Commerce, Tallahassee).

Visitor Services Project (1989, 1996), *Everglades National Park Visitor Study*. Moscow, Idaho: Cooperative Park Studies Unit, University of Idaho.

Wade, Dale, John Ewel, and Ronald Hofstetter (1980), *Fire in South Florida Ecosystems*, US Department of Agriculture, Forest Service General Technical Report SE-17, Asheville, NC: Southeastern Forest Experiment Station.

Walker, Robert (2001), 'Urban sprawl and natural areas encroachment: linking land cover change and economic development in the Florida Everglades,' *Ecological Economics*, **37** (3), 357–69.

Wanless, Harold R., R.W. Parkinson, and L. P. Tedsco (1994), 'Sea level control on stability of Everglades wetlands,' in S.M. Davis and J.C. Ogden (eds), *Everglades: The Ecosystem and Its Restoration*, Boca Raton., FL: St Lucie Press, pp. 199–223.

Watercourse and South Florida Water Management District (1996), *Discover a Watershed: The Everglades*, Bozeman, MT: Montana State University.

Wear, David N. (2002), 'How have land uses changed in the South, and how might changes in the future affect the area of forests?' in David N. Wear and John G. Greis, *Southern Forest Resource Assessment Summary Report*, USDA Forest Service, Southern Research Station and Southern Region, accessed at http://www.srs.fs.usda.gov/sustain/report/socio1/socio1.htm.

Weisskoff, Richard (1971), *A Multisector Simulation Model of Employment, Growth and Income Distribution in Puerto Rico: A Re-evaluation of 'Successful' Development Strategy*, New Haven, CT: Research Report to the US Department of Labor, Manpower Administration.

Weisskoff, Richard (1976), 'Income distribution and export promotion in Puerto Rico,' in K. Polenske and J. Skolka (eds), *Advances in Input–Output Analysis*, Cambridge, MA: Ballinger, pp. 205–28.

Weisskoff, Richard (1985), *Factories and Food Stamps: The Puerto Rico Model of Development,* Baltimore, MD: Johns Hopkins University Press.

Weisskoff, Richard (1993), 'Basic human needs and the democratic process in Latin America,' *North-South Issues*, **2** (2), 1–6.

Weisskoff, Richard (1998), 'Regional Economic Impacts,' in US Army Corps of Engineers, *Central and Southern Florida Project Comprehensive Review Study*, Jacksonville, FL, Appendix E, pp. 281–310.

Weisskoff, Richard (2000), 'Missing pieces in ecosystem restoration: the case of the Florida Everglades,' *Economic Systems Research*, **12** (3), 271–303, http://exchange. law.miami.edu/everglades/science/weisskoff/missingpieces.pdf.

Weisskoff, Richard (2003), 'A tale of two models: IMPLAN and REMI on the economics of Everglades restoration,' in D.J. Rapport, W.L. Lasley, D.E. Rolston, N.O. Nielsen, C.O. Qualset, and A.B. Damania (eds), *Managing for Healthy Ecosystems*, Boca Raton, FL: Lewis Publishers, pp. 1303–24, see also http://exchange.law. miami.edu/everglades/.

Weisskoff, Richard and Edward N. Wolff (1975), 'Development and trade dependence: the case of Puerto Rico, 1948–1963' *Review of Economics and Statistics*, **57** (4), 470–77, reprinted in Ira Sohn (1986), *Readings in Input-Output Analysis: Theory and Applications*, New York: Oxford University Press, pp. 406–16.

Weisskoff, Richard and Edward N. Wolff (1977), 'Linkages and leakages: industrial tracking in an enclave economy,' *Economic Development and Cultural Change*, **25**, 607–28.

West, Carol T. and David G. Lenze (1994), 'Modeling the regional impact of natural disaster and recovery: a general framework and an application to Hurricane Andrew,' *International regional Science Review*, **17** (2) 121–50.

Will, Lawrence E. (1968), *Swamp to Sugar Bowl: Pioneer Days in Belle Glade*, reprinted (1984), Belle Glade, FL: Glades Historical Society.

World Commission on Environment and Development (1987), *Our Common Future*, Oxford and New York: Oxford University Press.

Yaffee, Steven L., A.F. Phillips, I.C. Frentz, P.W. Hardy, S.M. Maleki, and B.E. Thorpe (1996), Ecosystem Management in the United States: An Assessment of Current Experience, Washington, DC and Covelo, CA: Island Press.

Index

A

age distribution, Southern Florida 115–18
agriculture 113–15, 143–61, 191–209
  acreage 146, 153–5
  correcting for "missing pieces" from
    REMI base model 22, 23
  drainage and irrigation 148–9, 155–7
  employment correction 193–7,
    200–202
  environmental impacts 145
  Everglades restoration impact
    scenarios 251
  farm employment 151, 158–60
  farm income correction 195, 198,
    203–4, 208
  farmland conversion 290
  farm size distribution 113, 114, 143,
    147
  growth trends 155
  IMPLAN model 198–9
  indirect inputs correction 198
  irrigated farmland 114, 143
  livestock and cropping patterns 152,
    158
  need for integrating in Everglades
    restoration planning 6
  number of farms 147
  problematic forecasting issues 191–2
  products by sub-region 152
  projected contribution to growth
    (2030) 28–9, 34
  REMI model 192–3
  sugarcane prices 207
  summary of forecast scenarios 296,
    299, 302
  summary table 144

USDA outlook projections 199, 206–8
value of production 114, 150, 155,
    194
water use 71
Alligator Alley 126, 127
aquifer storage and recovery (ASR) wells
    17, 246, 247

B

Babbit, Bruce 6–7, 11
Bacchus, Sydney 98
beach privatization 283
BEBR, *see* Bureau of Economic and
    Business Research (BEBR)
    projections
benefit–cost ratio 5
Big Cypress Swamp 101, 121
bonds, Everglades restoration financing
    11, 248
Broward County 25
  urban compression 83
  see also Lower East Coast
Broward, Napoleon Bonaparte 121
Brown, Mark T. 99
Brundtland Report 4
Burchell, Robert W. 89–92
Bureau of Economic and Business
    Research (BEBR) projections 29,
    34–5, 38–51, 188–90, 261–3
  construction permit data 212
  population under-forecasting 134,
    136–7
  REIS employment base 39
  USGS water use forecast 54–5

K

L